LEGO® PLAY BOOK

IDEAS TO BRING YOUR BRICKS TO LIFE

Written by Daniel Lipkowitz

BUILDER TALK

The fan builders pop up in their chapters to give insider tips and expert LEGO building advice.

LOOK OUT FOR THESE SPECIAL FEATURES!

COOL BRICK

The Cool Brick boxes show you versatile pieces and explain why they're so cool.

QUICK BUILD

If time is of the essence or you're looking for ideas for simpler builds, check out the Quick Build features.

CHALLENGE

Flip to the Challenge panels and pages to find ideas for activities to play with friends and a few LEGO bricks.

HANDFUL OF BRICKS

On the Handful of Bricks pages, you'll find the fan builders' attempts to prove that you can build just about anything with a handful of bricks and a little imagination! Look up the list of bricks in each "handful" on p.200.

CONTENTS

HI

Once Upon a Time

MEET THE BUILDER: BARNEY MAIN

Age: 20

Day Job: Engineering design student

LEGO® Specialities: Castles, pirate ships

Brick Collection: 25,000 parts

Favourite Brick: Round LEGO® Technic connector

Did You Know? Barney once built some weighing scales using a LEGO plane model when he was baking a cake and needed to weigh out the ingredients.

A SMALL WORLD

GO WILD!

PLEASED TO MEET YOU!

MEET THE BUILDER: TIM GODDARD

Age: 36
Day Job: Analytical chemist
LEGO Speciality: Microscale
Brick Collection: No idea, but it's pretty big!
Favourite Brick: 1x1 round plate (at least it is today!)
Did You Know? Tim took part in a workshop at LEGO headquarters to help with the initial planning of the LEGO® Legends of Chima™ theme.

MEET THE BUILDERS: PETE REID AND YVONNE DOYLE

Ages: Both 38
Day Jobs: Postman (Pete); IT support (Yvonne)
LEGO Specialities: Robots, spaceships (Pete); buildings, interiors (Yvonne)
Brick Collection: A shared collection of 250,000 pieces
Favourite Bricks: 2x2 octagonal plate (Pete); 1x1 tile (Yvonne)
Did You Know? Pete and Yvonne fell in love at a LEGO event. Their eyes met over a pile of LEGO bricks.

HELLO, HELLO

GO WILD! CONTENTS continued

THINGS THAT GO BUMP IN THE NIGHT

GREETINGS!

MEET THE BUILDER: ROD GILLIES

Age: 42

Day Job: Innovation and marketing for a big beer company

LEGO Specialities: Sci-fi vehicles, castles, micro-scale

Brick Collection: Lots!

Favourite Brick: Headlight brick

Did You Know? Rod sometimes goes to work with plasters all over his hands to cover cuts caused by him frantically rummaging through brick bins!

Wish You Were Here

G'DAY!

MEET THE BUILDER: TIM JOHNSON

Age: 42
Day Job: Digital producer
LEGO Speciality: Microscale architecture
Brick Collection: 120,000 pieces
Favourite Brick: 1x2 tile with grille
Did You Know? Tim used to keep all his empty LEGO boxes as a child, and still has them 30 years later.

CHALLENGE

Meet the fan builders behind the Challenge features in each chapter. Stephen designed the challenges, then Andrew brought them to life!

CONCEPTS: STEPHEN BERRY

Age: 22
Day Job: Mechanical engineering student
LEGO Specialities: Games, vehicles
Brick Collection: 10,000 parts
Favourite Brick: Angled plate
Did You Know? Ever since Stephen first began building with LEGO bricks, he has been inventing challenges and games to play with friends.

HOWDY

BUILDER: ANDREW WALKER

Age: 46
Day Job: Accountant
LEGO Specialities: Castles, pirate ships
Brick Collection: Too many!
Favourite Brick: 1x3 tile
Did You Know? Andrew is building a collection of Santa minifigures. He has one of every LEGO Santa ever produced and is now busy collecting all the accessories!

HEY

BUILDING BRICKS

Are you ready to build? What will you create? Here are a few hints and tips to get you started, but all you really need to know is that you can build just about anything!

WHAT BRICKS DO YOU HAVE?

Organising your bricks into type or colour can really get the creative juices flowing. However many bricks you have, and whatever colour or type they are, you can get building!

LOTS OF THE SAME COLOUR

Build models in all one colour, like this black alphapet. (See p.108.)

NOT MANY BRICKS

Make something small and simple, or try building in micro-scale. Turn to the Small World section on pages 52–93 for inspiration!

WHAT WILL INSPIRE YOU?

Inspiration is all around you – so start looking! Perhaps your ideas will spring from a little research, a single piece or through play with friends.

LOTS OF THE SAME TYPE

Make a model with lots of similar sections, like this slithering snake. (See p.116.)

HOW MUCH TIME DO YOU HAVE?

It doesn't matter! You can build for the whole day, or for the last ten minutes before dinnertime. The important thing is to start.

ONE PIECE

Just one piece can inspire many models. This octagonal plate with bars is part of a flower (p.18), an octopus (p.74) and a spider (p.112). Look for the Cool Brick features in this book for more inspiring bricks.

RESEARCH

Be inspired by images of the kinds of thing you want to build, in books or online.

PLAY

Think about *how* you want to play with your LEGO® bricks and invent models you can use in play with friends. See the Challenge features in this book for inspiration!

NOT LONG

Whiz through the speedy and simple Quick Build models in this book – they can be built in next to no time. On your marks, get set, BUILD!

WHAT IF IT GOES WRONG?

If it seems like you have hit a LEGO brick wall, don't panic! Even the most accomplished builders have to try several ways of building something before getting it right.

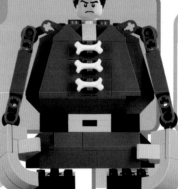

LOADS OF TIME

Try out a big model or scene, or devise a fun challenge to play with friends.

TAKE IT APART AND TRY AGAIN

Sometimes, you just have to grab your brick separator and start again! See it as a learning experience. You will get it right in the end!

CHANGE IT TO SOMETHING NEW

Maybe your creation could become something else. If your elephant model's head isn't working out, could the model become a rhino instead?

HOW MUCH DETAIL SHOULD I ADD?

It's up to you! The interesting thing about building in a small scale is that you don't need much detail to create the image of something; on the other hand, adding lots of intricate details to your models can be really fun, too.

SHOULD I PLAN MY BUILDS?

Some builders like to plan out their models, while others prefer to just dive into their bricks and see what happens! Either way, the results can be amazing. What kind of builder are you?

LOTS

These beautiful beach huts have lots of delicate details that really bring a laidback beach scene to life.

LITTLE

Despite not having buckets (and spades) of detail, this row of tiny beach huts paints a perfect picture.

PLAN IT OUT

If you want to build a large-scale model or an elaborate scene, it can be helpful to do a rough sketch of your creation and gather your bricks before building.

TRY IT OUT

Sometimes, just starting to build can lead to the most inspiration, especially when creating smaller models or delicate details – though you might reach a few stumbling blocks along the way!

WHAT IF I DONT HAVE THE PERFECT PIECE?

If your collection seems to be missing that one piece that will make your model your showpiece – never fear! It's just another chance to test out your building and creativity skills.

BUILD YOUR OWN

If nothing else will do, try building a piece yourself! No flame pieces to heat up your minifigures' dinner? Make a fire from whatever orange, red or yellow bricks you have.

HOW WILL YOU PLAY WITH THE MODEL?

Remember that LEGO bricks are meant to be played with. Half the fun of building is getting to have fun with your models afterwards! Think about the purpose and function of your model as you build it, so it has ultimate playability.

GET CREATIVE

You might not have *the* brick, but there will be other bricks that achieve the same effect. These bugs have a similar look, but they're made from completely different pieces.

MAKE A MOVE

Making models with moving parts can really bring them to life. This fairy tale dragon wouldn't be quite so scary if it didn't have chomping jaws, flapping wings and fast-moving legs!

TAKE A CHALLENGE

Get competitive with your creativity and build models that can form a game to play with friends. This book's Challenge features should give you some ideas.

TELL A TALE

Build scenes and models with a story in mind. Each chapter in this book tells a tale – use them as inspiration for your own LEGO stories!

BRICK-SPOTTING

Do you know a LEGO® plate from a LEGO tile? If not, don't worry! This book will show you all kinds of pieces, how they function and how they can be used with other parts. To get you started, here are some of the most frequently used or interesting pieces that you will see on the pages of this book. These are good parts to look out for in your own collection. What else can you find?

1x1x6 round column

Tube

1x6x2 curved arch

1x1 cone

2x2 cone

BRICKS
The humble 2x4 brick is the classic LEGO piece, but bricks come in all shapes and sizes. They can all connect to other bricks at the top and bottom. The bumps on the top of a brick, known as "studs," connect to the "tubes" on the bottom of another.

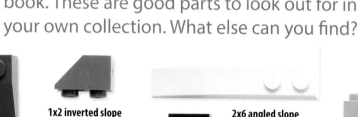

1x2 inverted slope

2x6 angled slope

2x3 slope

1x2 brick

2x2 inverted slope

1x3x2 curved arch

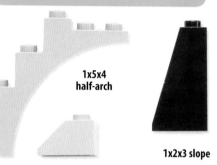
1x5x4 half-arch

1x2 curved half-arch

2x3 slope

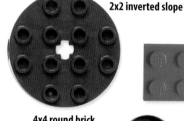
4x4 round brick

2x4 brick

1x3 arch

1x2 slope

1x2x3 slope

1x1x5 brick

2x2 domed brick

1x3x2 half-arch

1x2 log brick

Small wagon wheels and 1x4 axle plate

Ball joint socket

2x2 brick with ball joint

2x2 turntable

1x2 brick with axle hole

1x2 brick-with-hole

1x2 plate with click hinge

MOVING PIECES
Building moving parts into your LEGO models can really bring them to life. LEGO® Technic connecting parts and regular pieces, such as turntables, hinges and winches, can all help you to do this.

Hinged plates

LEGO Technic cross-axle 8

Hinge cylinder

1x1 plate with vertical clip

LEGO Technic pin

1x2 plate with handled bar

LEGO Technic half-pin

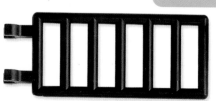
Ladder with 2 clips

2x4 winch

1x2 plate with click hinge

2x2 brick with side pins and axle hole

Tap

Bat

2x2 flower

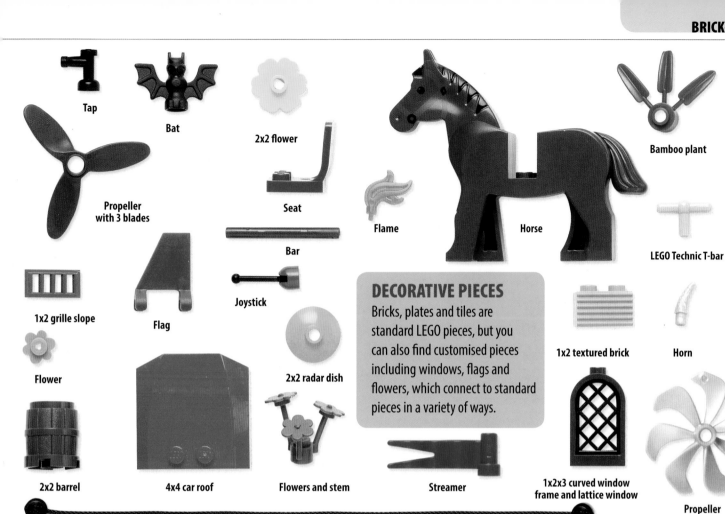
Horse

Bamboo plant

Propeller
with 3 blades

Seat

Flame

LEGO Technic T-bar

Bar

1x2 grille slope

Flag

Joystick

Horn

Aerial

Flower

2x2 radar dish

1x2 textured brick

DECORATIVE PIECES
Bricks, plates and tiles are standard LEGO pieces, but you can also find customised pieces including windows, flags and flowers, which connect to standard pieces in a variety of ways.

2x2 barrel

4x4 car roof

Flowers and stem

Streamer

1x2x3 curved window
frame and lattice window

Propeller

String with studs

SNOT PIECES
Most LEGO models are built from the ground up. The term "SNOT" stands for Studs Not On Top, a building style using bricks that allow you to build any which way but up! Pieces with studs on their sides, like the headlight brick and angle plates, are useful for building sideways or upside down.

Headlight brick

2x2 corner plate

2x6 plate

1x1 plate with
horizontal clip

1x1 plate with ring

1x2 jumper
plate

1x1 brick with
1 side stud

1x1 round plate

PLATES
Just like bricks, plates have studs on the top and tubes on the bottom, but plates are much thinner. Did you know that three plates stacked together are the same height as a standard brick?

2x3 curved plate
with hole

1x1 round plate

1x2/2x2 angle plate

1x2/1x4 angle plate

1x1 brick with
4 side studs

1x1 brick with
2 side studs

1x6 tile

2x4 plate

1x1 tile

TILES
Tiles are thin, like plates, but they only connect to other bricks at the bottom. The top of a tile has no studs on it, so tiles are great pieces for creating perfectly smooth surfaces.

1x2 grille

1x1 tooth plate

1x1 slope

2x2 tile

2x2 tile-with-pin

3x8 angled plate

Once Upon a Time

How do you create a fairy tale adventure?
You'll need a place where the tale begins, and
scenes that take place along the way. Make up
some fantastic creatures to be ferocious monsters
or brand-new friends. Don't forget some tricky
traps and puzzles, too. Get out your bricks and
start building your own story!

FAREWELL, MOTHER! I'M OFF TO FACE DIRE PERILS IN THE WILDERNESS.

HAVE FUN, DEAR.

COUNTRY COTTAGE
Goodbye, home-sweet-home! Jack lives with his mother in a country cottage deep in the woods. Jack doesn't know what lies beyond the woods – but he can't wait to find out! (See p.16.)

TELLING A FAIRY TALE
BARNEY MAIN

"I really enjoyed working on my chapter, as I got to read loads of children's books as my research! I also used cartoons and history books for inspiration. I had a good idea of how I wanted each fairy tale model to look, but I made lots of changes as I went along. I especially like how the larger fairy tale characters (pp.20–21) came out, as I'd never built anything like them before."

WE CENTAURS HAVE NO NEED OF GOLD.

JACK'S JOURNEY

Little Jack has spent all his young life in one place and longs to have an adventure. When a cry goes up across the land that the King's Royal Nugget has been stolen, Jack knows that at last this is his chance to see the big, wide world. The King requests that all heroes in the kingdom go in search of the Royal Nugget. The one to return it to him will be granted a rich reward. Jack decides to pack his backpack and set out to find the Royal Nugget – and his fortune!

"Hear ye, hear ye, the Royal Nugget is missing. Whoever finds it will be granted stuff." – Signed, The King

ALAS! WHERE COULD IT BE?

WOODLAND WONDERS

Jack discovers mythical woodland realms on his travels. Will the strange plants and creatures he finds there be his friends or his foes? (See p.18.)

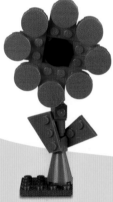

FEE-FI-FO-FUM, I'VE GOT SOME ROAST CHICKEN. YUM!

GIANT TROUBLE

Nowhere is out of reach for little Jack – even the kingdom of the giants, way up in the clouds. Will Jack become the giant's next dinner? (See p.28.)

NO NUGGET HERE, KID. SCRAM!

TROLL TERROR

Jack's quest to find the Royal Nugget takes him over a troll-guarded bridge. Better run, Jack – that troll doesn't look too happy! (See p.24.)

SQUEAK!

This door was built first, then the frame was constructed around it

Fancy window is the bottom of a small turntable piece

FRONT VIEW

Latticed windows lend a rustic feel

FAIRY TALE COTTAGE

Jack is setting out on his adventure, and where better to start his story than the quaint country cottage where he grew up? A cottage is a nice place to stop and rest after a long day of walking. Will your cottage be on farmland, or deep in the woods? You could even make extra cottages and change their colours around to create an entire village!

A roof of stepped yellow bricks looks like it's made out of straw. Make sure it's built to support its own weight so it doesn't collapse!

Try building a secret hiding place inside your cottage's roof.

KITCHEN

Give your minifigures everything they could need, including the kitchen sink! In the cottage kitchen there are jars of food on the shelves, a powerful oven and a nice mug of LEGO® broth waiting on the table.

The oven door is made from a tile with clips

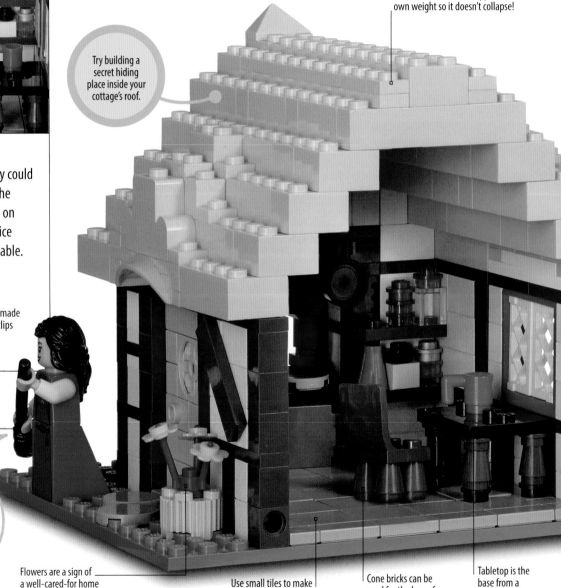

Pose and accessorise your characters so they're doing something, like gardening or repairing the house

IT'S SO HARD TO KEEP A COTTAGE WARM WHEN IT SPLITS OPEN IN THE MIDDLE!

Flowers are a sign of a well-cared-for home

Use small tiles to make a tiled floor, or long brown ones for wooden floorboards

Cone bricks can be used for the legs of a chair, table, or stool

Tabletop is the base from a LEGO® Minifigures collectible character

COSY HOME

Building from reference can really inspire your choice of colours and shapes for your fairy tale cottage, so take a look at your favourite fairy tale books for ideas! Brown timber frames around white plaster walls give this building a half-timbered style.

LIVING SPACE

Fill your cottage with furniture and decorations that fit a pastoral setting, like a rug, a picture and a fireplace. Use transparent orange elements to make a roaring fire, and have some firewood at the ready for when it starts to go out!

What will your occupants need in their home? Build in details to suit your minifigures.

Attach a 1x4 tile to a 1x1 brick with side stud for a diagonal brown beam

Stack white plates like a staircase to make a plume of puffy smoke

REAR VIEW

Use more than one hinge plate for strength and stability

Decorated and stickered tiles make great paintings. Attach them to bricks with side studs

Windows and curtains help make a house into a home

An auto mudguard can also be a shady window overhang

SIDE VIEWS

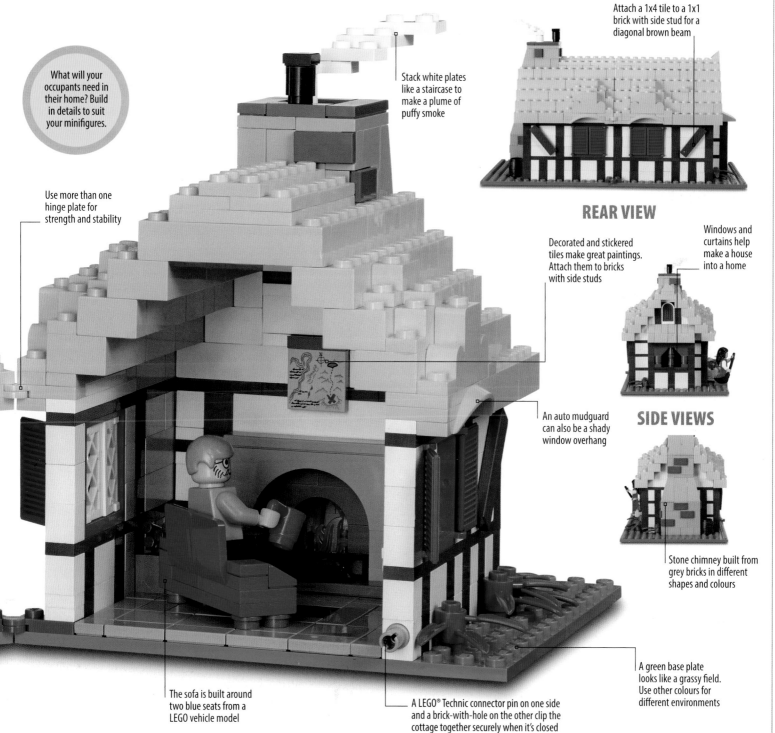

Stone chimney built from grey bricks in different shapes and colours

The sofa is built around two blue seats from a LEGO vehicle model

A LEGO® Technic connector pin on one side and a brick-with-hole on the other clip the cottage together securely when it's closed

A green base plate looks like a grassy field. Use other colours for different environments

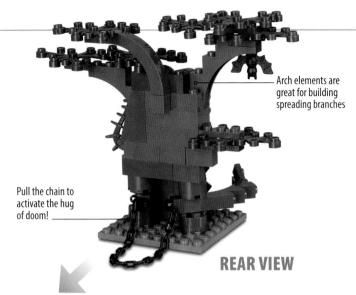

Arch elements are great for building spreading branches

Pull the chain to activate the hug of doom!

REAR VIEW

ENCHANTED FOREST

A walk in the woods sounded like fun, but Jack has gotten lost. Yikes, did that tree just move? Storybook forests are always full of mystery and adventure. They can be home to ferocious monsters and beasts, or helpful fairies and magical creatures. Build a forest with caves, rocks, rivers, and lots of trees in different shapes and sizes!

What is this tree protecting? Or does it just not like minifigures?

If you don't have LEGO leaf pieces, use any green bricks and plates – or just leave the branches bare!

Pieces with unusual curves and shapes make a forest creation look organic and growing

Two barrels attached with LEGO Technic cross-axles make a pair of creepy, hollow eyes

HUG OF DOOM

The tree's grabbing arms are half-arch pieces built on their sides, with L-shaped plates for the branch-hands on the ends. They move on pivot points made with LEGO Technic bricks and axles.

Use slopes and bricks to build up the shape of a big, sturdy tree trunk

MONSTER TREE

This tree's arm-like branches can close to capture a LEGO minifigure. To make your own living tree, just build a regular one and then add creature features like eyes, hands or even big pointy teeth!

Build in roots for a natural look

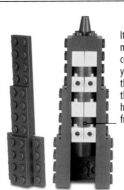

It doesn't matter what colour pieces you use on the inside – they'll be hidden from view!

INSIDE THE PINE

This pine tree is built around a central core of bricks with studs on their sides, and plates attached to them sideways. Stacking more plates on the bottom creates a tapered shape.

Studs pointing outwards make the tree look bristly

PINE TREE

Some LEGO sets include single-piece pine trees, but you can build your own versions to plant in your forest! This pine tree is built to fit into the same base as the chopping tree below, so the two are interchangeable.

Try blue trees for a magical forest, or white for a snowy one.

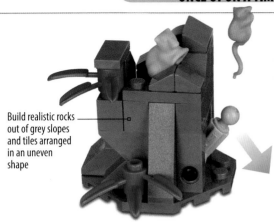

Build realistic rocks out of grey slopes and tiles arranged in an uneven shape

SECRET SURPRISES

What would a fairy tale forest be without a few surprises? This "ratapult" launches a rat out of a hollow rock to scare unwary adventurers! You can build all kinds of fun tricks and traps into your forest creations.

CHOPPING TREE

Some people work in forests – even enchanted ones! A woodcutter makes his living by cutting down trees. This chopping tree is perfect for lumber as it's straight, tall and thin enough to be cut up and hauled away. Its trunk is made from stacked 2x2 round bricks, with plant leaves built in.

Light green leaves look healthy and vibrant

OH BOY! I HOPE I GET MADE INTO SOMETHING REALLY COOL...LIKE A BATTERING RAM!

A LEGO Technic towball inside the hollow base pushes up on the trunk to dislodge it

Build the trees for your forest with different heights and leaf patterns to make them look unique

Push down here to topple the tree

TOPPLING TREE

This tree is built with a special action feature: when you push down on the LEGO Technic towball at its base, it topples over as if the woodcutter has just chopped it down.

TIMBER!

Stacked 2x2 round bricks

FOREST FLORA

Strolling through the woods, Jack spots all sorts of strange and wondrous things. Maybe getting lost isn't so bad after all! When building flowers and mushrooms for an enchanted forest, look at real plants for inspiration – but don't stop there. Let your imagination take root and grow by giving your creations new shapes, wild colours, and magical features.

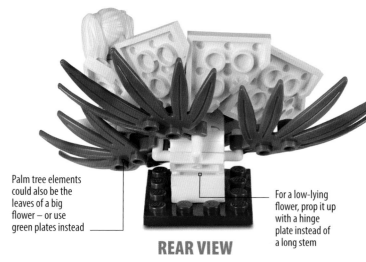

Palm tree elements could also be the leaves of a big flower – or use green plates instead

For a low-lying flower, prop it up with a hinge plate instead of a long stem

REAR VIEW

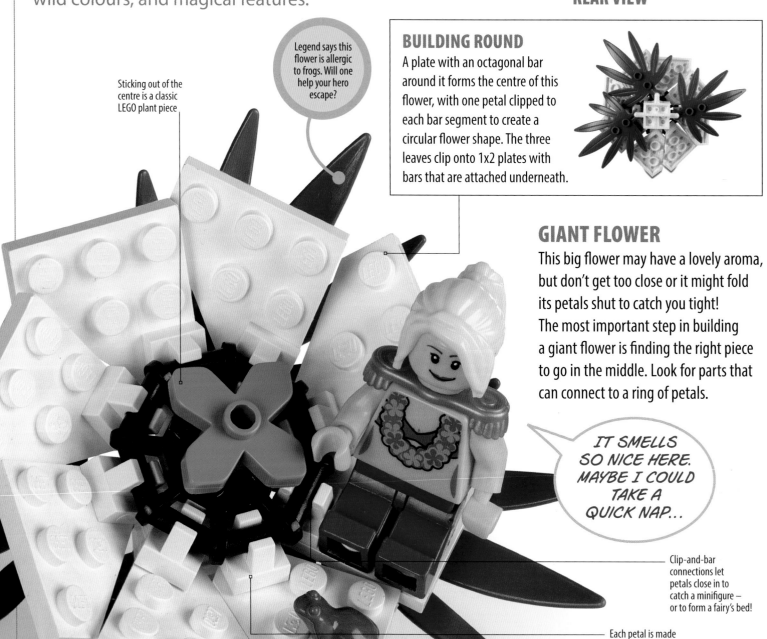

Legend says this flower is allergic to frogs. Will one help your hero escape?

Sticking out of the centre is a classic LEGO plant piece

BUILDING ROUND

A plate with an octagonal bar around it forms the centre of this flower, with one petal clipped to each bar segment to create a circular flower shape. The three leaves clip onto 1x2 plates with bars that are attached underneath.

GIANT FLOWER

This big flower may have a lovely aroma, but don't get too close or it might fold its petals shut to catch you tight! The most important step in building a giant flower is finding the right piece to go in the middle. Look for parts that can connect to a ring of petals.

IT SMELLS SO NICE HERE. MAYBE I COULD TAKE A QUICK NAP...

Clip-and-bar connections let petals close in to catch a minifigure – or to form a fairy's bed!

Each petal is made from two pieces: an angled plate and a 1x1 plate with a clip on top

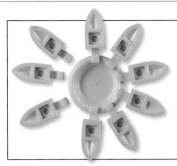

PETAL POWER

To build this flower, you only need a few types of LEGO pieces: a dinner plate element for the circular centre, and a set of petals made from tooth plates attached to 1x1 plates with clips.

TALL FLOWERS

Flowers can be even more realistic if you build them on top of stems. It may be tricky to make a stem that is tall and thin, but also sturdy and well-balanced. Here are some different ways to create them.

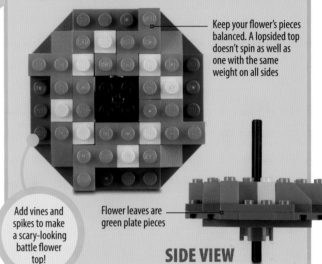

Stacked 1x1 round bricks, with slope bricks for leaves

Petals are double angled plates connected to plates with clips, which clip on to handled bars around the centre

Angled-plate leaves attach to a brick with side studs

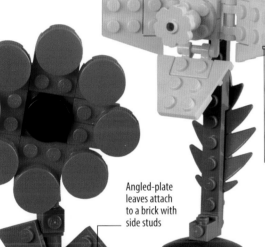

FOREST FUNGI

Decorate your fairy tale forest with mushrooms and toadstools in many sizes and colours. You could make tiny ones with small radar dishes and round bricks, or build your own giant mushrooms like this one out of bigger bricks and plates.

Build from the top down, creating descending steps in all directions

Jumper plates help to line up the pieces at the bottom

Use textured bricks for a stalk

SPINNING FLOWER TOPS

In a magic forest, flowers don't have to be attached to the ground! Why not build a flower that can spin around like a spinning top? Build some with your friends and see whose spinning tops can spin the longest, travel the furthest or knock the other forest flowers down.

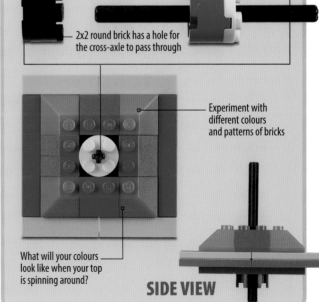

Keep your flower's pieces balanced. A lopsided top doesn't spin as well as one with the same weight on all sides

Add vines and spikes to make a scary-looking battle flower top!

Flower leaves are green plate pieces

SIDE VIEW

SECURE SPIN

Push a LEGO Technic cross-axle through the centre of your spinning top for a point on the bottom and a spinning-handle on top. Use bricks with axle holes through them to hold the cross-axle in place.

2x2 round brick has a hole for the cross-axle to pass through

Experiment with different colours and patterns of bricks

What will your colours look like when your top is spinning around?

SIDE VIEW

FAIRY TALE CREATURES

The world is an incredible place when you're on an adventure. Jack bumps into all kinds of amazing creatures on his quest! Animals and fantasy creatures bring lots of new storytelling possibilities to fairy tale models. You can add extra parts to your minifigures to make some, or build them entirely out of your bricks.

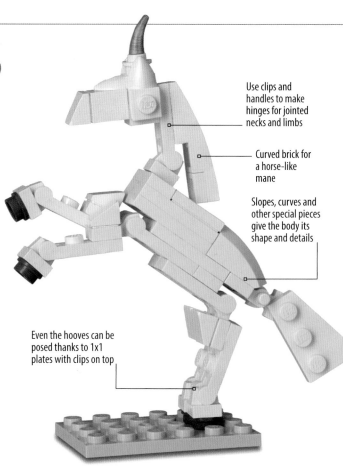

Use clips and handles to make hinges for jointed necks and limbs

Curved brick for a horse-like mane

Slopes, curves and other special pieces give the body its shape and details

Even the hooves can be posed thanks to 1x1 plates with clips on top

UNICORNS

Unicorns are usually portrayed as white horses with horns growing from their foreheads. Beyond that, the details are up to you. This posable unicorn looks like it's ready for battle!

HONK!

FEATHERED FORM

The adult swan's wings are built separately to the body. They are made up of curved bricks on top, slope bricks below, and a stacked pair of tooth plates for feathers in the back.

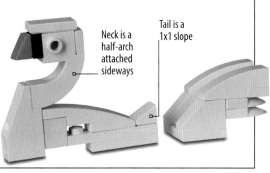

Neck is a half-arch attached sideways

Tail is a 1x1 slope

ELVES

Your stories can involve different kinds of elves, from tiny cobblers to tall and graceful warriors. These Fair Folk of the woods wear green and brown so they blend in with the trees. Will they help your hero or play mischievous tricks?

Both swans use the same bricks for their eyes and beaks, but extra pieces make the adult's head longer

A hinge base for a stubby tail

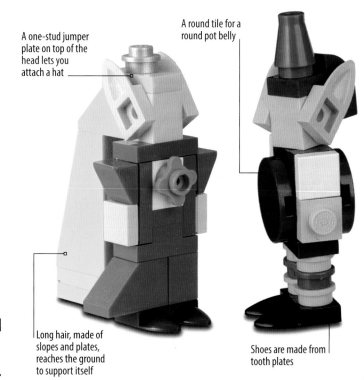

A one-stud jumper plate on top of the head lets you attach a hat

A round tile for a round pot belly

Feet are minifigure flippers

Long hair, made of slopes and plates, reaches the ground to support itself

Shoes are made from tooth plates

SWANS

Remember the ugly duckling that turned out to be a swan? You can build both! Baby animals often look cute and clumsy, with big heads, eyes and feet. A grown-up swan should have graceful curves and smooth features.

ADVENTURE ACCESSORIES

Use your bricks to create unique items for your story's minifigures. For a staff, all you need is a long handle, antenna or bar. Attach other elements to the end or clip them to the sides to make different styles.

A skull and axe blades make this look like a villain's weapon

You can include magical special effects, too!

A wise wizard might carry this ancient stone walking stick

This could be a sorcerer's staff...or add a flame in the middle for a tall torch

Try to match the colours of the hair piece and the horse body

CENTAURS

Half-horse and half-human, these galloping creatures of myth can be created by building new four-legged lower bodies with two-stud attachments on top for minifigure torsos.

Two pairs of minifigure legs make great horse legs!

Round plates for hooves

Is your centaur a scholar or a fighter? It's all in the choice of minifigure parts and accessories!

Stacks of plates and bricks for legs — or make them posable like the unicorn's

QUESTS

As your heroes travel on their fairy tale adventure, they're sure to discover challenges that test their courage and skills. They might have to cross a rickety bridge high above a lava-filled chasm, face a monster in its den or track down a king's missing treasure. Whatever quests you can imagine, you can make them come to life with your LEGO bricks.

MAGIC WELL

This could be an enchanted well that grants your wish if you drop in a brick. Or maybe it has a curse on it that turns anybody who drinks from it into a frog. Better ask the witch, to be on the safe side!

Roof shingles built from brown plates

Plates with clips make nice decorations

DOUBLE, DOUBLE, TOIL AND TROUBLE... I'VE FORGOTTEN WHAT I PUT IN THIS ONE!

OKAY, I'VE GONE UP THE HILL AND FETCHED A PAIL OF WATER. NOW WHAT?

Make a deeper well by building your structure on a raised platform

For a bucket, you could also use a barrel or a 2x2 brick

Tiles on top hold the walls together

THE MAGIC REVEALED

Just turn the lance to wind up the chain and discover the magic potion inside the well. The lance goes through bricks with holes at the tops of the support posts, and has a cone over its end at the far side so it won't slide out.

Bricks with side studs hold the roof at an angle on both sides

1x1 brick-with-hole

The round shape of the well is built with curved bricks

If you don't have a chain, try using a string

Tan side-by-side 1x4 plates blend in with the rest of the surface

Strange plants and dangerous animals make a scene appear weird and foreboding

Skull and crossbones tile from a LEGO pirate game

I WONDER WHAT THAT SIGN SAYS. OH WELL, IT CAN'T BE TOO IMPORTANT.

Use brown pieces to make a dirt trap, or white for a pit full of snow.

QUICKSAND

In a fairy tale world, you never know where you'll encounter a trick or a trap. What looks like a stretch of solid ground might really be a treacherous pit full of quicksand!

It's a good thing this adventurer checked the sand with his walking stick first!

Pull this slider to release the trap

To reset the trap, just take the 1x4 plates out and push the slider back in again

ACTION VIEW

Smooth tiles keep trap pieces from snagging on studs when you slide it out

A T-shaped end keeps the slider from being pulled out too far

SAND, QUICK!

When you pull the plate with handle on the slider, the loose 1x4 plates that are resting on top fall into the deep pit beneath – taking anyone standing there along with them!

ARGHH!

TROLL BRIDGE

"Hold it right there! If you want to cross this bridge, you'll have to pay the troll." Jack has come upon a classic fairy tale peril: an evil troll that lives under a bridge. To get past it, he might have to solve a riddle, battle his way across or distract the troll with a tasty snack. But step carefully, because this bridge has a built-in surprise!

Top plate rests on a thin lip at one end and smooth tiles at the other. Nudge it out of place and gravity takes care of the rest!

You could also make a hinged trap door, or one that works like the quicksand trap on p.23.

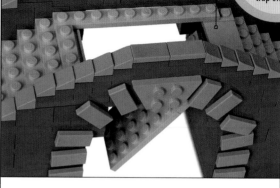

TRAP DOOR

Step in the wrong spot on top of the bridge and the secret hatch falls down, sending you tumbling into the clutches of the troll below! Some LEGO sets include trap door elements, but you can also build your own in whatever style you like.

THE BRIDGE

A bridge should be built like an arch — good and strong. This one is made out of dark grey bricks with lighter grey bricks for accent stonework. Tan bricks form steps to let a minifigure (or goat) walk up and across the span.

I CAN SEE MY HOUSE FROM HERE!

A 2x4 double angled plate for a keystone

1x1 slopes turn jagged bumps into smooth curves

Use an antenna or spear with a round brick on the end to make bulrushes

Include wetlands details such as muddy banks, plants and frogs

Does your bridge go over water? Then build a base of transparent and solid blue plates!

TROLL

This mean-tempered troll is big enough to bully a minifigure, but small enough to hide under the bridge. Add a plate with clip to his hand so he can hold a spiked club — and shake it angrily at any trespassers!

WHO'S WALKING ON MY BRIDGE? I'LL GOBBLE THEM UP, BRICKS AND ALL!

TROLLISH FEATURES

Four headlight bricks with hollow side studs make up most of the troll's square head. His little round nose is a folded-up hinge plate.

Horn pieces from a LEGO cow plug into the headlight bricks' hollow studs

Eyes are round plates from a LEGO® Games set

Hinge plate

FRONT SIDE VIEW

Spiked club comes from the LEGO Minifigures line

Arms are built out of hinges, clips and plates with handles

Clawed fingers and toes are made from tooth plates

Legs are made from 2x2 round bricks and plates

Set one foot in front of the other for a sense of movement and action

Big feet make a two-legged model more stable

QUICK BUILD

BILLY GOATS GRUFF

Each of these three billy goat brothers is bigger and tougher than the last. You can build them in two shakes of a goat's tail if you have similar pieces! First design your goat's head, then use slopes or arches lined with plates for the body, and cones and round plates for legs and feet.

Horn piece for a stubby tail

Tail piece used as a horn

Don't forget a beard for the biggest billy goat

Include features in common, like headlight brick eyes and little clippity-clop hooves

Attach cow horns to 1x1 round plates with open studs

You can use these same techniques to make little versions of big animals or big versions of little ones!

Hooves are flowers with open studs

CASTLE SIEGE

Jack hears a rumour about a kingdom that is under siege. Some people say the attackers are bandits. Some say it's a gold-hungry dragon! Here's a challenge to test both your building skill and your aim. Build a castle and use catapults to launch LEGO pieces inside. Who amongst you and your friends can get the most bricks over the wall?

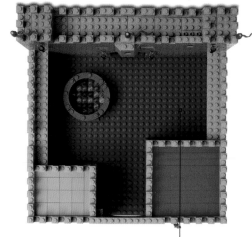

TOP VIEW

Get 1 point for landing your brick in the courtyard

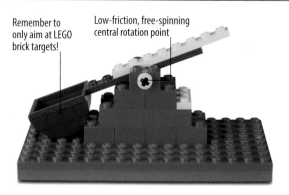

Remember to only aim at LEGO brick targets!

Low-friction, free-spinning central rotation point

SIEGE PLANS

Your castle should have a high wall and a central courtyard where you want the launched pieces to land. For an extra challenge, build coloured tower platforms and award extra points for hitting more difficult targets!

See p.40 for more tips on building castles!

CATAPULTS

Assemble a catapult and use it to toss 1x1 round bricks over the castle walls. Here are some ideas to get you started – what will yours look like?

Experiment with different heights and arm lengths to get your catapult just right

Wheels let you move a catapult around quickly

Use 1x1 round bricks for your catapult ammunition

Include a basket or bucket to hold the ammunition

A sturdy base keeps a catapult steady when it's fired

A long throwing arm acts like a lever to fling the bricks

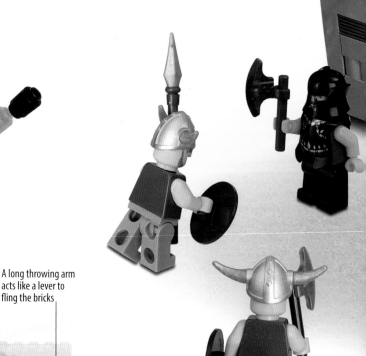

If you don't have the pieces to build a castle, you could make anything you like – even just a simple ring.

Get 4 points for getting your brick through the castle door

What happens if you hit these torches? That's up to you!

Get 5 points for landing your brick in the little well – the toughest shot of all!

Get 3 points for landing your brick on the green tower

Get 2 points for landing your brick on the red tower

INCOMING BRICK... EVERYBODY DUCK!

IT'S YOUR JOB TO SNEAK INTO THE CASTLE AND BRING BACK THE MISSILES.

BAH!

Get a bonus point if your brick goes through the gateway instead of over the wall

Building on a big base plate will help keep your castle walls stable

Use coloured plates or tiles to mark special target zones

Try attaching ammunition-blocking defences to the castle battlements, such as knights with shields.

GIANTS

When Jack climbed up a beanstalk, he never expected that he'd discover a land in the clouds, much less one filled with hungry giants! If you're tired of tussling with trolls, then try a giant on for size. These fee-fi-fo-fearsome creatures are really tough because they can be as smart as a human (or a minifigure), but they're a whole lot bigger and stronger.

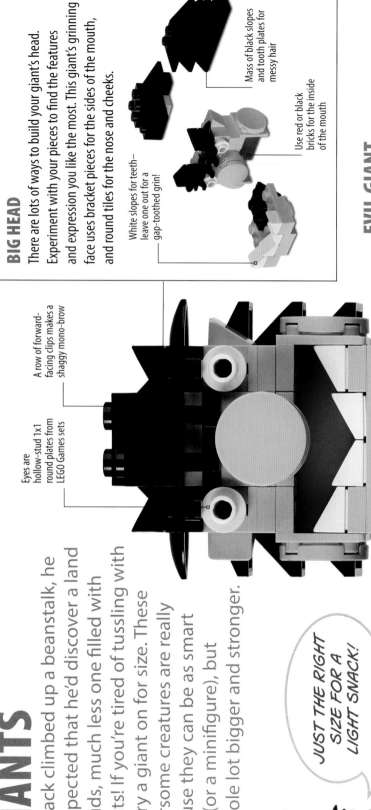

BIG HEAD

There are lots of ways to build your giant's head. Experiment with your pieces to find the features and expression you like the most. This giant's grinning face uses bracket pieces for the sides of the mouth, and round tiles for the nose and cheeks.

Mass of black slopes and tooth plates for messy hair

Use red or black bricks for the inside of the mouth

White slopes for teeth— leave one out for a gap-toothed grin!

A row of forward-facing clips makes a shaggy mono-brow

Eyes are hollow-stud 1x1 round plates from LEGO Games sets

EVIL GIANT

Better run, Jack — this giant's legs are a lot longer than yours! They are attached to LEGO Technic bricks with ball joints to make them posable. All giants are tall, but they are also individuals, so give your giants all kinds of different faces, clothes and body shapes.

Tunic is shaped by slope bricks

Bones for shirt toggles

Use ball-and-socket pieces from LEGO buildable action figures to create articulated arms

A giant-sized belt to hold up giant-sized pants!

SIDE VIEW

JUST THE RIGHT SIZE FOR A LIGHT SNACK!

EEK!

You can also use basic bricks and hinges for bendable arms

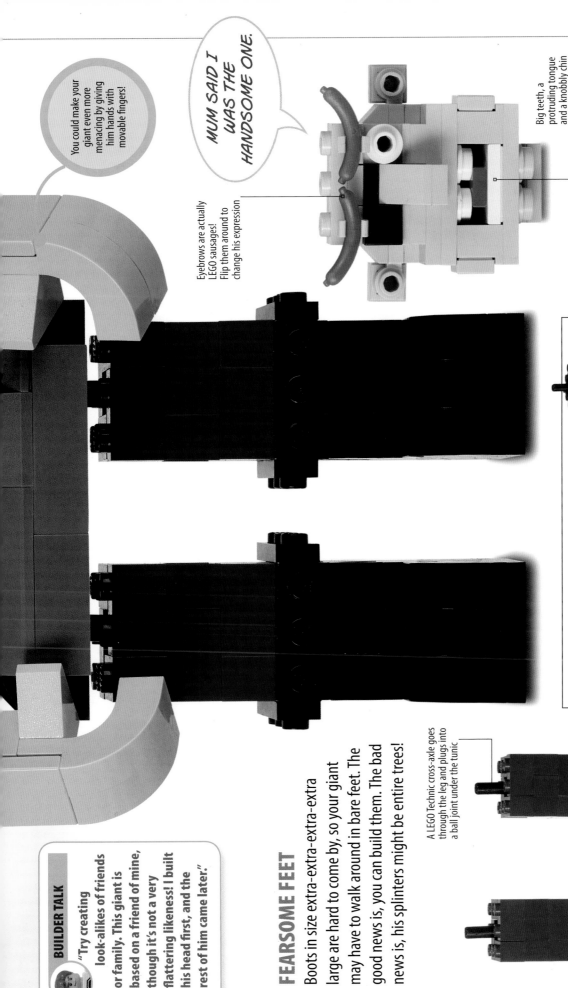

You could make your giant even more menacing by giving him hands with movable fingers!

MUM SAID I WAS THE HANDSOME ONE.

Eyebrows are actually LEGO sausages! Flip them around to change his expression

Big teeth, a protruding tongue and a knobbly chin give this giant a whimsical look

OFF WITH HIS HEAD

Here's another giant head made with a different selection of parts. You can build your own giants to be as mean, friendly or goofy as you want. It all depends on the pieces you have and the story you're telling.

Make the little toe shorter than the rest

Big toe is plugged into a small clip, which attaches to a bar on the end of a plate

ANATOMY OF A FOOT

The bottom of the foot is built like a wall flipped onto its side. It is attached to the top of the foot using bricks with side studs. The big toe is an undecorated minifigure head piece, and the other toes are 1x1 round bricks.

FEARSOME FEET

Boots in size extra-extra-extra-extra large are hard to come by, so your giant may have to walk around in bare feet. The good news is, you can build them. The bad news is, his splinters might be entire trees!

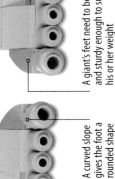

A LEGO Technic cross-axle goes through the leg and plugs into a ball joint under the tunic

A giant's feet need to be wide and sturdy enough to support his or her weight

A curved slope gives the foot a rounded shape

GIANT'S KITCHEN

As Jack explores the land of the giants, he starts to feel a bit like a mouse. Everything here is so huge! Don't just build a giant for your adventure – construct a whole world for it. What kind of furniture and tools would exist in a giant's home? Does your giant use regular-sized objects in new ways, like a sword for a butter knife or a lion for a house pet?

ROAST CHICKEN

For an appetising dinner, use curved bricks and tiles to hide the studs. LEGO Technic pins let the drumsticks attach at an angle, and pop right off if your giant is feeling hungry!

LEGO dinner plates will work for small dishes, but for big ones, make your own!

NOW WHERE HAS THAT LITTLE MORSEL GONE?

CHAIR

Can you match the look of your table and chairs? This chair has a wooden frame of brown bricks and plates, with tan grilles in the seat to make a wicker pattern. Just like the table, the legs are topped with minifigure skulls.

A radar dish, an antenna and a dome make a fine candlestick

A green LEGO® EXO-FORCE™ hair piece resembles a leafy head of cabbage

Bones are the remains of previous meals

A whole barrel can be a giant's drinking cup

GULP

Tabletop made from overlapping plates

DINNER TABLE

Building a giant table is just like building a small one: it needs four sturdy legs and a big flat top. Look for the biggest pieces in your collection, or assemble it in sections from lots of small bricks.

Attach transparent 1x1 round plates to one-stud jumper plates to make bubbles

Have you heard of being in hot water? This is even worse!

SOUP'S ON!

What's in the pot? An upper surface of green tiles, some vegetables made from more LEGO EXO-FORCE hair (this giant likes his greens!), and a secret ingredient or two. You can use any pieces and colours you like for your giant's stew.

LEGO carrots can be found in many farm and house LEGO sets

COOKING POT

No hero wants to land in a giant's pot, but imagine the adventure you can have getting back out! This pot could be found in the forest or the kitchen of the giant's castle. It could work for a witch's cauldron, too.

FIRE PIT

Build wood for a giant's bonfire just like you would make sections of a tree trunk (see p.16) – after all, that's exactly what they are! The logs and flames in this model are attached with brackets and clips.

You could build a roasting spit instead, or even some sticks with giant-sized marshmallows!

HEY! WHEN I ASKED IF I COULD HELP MAKE THE STEW, I WASN'T VOLUNTEERING TO BE PART OF IT!

Use plenty of flame pieces to make a roaring fire

A rough, uneven shape makes the fire pit look simple and crude

Use long LEGO Technic cross-axles to make poles, and hang the pot from them with chains

Iron pot built by stepping bricks up and out to make a cup shape

Include a pile of small black pieces in the centre for ash and charcoal

Build up the outside of the pit with angled plates and round bricks to contain the blaze

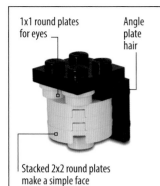

1x1 round plates for eyes

Angle plate hair

Stacked 2x2 round plates make a simple face

PLAY OPTIONS

Think about how you want to play with your brick character. Build some extra body parts to swap in and give your characters different looks and poses. This knight also has an unhelmeted head for when he doesn't have to stand guard at the castle!

There are lots of ways to build a helmet. Create some different designs of your own!

Armour built out of curved and angled pieces

FAIRY TALE CHARACTERS

Your fairy tale doesn't have to just star minifigures. You can use your bricks to build bigger and more detailed characters, too. They can be as colourful and as fantastical as you like! You can even mix them in scenes with minifigures so they become super-sized heroes.

Side stud bricks for hands allow the knight to hold his sword and shield

Sword blade is a long, round column, but you could build a stack of 1x1 round bricks

Small radar dish for the shield's central boss

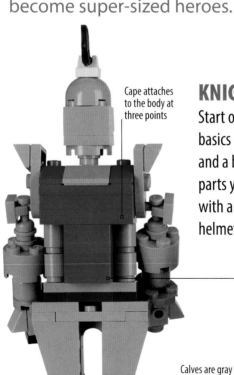

Cape attaches to the body at three points

KNIGHT

Start out a brick character with the basics – a head, two arms, two legs, and a body – and then add any other parts you want. This knight is equipped with a sword, a shield, a cape, and a helmet with a fancy feather plume.

Calves are gray minifigure heads

REAR VIEW

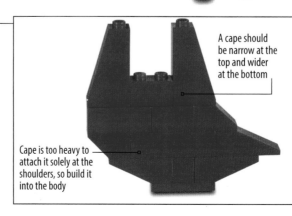

A cape should be narrow at the top and wider at the bottom

Cape is too heavy to attach it solely at the shoulders, so build it into the body

BRICKS IN MOTION

Solid bricks can be used to create dynamic motion. The knight's cape is built just like a LEGO brick wall, with slopes and inverted slopes to give it a swooshing shape, as if it is being blown by the wind.

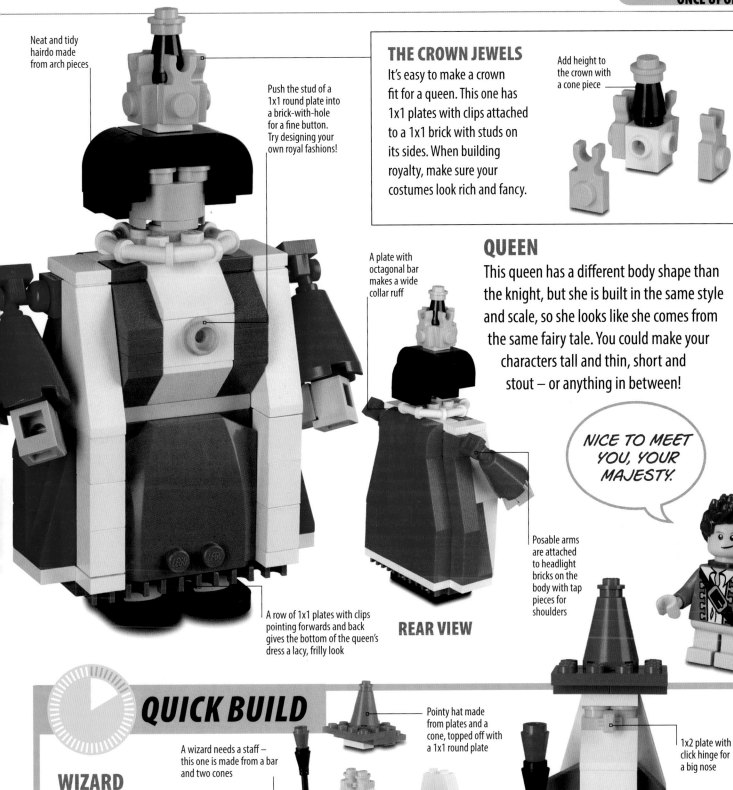

Neat and tidy hairdo made from arch pieces

Push the stud of a 1x1 round plate into a brick-with-hole for a fine button. Try designing your own royal fashions!

THE CROWN JEWELS

It's easy to make a crown fit for a queen. This one has 1x1 plates with clips attached to a 1x1 brick with studs on its sides. When building royalty, make sure your costumes look rich and fancy.

Add height to the crown with a cone piece

A plate with octagonal bar makes a wide collar ruff

QUEEN

This queen has a different body shape than the knight, but she is built in the same style and scale, so she looks like she comes from the same fairy tale. You could make your characters tall and thin, short and stout — or anything in between!

NICE TO MEET YOU, YOUR MAJESTY.

Posable arms are attached to headlight bricks on the body with tap pieces for shoulders

REAR VIEW

A row of 1x1 plates with clips pointing forwards and back gives the bottom of the queen's dress a lacy, frilly look

QUICK BUILD

Pointy hat made from plates and a cone, topped off with a 1x1 round plate

1x2 plate with click hinge for a big nose

A wizard needs a staff — this one is made from a bar and two cones

WIZARD

You don't need a magic wand to build this model! A simple wizard can be built in a flash if you have similar pieces. Slope bricks build up the majority of the body and the hair.

Create a cloak with a car roof

UNDERSEA CHARACTERS

While taking a swim, Jack is so surprised that he almost forgets to hold his breath…there are people living under the sea! The seas of a fairy tale world are brimming with mythical, magical creatures, from krakens and sea serpents to mermaids and mermen. If you don't have any mer-minifigures, don't flounder about – use your bricks to build some!

MY HAIRSTYLE? I LIKE TO GO FOR THE WET LOOK.

Curved and clip pieces make her hair look wild and wave-tossed

1x2 curved half-arch piece for a curving forearm

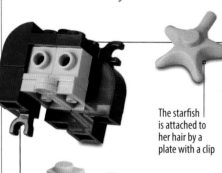

MER-CONSTRUCTION

The mermaid's mouth is three stacked jumper plates in front of two headlight bricks, her rounded nose is a folded hinge plate, and her eyes are two more headlight bricks.

The starfish is attached to her hair by a plate with a clip

A plate with side ring can hold a hairbrush

Seashells are a traditional underwater fashion

Build in a 1x1 round plate for a bellybutton!

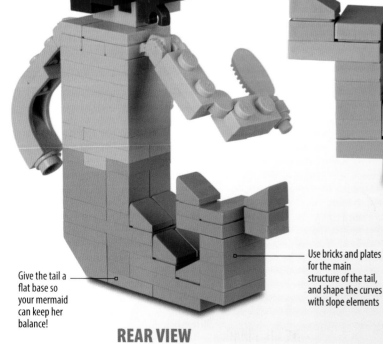

Use bricks and plates for the main structure of the tail, and shape the curves with slope elements

Give the tail a flat base so your mermaid can keep her balance!

REAR VIEW

MERMAID

Building a mermaid is like building any other fairy tale character, except that she has a tail instead of legs. Search through your collection for sea-themed accessories that you can use to give your mermaid her own unique, aquatic style.

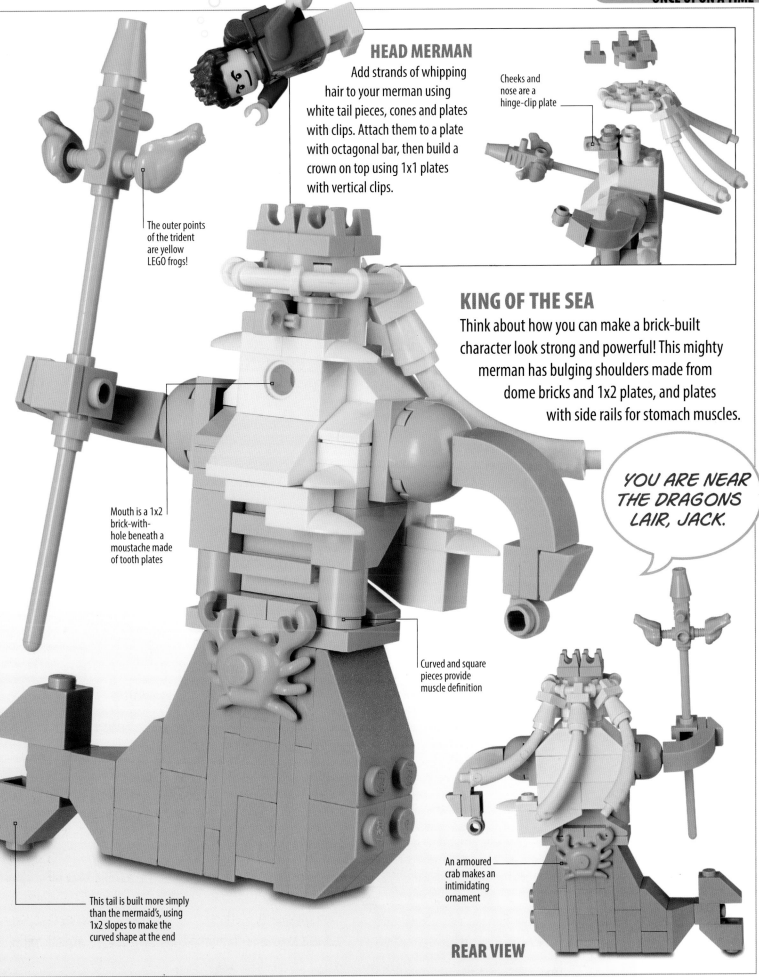

HEAD MERMAN
Add strands of whipping hair to your merman using white tail pieces, cones and plates with clips. Attach them to a plate with octagonal bar, then build a crown on top using 1x1 plates with vertical clips.

Cheeks and nose are a hinge-clip plate

The outer points of the trident are yellow LEGO frogs!

KING OF THE SEA
Think about how you can make a brick-built character look strong and powerful! This mighty merman has bulging shoulders made from dome bricks and 1x2 plates, and plates with side rails for stomach muscles.

Mouth is a 1x2 brick-with-hole beneath a moustache made of tooth plates

YOU ARE NEAR THE DRAGONS LAIR, JACK.

Curved and square pieces provide muscle definition

An armoured crab makes an intimidating ornament

This tail is built more simply than the mermaid's, using 1x2 slopes to make the curved shape at the end

REAR VIEW

DRAGON

Jack never dreamed that his search for the Royal Nugget would lead him to the cave of a fire-breathing dragon! He will have to rely on all of his luck and courage (and some help from a fearless dragon catcher) to get out of this in one piece. Defeating a dragon can be the ultimate quest for a hero. Build yours with lots of teeth, scales and spikes – and don't forget a big pair of wings.

Gems aren't just for treasure – these ones make the dragon's big, glowing eyes!

Horn elements can attach to clips and bricks with hollow studs to make spikes and frills

FIRE BREATH

Smaller LEGO flame pieces plug into small brick holes, and bigger ones can attach to LEGO Technic cross-axle holes. Build pieces with attachment points into your dragon's head for a fiery-breath attack!

Neck joints are made with clips and handles

What reason will your hero have to brave the dragon's lair?

HEY, BIG AND SCALY! LOOK OVER HERE!

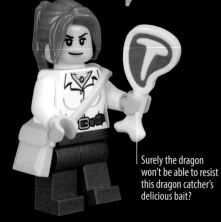

BUILDING A DRAGON

You can build a dragon in any size, shape or colour – it's your fairy tale! Design your dragon's head first, and then the neck and body. Add a tail, wings and legs next, making sure it isn't too heavy or off-balance to stand up. Then give it lots of spikes and other ferocious details!

Add taloned toes to your dragon's feet

Surely the dragon won't be able to resist this dragon catcher's delicious bait?

Look through your collection for gold and silver elements, jewels, swords, crowns and other precious items

HEAD DESIGNS

The dragon's head can inspire the rest of the body, so it's a good place to start building. Here are some head ideas for a long-horned blue dragon, an Asian-style green dragon and a majestic golden dragon.

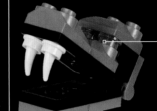

Neck spikes plug into 2x2 round plates

Use plenty of hinges to make your dragon super-posable!

Transparent round plates for eyes

Wings are built out of overlapping angled plates to give them their shape

Use pointy white pieces for horns or fangs

TOP VIEW

SHHHHHH!

Tail spikes plug into jumper plates

Jack has found the Royal Nugget under the dragon's foot!

LEGO Technic pin helps to rotate the knee joint

WINGS

All the scariest dragons have the power of flight! This dragon's vast wings are braced by LEGO Technic cross-axles inside the body, which hold the ball joints in place and allow them to pose and flap. The ball and socket pieces need to be locked in place solidly so they don't pop loose.

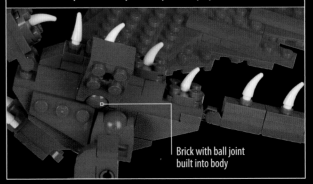

The tail is built out of segments held together by clip hinges to let each one swing up and down

Brick with ball joint built into body

HANDFUL OF BRICKS

Each of the fan builders was given a handful of common LEGO elements and asked to make as many different models as they could using only those pieces. Here's what Barney came up with.

Pieces with printed eyes are great for making expressive animals and people

Posing the tail at an angle gives it a sense of life and movement

WHO? WHO?

MINI DRAGON

You have already met Barney's evil dragon — now here's a much friendlier-looking one, made mostly out of red bricks. Perhaps it could keep Jack company on his adventures!

ME, THAT'S WHO!

OWL

With its big eyes and upraised wings, this owl looks pretty surprised! Barney used a printed radar dish element for its round, feathery tummy.

Placing the brick at an angle gives baby bird's shell a nice dimension

BABY BIRD

This baby bird has just popped out of its shell! A foot at the bottom will let it hop around until it's ready to hatch all the way.

A smaller 2x2 radar dish looks like a budding flower

BEE AND FLOWER

With a tap for a nose and an antenna for a stinger, Barney's bee is all abuzz about this flower. The same radar dish that gave the owl colourful feathers gives this flower delicate petals!

Sandwich a plate between two bricks to make a stripe

Angled plates are perfect for creating wings on small models

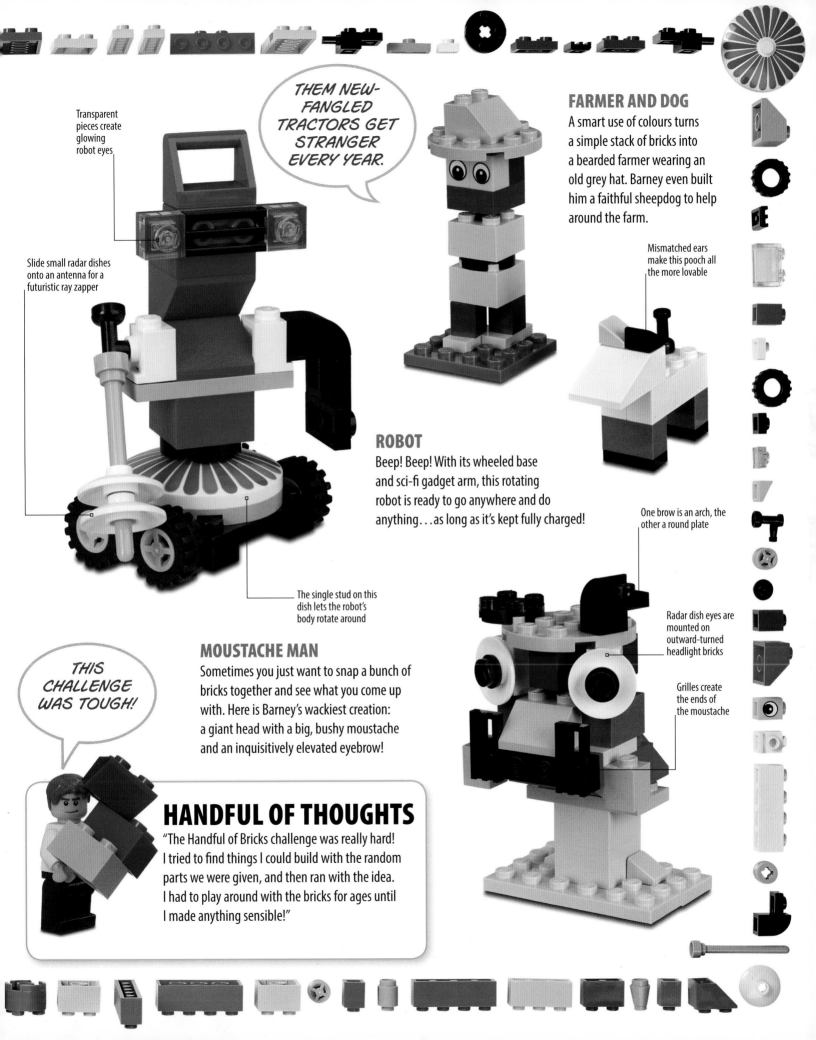

Transparent pieces create glowing robot eyes

THEM NEW-FANGLED TRACTORS GET STRANGER EVERY YEAR.

FARMER AND DOG

A smart use of colours turns a simple stack of bricks into a bearded farmer wearing an old grey hat. Barney even built him a faithful sheepdog to help around the farm.

Slide small radar dishes onto an antenna for a futuristic ray zapper

Mismatched ears make this pooch all the more lovable

ROBOT

Beep! Beep! With its wheeled base and sci-fi gadget arm, this rotating robot is ready to go anywhere and do anything...as long as it's kept fully charged!

One brow is an arch, the other a round plate

The single stud on this dish lets the robot's body rotate around

MOUSTACHE MAN

Sometimes you just want to snap a bunch of bricks together and see what you come up with. Here is Barney's wackiest creation: a giant head with a big, bushy moustache and an inquisitively elevated eyebrow!

Radar dish eyes are mounted on outward-turned headlight bricks

Grilles create the ends of the moustache

THIS CHALLENGE WAS TOUGH!

HANDFUL OF THOUGHTS

"The Handful of Bricks challenge was really hard! I tried to find things I could build with the random parts we were given, and then ran with the idea. I had to play around with the bricks for ages until I made anything sensible!"

FAIRY TALE CASTLE

Recovering the Royal Nugget has earned Jack an invitation to the king's castle. While real medieval castles were usually built to keep enemy armies out, and were more practical than beautiful, the castle of a fairy tale kingdom can be colourful and ornate. Give it elegant peaked turrets, festive flags and banners and decorative designs that show off the magic and majesty of your fantasy kingdom.

Pennant flags can be found in castle-themed LEGO sets – or build your own out of plates and clips!

TURRET

Make your castle's turrets hollow with strong walls and an opening door so you can easily place minifigures inside. Will you put a palace guard or a captured prisoner in there?

Arches support the weight of the turrets from underneath

Studs on the floor stop the door from swinging too far in

Turret cones are built from the top down, stepping out each lower layer

Battlement crenellations are 1x2 bricks topped with 1x1 slopes

Bricks in the middle of the turret cone keep it strong

Alternate round and square pieces to make columns around windows

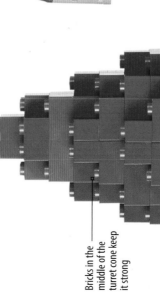

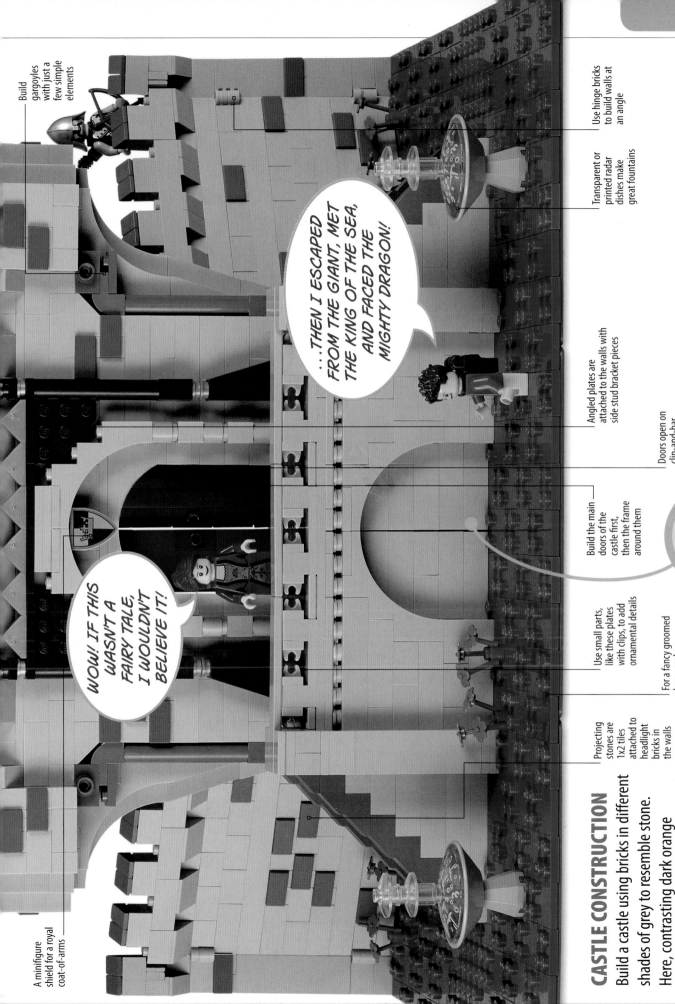

Build gargoyles with just a few simple elements

A minifigure shield for a royal coat-of-arms

Use hinge bricks to build walls at an angle

Transparent or printed radar dishes make great fountains

...THEN I ESCAPED FROM THE GIANT, MET THE KING OF THE SEA, AND FACED THE MIGHTY DRAGON!

WOW! IF THIS WASN'T A FAIRY TALE, I WOULDN'T BELIEVE IT!

Angled plates are attached to the walls with side stud bracket pieces

Doors open on clip-and-bar hinges

Build the main doors of the castle first, then the frame around them

What secret does this balcony hide? Turn the page to find out!

Use small parts, like these plates with clips, to add ornamental details

For a fancy groomed lawn, make a checkerboard pattern of green 2x2 plates and tiles

Projecting stones are 1x2 tiles attached to headlight bricks in the walls

CASTLE CONSTRUCTION

Build a castle using bricks in different shades of grey to resemble stone. Here, contrasting dark orange brickwork adds texture and realism. More light grey pieces will make it look friendly, while dark grey will create a foreboding appearance.

BUILDER TALK

"Take inspiration from a mixture of your favourite books. This castle design was inspired by the castle in the fairy tale *Cinderella*, with a lawn based on the Queen of Hearts's castle in Lewis Carroll's *Alice in Wonderland*."

MEET THE KING

Jack finds that even an old stone castle can be full of excitement. Not only does he meet a king, he is also given his very own fairy godmother! Building special features into your fairy tale castle will help you to tell even better stories with your bricks and minifigures. How about giving your castle a damsel in a tower, an ogre in the basement or a secret treasure chamber?

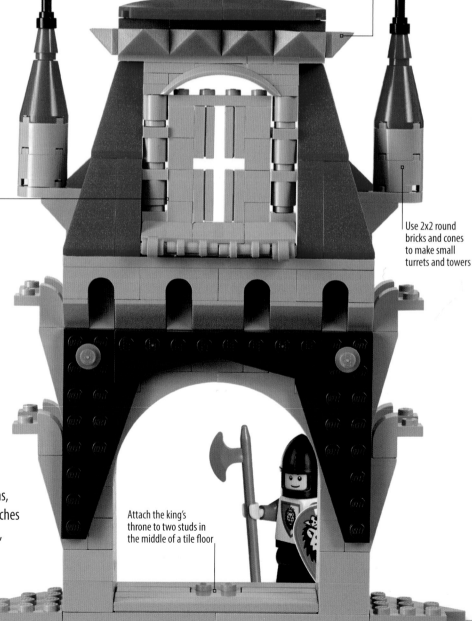

Steep pointed roof is made with slopes and cones on top of 4x4 car roof pieces

HIS MAJESTY'S TOWER

Some kings have huge throne rooms, but this one prefers a spot high in his castle where he can see the entire kingdom. The royal blue and gold around the archway tells all who behold it that their king is watching over them.

Gold, triangular slopes make a crown-like ring

ARROW SLIT

Many fairy tale castles have narrow windows to let archers inside fire at enemies outside. Combine 1x1 bricks and tiles, then add decorative columns built from 1x1 round bricks. Hold them in place with 2x3 curved plates with holes.

2x3 curved plate with holes

Use 2x2 round bricks and cones to make small turrets and towers

Jewels add the finishing touch to the royal throne

ROYAL THRONE

The royal throne is no mere chair! Flanked by gold swords and topped by a trio of jewels mounted on golden robot arms, this one is fit for a king. It attaches to the tower on just two studs, so it's easy to get in and out.

Attach the king's throne to two studs in the middle of a tile floor

PEGASUS

A messenger on a winged horse travels the length of the kingdom to spread the news that the nugget has been found by a boy named Jack! Build your own flying steed by adding wings made of angled plates and clip hinges to a LEGO horse.

HUZZAH FOR JACK THE HERO!

Angled plates held together with sliding plates

Minifigure attaches to studs on the horse's back

I GRANT YOU THREE WISHES!

A glowing magic wand, a crown and a kindly expression show that this fairy is a friend

Wings are overlapping angled plates attached to a minifigure neck bracket piece

If you don't have a decorated dress piece, you can use a plain slope brick instead

FAIRY GODMOTHER

This friendly fairy godmother will bestow Jack's reward for finding the nugget. She has three wishes for Jack to do with as he pleases! Your fairy could be good or evil. Use colours, faces and wing shapes to decide which yours is.

TREASURE CHAMBER

Sliding doors beneath the entrance conceal the castle's secret treasure chamber. Perhaps Jack's brave deeds will have earned him an item of his choice. Flickering candles and hanging spiderwebs can create a creepy atmosphere.

Instead of treasure, this chamber could house a powerful beast or knightly guardian to protect the castle!

Treasure chests are found in many LEGO castle and pirate sets – or build your own!

THANKS FOR GETTING OUR TREASURE BACK FROM THAT BIG LIZARD, JACK!

MOVING WALL

These secret panels are built to match the castle walls, but they're not locked into position. A base of smooth tiles beneath lets them slide back and forth, while pillars hold the sliding walls in place so they don't fall forwards.

A row of tiles conceals the top of the door but leaves it free to move

Pillars made from a 1x2x5 brick and two 1x2 bricks

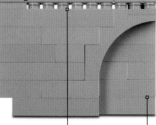

Add detail to the door with 1x1 round plates

Archway detail hints at the secret chamber beyond

CASTLE COMFORTS

Jack has never seen so much wealth in one place before. Palace life is definitely the life for him! Your castle's royal residents are used to luxury, so build them some of the finer things in life. A good use of colour goes a long way in making brick-built objects look expensive, and don't forget the fancy ornamentation.

FOUR-POSTER BED

For inspiration in building old-fashioned furniture, look in a storybook...or a history book! With its resplendently thick mattress, softly curving sheets, and sparkling gems, this covered bed is truly fit for a princess.

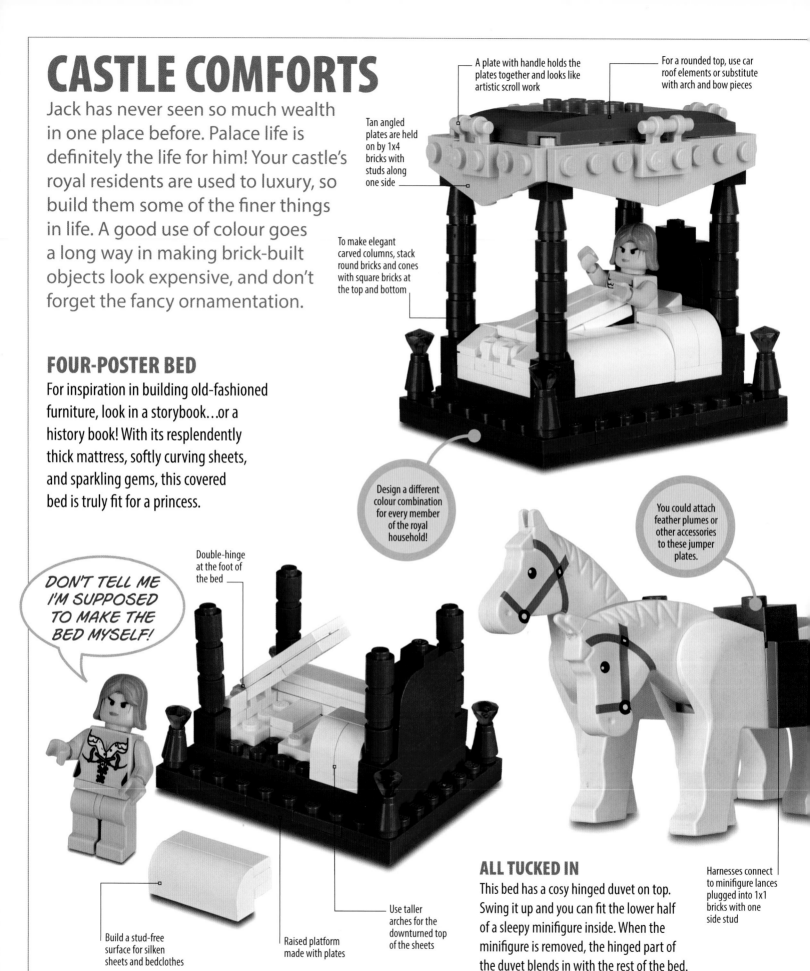

A plate with handle holds the plates together and looks like artistic scroll work

For a rounded top, use car roof elements or substitute with arch and bow pieces

Tan angled plates are held on by 1x4 bricks with studs along one side

To make elegant carved columns, stack round bricks and cones with square bricks at the top and bottom

Design a different colour combination for every member of the royal household!

DON'T TELL ME I'M SUPPOSED TO MAKE THE BED MYSELF!

Double-hinge at the foot of the bed

You could attach feather plumes or other accessories to these jumper plates.

Build a stud-free surface for silken sheets and bedclothes

Raised platform made with plates

Use taller arches for the downturned top of the sheets

ALL TUCKED IN

This bed has a cosy hinged duvet on top. Swing it up and you can fit the lower half of a sleepy minifigure inside. When the minifigure is removed, the hinged part of the duvet blends in with the rest of the bed.

Harnesses connect to minifigure lances plugged into 1x1 bricks with one side stud

COOL BRICK

"This versatile brick adds fancy decoration to the royal carriage. It has also been used on the cottage (p.14) and castle (p.40) – can you spot where?"

REMOVABLE ROOF

Make the roof removable by clicking it onto just a few studs, so that you can move your characters around inside the carriage. This one rests its weight on the front supports, but only attaches at the back.

A tile bears the weight of the roof at the front

Interior colour matches the outside trim

White bricks make a model look like it's made of polished marble, ivory or painted wood

Roof provides shade and privacy

Decorative flowers on top

ROYAL CARRIAGE

A basic carriage has big round wheels, horses to pull it and spots for the driver and passengers to sit. For a royal carriage, add lots of curves, slopes and decorations. You could make other modifications to create prison carriages, mail coaches and racing buggies.

Roof supports built like shorter versions of the four-poster bed columns

Make sure your carriage's wheels have enough clearance to turn without bumping the sides

STEERING WHEELS

This carriage is built in two sections. The front part where the coachman sits is connected to the passenger portion with a 2x2 turntable plate, allowing the front wheels to steer and navigate winding roads.

These large wagon wheels can be found in many castle-themed LEGO sets

A turntable plate lets the back half of the carriage move separately

1x1 bricks with side studs are under these tiles

The wheel is attached with a free-spinning LEGO Technic pin

CASTLE STABLES

Feed the horses…sweep the stables…
there's so much work for Jack to do
around the palace! Every good castle
has horses to pull its carriages and carry
its knights, and those horses need
somewhere to rest when they're not on
duty. Build a strong wooden stable to
house your kingdom's loyal steeds in
the safety and comfort
they deserve.

WATER TROUGH

This whole trough is built
around a core of two 1x1
bricks with four side studs.
For the trough's long sides,
use one 2x4 tile or two 2x2
tiles, and 1x2 tiles for the
short sides. Add water
for thirsty horses by
using a blue 1x4 tile.

Switch out the blue tile for
a different colour to make
a food trough instead!

LEFT SIDE VIEW

REAR VIEW

Yellow 2x2 bricks serve
as bales of hay for the
horses' mealtime

Rear wall mixes dark
grey bricks with dark
tan 1x2 log bricks for
a stone-and-wood
appearance

RAISE THE ROOF

Enhance the play potential of your stable by building it with a
removable roof. This stable's roof is only attached at two points
on the back wall, so it can be removed completely. The roof can
also be flipped back for play thanks to LEGO Technic bricks and pins.

You can use curved
barred fences to build
secondary enclosures

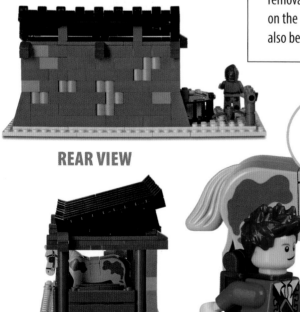

CAN THESE
HORSES
TALK?

RIGHT SIDE VIEW

The king's knights
can mount up at this
hitching post, built
from 1x1 round bricks
and headlight bricks

I LIKE TO FENCE!

FENCING

Add strong fencing to your stables so your horses don't bolt! The wooden slats of this stable's fences are made from brown tiles turned on their sides and attached to stacks of headlight bricks.

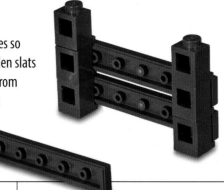

THE ROYAL STABLE

Stables are usually built to be plain and serviceable. Since the structure has so many open areas, take care to make the roof well-supported by the back wall and pillars. Include wide gates so the king's royal horses can get in and out with ease.

Roof is textured with a repeating pattern of tiles and 1x1 slopes

A farmer's stable might only have space for one or two horses, but a castle's stables need plenty of room for all the king's horses!

An overlapping framework of plates supports the roof and holds the pillars in place

NEIGH!

Single-piece round columns in the corners are stronger than stacks of individual bricks

A tan base looks like mud – or use yellow for scattered straw

Gates are attached to clips to let them swing open

47

CASTLE ENTERTAINMENT

Walking through the castle grounds, Jack stumbles upon the preparations for the grand ball that will be held in his honour. When he hears the musicians practising their songs, he can't help but join in! Kings and queens have a lot of responsibilities, and one of them is keeping all of their guests entertained. Make sure your fairy tale castle is well-stocked with food, entertainment and party supplies.

Lay long tiles across for a flat top

A yellow 1x1 plate with clip stands in for pedals

Keys are a row of white grilles

UPRIGHT PIANO

An upright piano is built like a series of walls assembled together, so use bricks and shape elements such as slopes and cones to recreate its design.

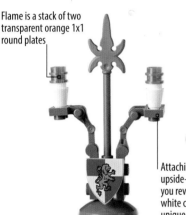

Flame is a stack of two transparent orange 1x1 round plates

Candle stand is a small barrel

Attach stand and side-branches to bricks with side studs

Attaching this plate upside-down lets you reverse the white cone for a unique candle shape

Almost any piece can become part of a candlestick. These arms are handles from a pair of ninja nunchuks

CANDLESTICKS

To make candlesticks, look through your smallest pieces and see what you have in the same colour, then combine them in interesting ways. Use white 1x1 round bricks or cones as candles, and transparent orange, red or yellow pieces for flames.

HIC!

A LEGO Technic half-beam holds the stand and barrel together

EVERYBODY READY? A-ONE, A-TWO AND...

Make sure your musicians have a way to hold their instruments!

BEVERAGE BARREL

On its own, a half-barrel piece makes a handy washing basin or medieval bathtub. When you connect two together with a LEGO Technic axle-with-stud, then add a tap and stand, you've got a beverage barrel large enough for the biggest castle party!

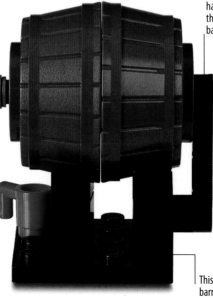

This stand stops the barrel from rolling away

GRAND PIANO

A grand piano takes a little more work. If this design is too complex, you can simplify things by using regular bricks. Give the pianist somewhere to sit, and provide a few refreshments for long performances!

A small radar dish does double-duty as the teapot's lid and base

Teapot has a cow's horn for a handle and a horn for a spout

Use white elements for fine china

> IF YOU CAN HUM IT, I WILL PLAY IT!

A pianist's stool can be made with tiles, a plate beneath and a radar dish for a stand

Keys are black grilles and a white tile

CASTLE BAND

Build your own musical instruments for the band. Look at real instruments and see how you can copy their shapes with your LEGO elements. You can stick to authentic medieval instruments, but since this is a fairy tale, you don't have to!

Use screwdrivers or bars as drumsticks

Centre drums are made from sliding plates and upside-down domes

MAKE SOME MUSIC

The front and middle of the grand piano are fairly basic builds. The back is constructed sideways, using bricks and plates for the core. The curves are made from small and medium arches.

A tile with a printed scroll works well for sheet music

Each leg is built with a 1x1 round brick, round plate and a square plate

Saxophone is made from two taps, a goblet, a 1x1 plate with clip, and a round plate on the bottom

> ♫ JACK! JACK! I'M A LEGO MANIAC! ♫

CASTLE BALLROOM

Here in the castle's grand ballroom, Jack almost feels like a prince himself. A ballroom makes a great story setting for medieval minifigures who want to party. It can include places for characters to sing and dance, eat and drink, and give speeches or play music. It's also a good location for daring swordfights and rescuing damsels in distress.

Attach tiles to bricks with side studs for trim around columns and wall edges

STAIRCASE

This railing design is made of 1x1 slopes on top of pairs of 1x1 round plates, with a 1x1 square plate underneath

Your ballroom's staircase can be as tall, wide, long or short as you want it to be. Build the sides a little higher than the steps, and add detail bricks on top for a decorative railing.

Each level of the staircase is two plates higher than the last one

Create mood with colour. A bold black-and-red ballroom could belong to an evil tyrant!

THEY CALL ME TWINKLE TOES ON THE DANCE FLOOR.

BUILDER TALK

"I got the idea for this ballroom model from an animated fairy tale movie. I had to stop myself from putting in even more detail!"

HELP! CAN ANYONE READ SHEET MUSIC?

HAVE A BALL!

A castle ballroom should be vast and well-lit. Create a wide-open look by building your ballroom's floor and walls in light colours. Add lavish decorations such as carpets, statues, and wall hangings – plus a big central staircase so your guests can make a royal entrance.

Make a pattern with studded plates for a thickly carpeted dance floor, or use smooth tiles for something a little shinier

Use a different colour and some inverted-slope elements to turn a projecting layer of wall into a big curtain around the window

Telescopes make great hanging tassels!

GREAT WINDOW

Build a big window to let light flood in! Try stacking small windows together to make a large one, or build a wall out of coloured transparent bricks for a beautiful stained glass window.

If you don't have enough small window pieces, build a hollow frame instead

STATUES

Combine minifigure parts in solid colours to make gargoyles and other statues for your castle interior. Grey, for stone, looks most realistic, but you can use any colour you like.

Lampstand is built out of an upside-down spear, two LEGO® Space laser guns, and a brick with studs on its side to hold them together – plus matching flames!

Gargoyle's face is an alien mask from the LEGO® Space Police theme

A TOAST TO OUR NEW FRIEND JACK!

Roll out the red carpet for your minifigures by building a strip of red plates down the centre of the stairs

A double-layered base gives your model strength and stability, and lets you make the carpet on the same level as the ballroom floor

Have you ever wanted to build something big, but didn't have enough bricks? Try making it in micro-scale! By shrinking down the scale of your models, you can create vehicles, buildings and entire landscapes, all in a smaller size. In this section, you'll find ideas for making the most of even your tiniest LEGO® elements.

A SMALL WORLD

TINY TRAVEL

When you are as small as the Gnome, it's easy for people to overlook you. That's why he likes micro-scale building so much. It makes him feel like he is enormous! The Gnome might usually be a tiny creature in a big world, but when he switches to micro-scale, he can be the biggest thing around. Join him on his travels through LEGO® models that recreate the past, present, and future…all in miniature form!

> GNOME TO MARS BASE: I'M ABOUT TO LAND.

> FROM SMALL BEGINNINGS COME GREAT THINGS!

MAKING A MICRO-WORLD
TIM GODDARD

"For this chapter, I could build pretty much anything I wanted, as long as it was in a small scale. I began by coming up with lots of different ideas of what would work well, and then I started building. I don't tend to plan my builds much beyond a rough idea; I just let the bricks guide me. I'm particularly happy with the way the modular city (pp.56–61) came out. Being able to make a building and then add it to a bigger city, or have your friends add to it, really appeals to me."

MICRO-MARS
Take a trip into micro-space and join the Gnome on a visit to the Red Planet! Its futuristic cityscape of shining hi-tech towers and spaceship landing platforms is out of this world. (See pp.92–93.)

ROOOOAAAR!

POCKET-SIZED GIANTS

Journey to a prehistoric world full of giant reptiles that are small enough to fit in your pocket! Just don't blame the Gnome if they escape while you're at school... (See pp.80–83.)

THE LITTLE CITY

Skyscrapers short enough for a minifigure to climb? You'll find them in a micro-metropolis, along with an office building, a construction site, a hospital and police headquarters. (See p.88.)

EVEN IN MINIATURE, THEY STILL SEEM PRETTY BIG TO ME.

MICRO-SCALE MODELS ARE A BIG DEAL TO ME!

I'M THE KING OF THE MICRO-WORLD!

CITY LIFE

Recreate the hustle and bustle of city life by building in micro-scale. Cities are full of structures with different shapes and colours, making them a lot of fun to design with your LEGO bricks. They're also made up of lots of smaller block sections, so you can build your city in separate parts and then combine them to make an entire micro-scaled metropolis.

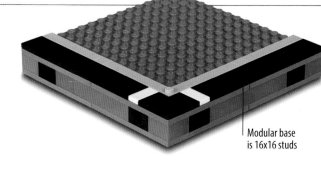

Modular base is 16x16 studs

BACK TO BASICS

Try constructing your buildings on modular bases like this one. You could make each of your city's bases the same size and shape, and connect them all with LEGO Technic bricks and pins. You can assemble as many as you like – and take them apart to rearrange them whenever you want a change!

WHIZZ!

Grey LEGO Technic connector pin allows the top rotor to spin freely

HELICOPTER

This helicopter carries patients to the hospital in super-fast time. To make the tail rotor, attach a LEGO® Technic half-bush to a tap. Two 1x1 plates with clips hold the landing skids in place.

Use tiles to make a helipad for your helicopter to land on

Search your collection for printed pieces to add detail to your building

You could add a bench and some colourful scenery outside the hospital.

Tiny square windows are the backs of headlight bricks

Add pavements in a contrasting colour to the base so they can be seen clearly

HOSPITAL

A hospital is a functional building that every city should have, but that doesn't mean it has to be boring! Include little details, like some shrubbery, street lights and pavements to make your hospital a pleasant place to visit.

Thin layer of coloured stripes visually separates floors

PLASTIC FLOWERS ARE A MUST WHEN VISITING THE HOSPITAL.

AIRPORT

How about adding an airport to your city so that your micro-scale citizens can travel to other places? Prepare for take-off on this (not so) jumbo jet! You can add some mobile boarding steps to your jet by building a staircase of jumper plates with a tile on top, and wheels at the base.

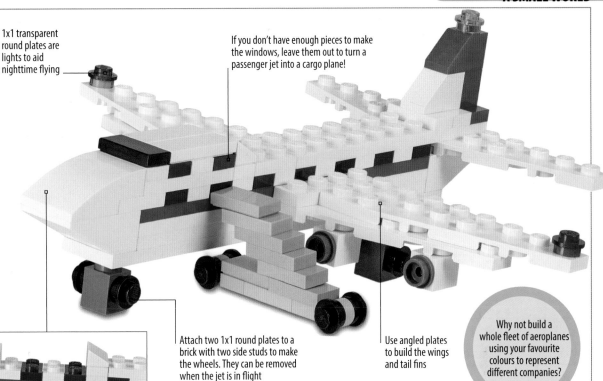

1x1 transparent round plates are lights to aid nighttime flying

If you don't have enough pieces to make the windows, leave them out to turn a passenger jet into a cargo plane!

Attach two 1x1 round plates to a brick with two side studs to make the wheels. They can be removed when the jet is in flight

Use angled plates to build the wings and tail fins

Why not build a whole fleet of aeroplanes using your favourite colours to represent different companies?

WINDOW SEATS

Place blue plates at intervals through the body to make windows that appear on both sides of the jumbo jet.

Sleek, aerodynamic nose made with slopes and curves

CONTROL TOWER

A tall air traffic control tower keeps track of the aeroplanes in the sky and on the runway. The controllers inside need to see all around, so give them windows facing in all directions using headlight bricks. A radar tower will help the controllers to track air traffic at any altitude.

Radar panels are made with grilles, but you could use tiles or plates instead

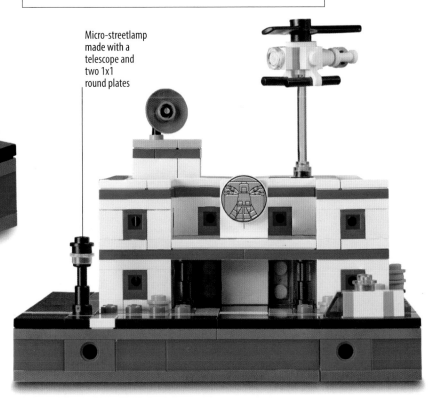

Micro-streetlamp made with a telescope and two 1x1 round plates

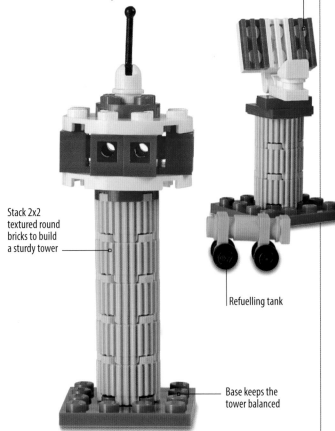

Stack 2x2 textured round bricks to build a sturdy tower

Refuelling tank

Base keeps the tower balanced

HOSPITAL FRONT VIEW

DOWNTOWN

As you build up your micro-sized city, you can add offices, stores and important civic structures such as schools, fire stations and a police headquarters. Keep the height of the storeys equal so that all of your buildings look like they are in the same scale, but use your imagination to create the rest of their details.

OFFICE BUILDING

This building is home to Octan – the imaginary fuel brand of LEGO autos everywhere – but you could become owner of your very own business by choosing your own colour scheme and decorations. If you don't want to use a printed tile as a company logo, then build any sign you like.

Air conditioning units on the roof keep the office workers cool

GOING UP!

Build each level above the ground floor in exactly the same way to make the office building look neat and professional. Use transparent pieces for big glass windows, and include vents and other details on the roof.

GREENERY

These decorative trees are constructed by stacking three 2x2 round plates for pots, and then alternating 1x1 round plates and small radar dishes to make trunks and leaves.

Pots are in the Octan company colours

An overhang above the door provides shade and shelter

Window washers make the exterior look pristine

A printed tile from a classic LEGO® Town set shows that this office belongs to Octan

Vehicles add detail to your micro-city and can be built with just a few pieces!

Don't be square. Add a doorway or a wall to the front of your building at a different angle

Make communications gear with a radar dish, a plate with a clip on top, and a tap

POLICE STATION

A micro-city's citizens may be too small to see, but they still need to be served and protected! This police station is built like the hospital (see p.56), but with more storeys and a white-and-blue colour scheme.

CALLING ALL UNITS: THERE ARE REPORTS OF A GIANT GNOME!

Include support walls between windows

Different colours and combinations of round and square 1x1 plates give vegetation a realistic look

Police vehicles can park under the elevated building

ARRESTING ARCHITECTURE

There's no law to say that your buildings have to be basic boxes. This police station has two separate buildings connected with a covered bridge that runs between them!

I HOPE THERE ISN'T A LAW AGAINST BEING TOO TALL IN THIS MICRO-CITY.

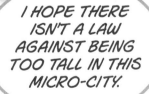

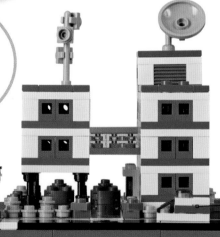

Police van is a stack of 1x1 pieces, with a 1x1 slope for the windscreen

FRONT VIEW

CITY PARK

Life in the big city can be hectic – sometimes you need to get away from it all for a bit of peace and quiet. That's why every city should have a park. But before it can be enjoyed, your park needs to be built. Here are before-and-after versions of this vital addition to your micro-city.

BUILDER TALK

"There are lots of different scales you can use when building smaller than minifigure scale. Think about what size a person would be for the building or vehicles you are making. This will help the small worlds that you build look like they fit together."

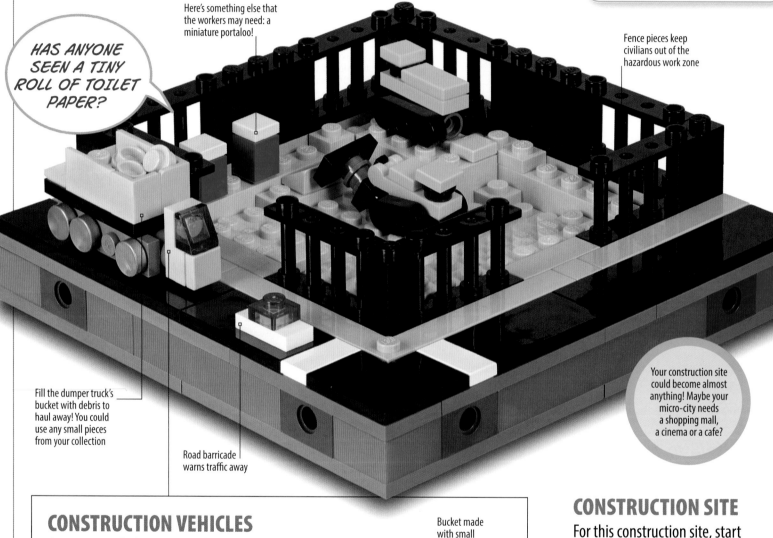

HAS ANYONE SEEN A TINY ROLL OF TOILET PAPER?

Here's something else that the workers may need: a miniature portaloo!

Fence pieces keep civilians out of the hazardous work zone

Fill the dumper truck's bucket with debris to haul away! You could use any small pieces from your collection

Road barricade warns traffic away

Your construction site could become almost anything! Maybe your micro-city needs a shopping mall, a cinema or a cafe?

CONSTRUCTION VEHICLES

Construction vehicles come in different colours, but yellow is the most classic look. Despite their size, these micro-models are very recognisable thanks to a clever choice of pieces.

Bucket made with small corner wall elements

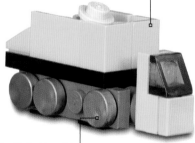

Digger is built around a droid torso piece

1x2 jumper plate

1x1 round tiles attached to a plate and a brick with side studs

CONSTRUCTION SITE

For this construction site, start with the modular base used for the hospital and police station. Remove the top plates so that it looks dug up and arrange bricks, plates and tiles to make mounds of freshly excavated earth.

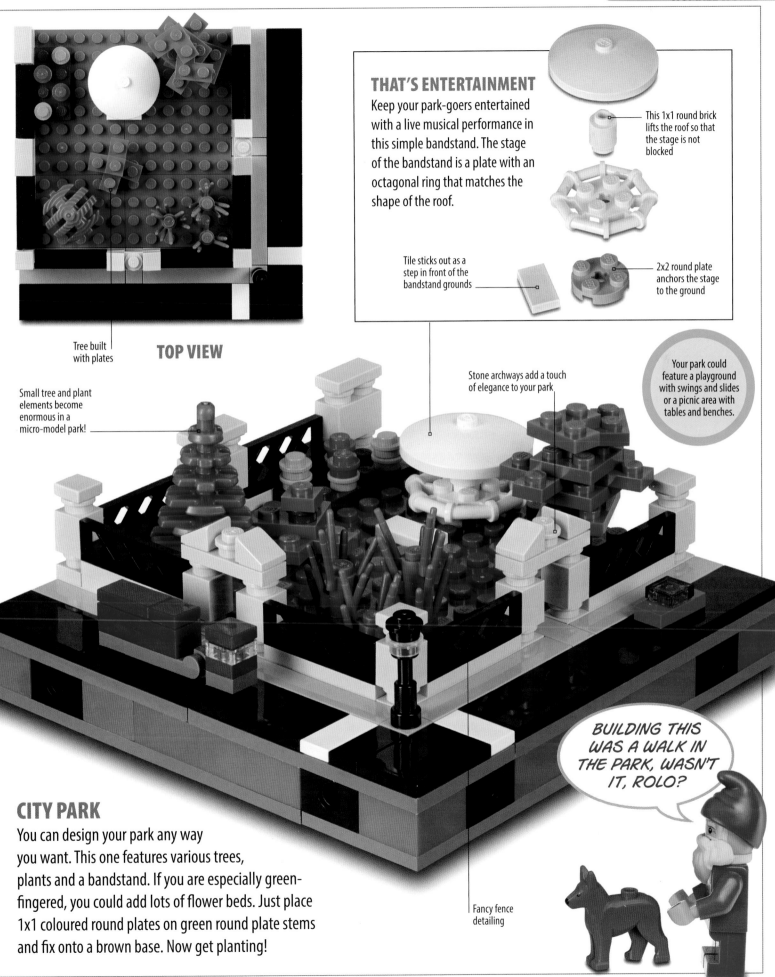

Tree built with plates

TOP VIEW

THAT'S ENTERTAINMENT

Keep your park-goers entertained with a live musical performance in this simple bandstand. The stage of the bandstand is a plate with an octagonal ring that matches the shape of the roof.

This 1x1 round brick lifts the roof so that the stage is not blocked

Tile sticks out as a step in front of the bandstand grounds

2x2 round plate anchors the stage to the ground

Small tree and plant elements become enormous in a micro-model park!

Stone archways add a touch of elegance to your park

Your park could feature a playground with swings and slides or a picnic area with tables and benches.

CITY PARK

You can design your park any way you want. This one features various trees, plants and a bandstand. If you are especially green-fingered, you could add lots of flower beds. Just place 1x1 coloured round plates on green round plate stems and fix onto a brown base. Now get planting!

Fancy fence detailing

BUILDING THIS WAS A WALK IN THE PARK, WASN'T IT, ROLO?

RACETRACK

Get out your biggest base plate and use your smallest LEGO elements to build a micro-scale racetrack! Give it all the features of the real thing: a circular course with side barriers, a starting and finish line, stands full of spectators and a set of miniature race cars. When you're done, think up rules for a racing game to play with your friends!

2...4...6...8... WHO DO WE APPRECIATE? MICRO-RACERS!

Build special obstacles like water traps, sand dunes, ramps and tunnels to change the game-play!

Use red round plates to make corner barriers that keep cars inside the track

Around the back are buildings for the pit crews who repair and maintain the cars

1x2 and 1x1 tiles make stripes that could work like the spaces on a game board

Build the road out of smooth tiles so the cars can slide along its surface

Black and white pieces mark the beginning and end of the race

COOL BRICK

"This little 1x1 round plate can be used for all sorts of things! When I built the mini cars, I knew I'd have to use this part as the wheels and it dictated the size of the cars. You can also find it used as a nose for the mini lion on p.79."

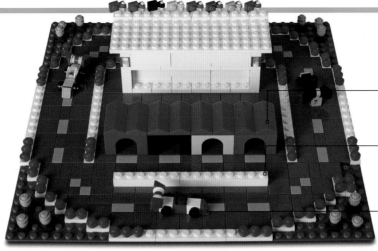

The pit buildings are made from roof tiles and arch bricks. If you don't have these, use bricks and plates instead

A long brick or panel works for the pit wall

A race car only seats one, so you only need one window!

REAR VIEW

GRANDSTAND

What's a race without the fans? Minifigures are way too big for a micro-scale crowd, but rows of colourful stacks of two 1x1 round plates create just the right look.

Use transparent bricks for windows on the sides of the grandstands

Attach 1x1 plates with side clips to pieces with bars for tiny pennant flags

Decorate the outside with trees and bushes made from 1x1 square and round plates

TOP VIEW

I'M ASKING FOR DIRECTIONS!

WHY DO YOU KEEP STOPPING?

Wheels are 1x1 round plates attached to 1x1 bricks with studs on two sides

TINY RACERS

Build these racing cars in a similar way to the micro-cars on p.65. Removing the 2x4 plate in the middle and adding a spoiler at the back increases the car's speed.

VEHICLES

Build some micro-scale automobiles and a truck to haul them around. If it were scaled to minifigures, this car carrier would be a truly massive model, but as a micro-build, it can be made in a much more manageable size. Load up its trailer with colourful cars and take them on a road trip.

Transporter trucks come in different sizes, so try building a trailer that holds one, two or even 20 autos!

NOW THIS IS THE WAY TO TRAVEL!

Make sure your hinges are well attached as you build

Top bars are lances from minifigure knights

Wheels are from a small LEGO race car set

TRANSPORTER TRUCK

Building a fairly large micro-scale model means that you get to add in special features, such as a turning cab, spinning wheels, and a trailer that works like the real thing.

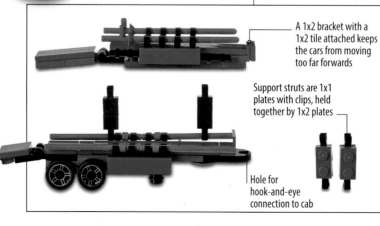

A 1x2 bracket with a 1x2 tile attached keeps the cars from moving too far forwards

Support struts are 1x1 plates with clips, held together by 1x2 plates

Hole for hook-and-eye connection to cab

DESIGNING A TRAILER

Your trailer needs to be long, wide and tall enough to hold your micro-cars. That's why it's a good idea to build the autos first and then design the trailer to fit them.

MICRO-CARS

Here are a few simple ways to use small LEGO pieces to create micro-scale automobiles. You can use the same techniques to make boxy vans, racing cars (see p.63) and stretched limousines.

Use 1x1 bricks with one side stud between the wheels and attach to the bottom of the plate

Each one of these micro-cars is built around a 2x4 plate

CAB CONSTRUCTION

The truck's cab can be long-nosed or flat-nosed, and any colour you like. This cab's window is three 1x2 transparent bricks side-by-side, with a 2x3 plate as a roof. Attach slopes to the side of the bonnet to create an angled shape.

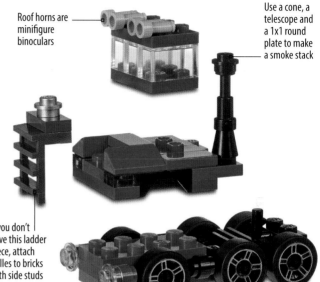

Roof horns are minifigure binoculars

Use a cone, a telescope and a 1x1 round plate to make a smoke stack

If you don't have this ladder piece, attach grilles to bricks with side studs

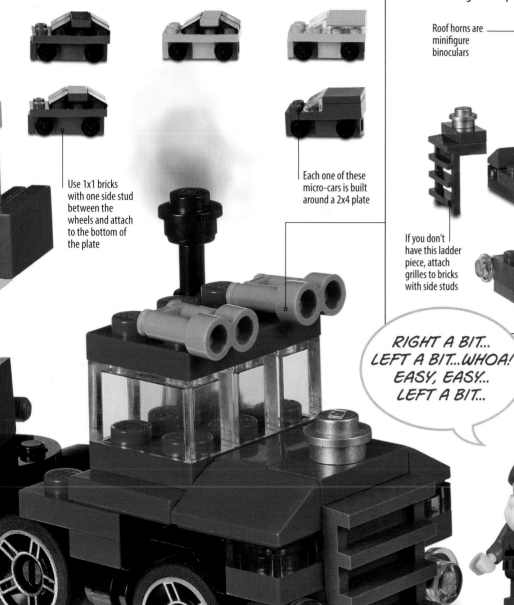

RIGHT A BIT...
LEFT A BIT...WHOA!
EASY, EASY...
LEFT A BIT...

BUILDER TALK

"The trailer was the challenging part of this model. It was tough to make it as small as possible, while still keeping it functional. I used a hook-and-eye connection to allow the truck to make turns and the trailer to be easily removed."

LOAD 'EM UP!

Each level of the trailer has its own hinged ramp to let the cars drive on and off. When folded back up, the ramps lock the cars in place.

Wheels are black 1x1 round plates attached to 1x1 bricks with studs on two sides

Smooth tiles let autos slide into place without sticking on studs

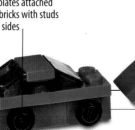

CARGO HAULERS

With so much micro-scale construction going on, you'll need a way to transport your precious pieces from place to place. Build a freight train to move them around the country, and a cargo ship to carry them across the sea.

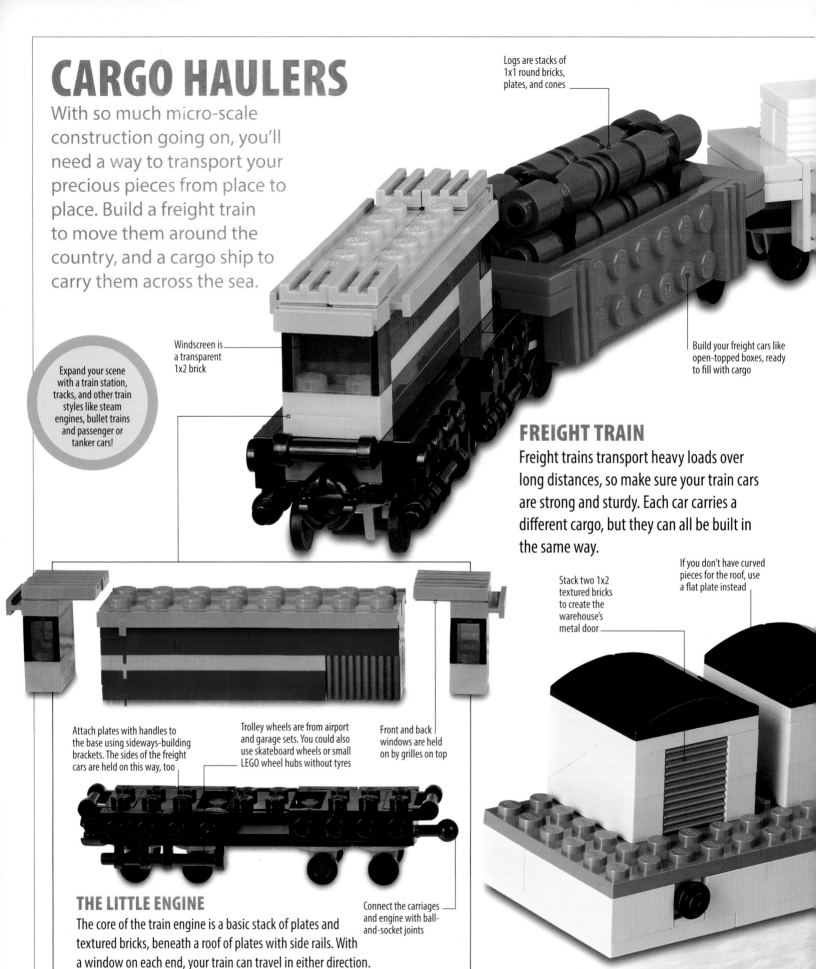

Logs are stacks of 1x1 round bricks, plates, and cones

Expand your scene with a train station, tracks, and other train styles like steam engines, bullet trains and passenger or tanker cars!

Windscreen is a transparent 1x2 brick

Build your freight cars like open-topped boxes, ready to fill with cargo

FREIGHT TRAIN

Freight trains transport heavy loads over long distances, so make sure your train cars are strong and sturdy. Each car carries a different cargo, but they can all be built in the same way.

If you don't have curved pieces for the roof, use a flat plate instead

Stack two 1x2 textured bricks to create the warehouse's metal door

Attach plates with handles to the base using sideways-building brackets. The sides of the freight cars are held on this way, too

Trolley wheels are from airport and garage sets. You could also use skateboard wheels or small LEGO wheel hubs without tyres

Front and back windows are held on by grilles on top

THE LITTLE ENGINE

The core of the train engine is a basic stack of plates and textured bricks, beneath a roof of plates with side rails. With a window on each end, your train can travel in either direction.

Connect the carriages and engine with ball-and-socket joints

Containers are 1x2 textured bricks held together by a 2x4 tile on top

OH WOW. NOW I'M ON A TRAIN!

Use your micro-cars from p.65 as train cargo!

HARBOUR CRANE

The crane's boom arm is attached with a click hinge, which can hold an extended position and support the weight of cargo bricks without drooping.

MICRO-HARBOUR

Build a ship, then construct a whole harbor where it can dock and resupply. Add warehouses, fuel tanks and a big crane for loading and unloading cargo.

Fuel tanks are made with 2x2 round bricks, plates and domes, with 1x1 round tiles on top

Crane operator sits behind this 1x1 slope window

Headlight brick weighs down the end of the string and attaches to the studs on top of cargo bricks

Crane legs are built with clips and plates with handled bars

ALL ABOARD! BE CAREFUL, IT'S A TIGHT FIT.

To prevent your ship from crashing into the dock, attach 1x1 round plates to headlight bricks to create rubber bumpers

Grey bricks resemble bare metal, but you could use other colours for a painted hull

Add a plate stripe for decoration

OIL PLATFORM

Take your building offshore and construct a miniature oil platform to collect oil and natural gas from beneath the ocean floor – those tiny cars and trucks need to get their fuel from somewhere!

SPINNING DRILL

Think about how you can use your LEGO Technic parts to build special moving functions into your micro-models. Spin the black gear on the side of the rig, and its long drill and the flame on top rotate right along!

Use any flame piece from your collection, or build your own out of transparent pieces

CAN WE ORDER A PIZZA FOR DELIVERY HERE?

A joystick, a tap, and a small radar dish create an array to communicate with the mainland

Crew quarters is built by stacking white and transparent pieces, with dark grey for rooftops

MINI VEHICLES

The mini-helicopter carries workers to and from the oil platform. Its main rotor is a small tail rotor from a bigger helicopter model. The mini-sub dives under the water to check the rig and repair any problems. It is built in yellow for high visibility and uses several one-stud jumper plates.

Cockpit is built with two 1x1 slopes attached sideways

A 1x1 round plate is just the right size for a tiny propeller

Transparent element acts as a spotlight to navigate the murky seas

Pontoons are fire hose nozzles held on by clips

Helipad has a 2x2 yellow tile on top to prevent the helicopter from sliding around

FUELLED AND READY FOR TAKE-OFF!

PINT-SIZED PLATFORM

This model is based on a fixed platform oil rig, with legs that are anchored to the seabed. Most of the oil rig stays underwater, with the platform near the top sticking up above the surface. The tapering drill frame at the top of the oil platform is built like the harbour crane (see p. 67), using narrow clip-and-bar hinges.

Grey pieces look like strong steel

Try building a tanker ship or a pipeline to transport the oil back to land!

Angled supports are made with clips and plates with handles, joined together by narrow tiles

Yellow cranes move on clip hinges to lift supplies or lower the mini-sub into the water

Plates with holes lock the rig levels together, while letting the cross-axle drill pass through

Use single-piece columns for strength and stability

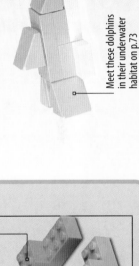

REAR VIEW

Meet these dolphins in their underwater habitat on p.73

PUZZLE PLAY

This micro-puzzle is small in size, but big on fun! Build a frame using simple bricks, then combine other pieces to make shapes to fit inside it – just like a jigsaw puzzle. Ask your friends and family to complete the puzzle. Try timing them to see who can fit the bricks inside the frame the fastest!

A puzzle shouldn't just be functional – make it decorative, too

Frame can be any shape you like!

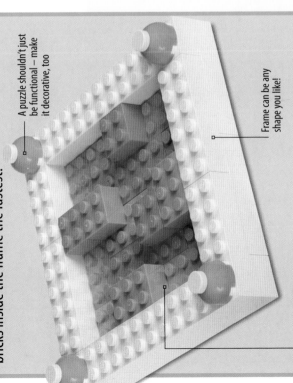

BRICKS AND PIECES

The brick pieces you build need to fit perfectly into your frame, but create different shapes and sizes to make the puzzle a real challenge.

Join your brick shapes with 2x2 bricks, which will also make the shapes easier to move around the puzzle

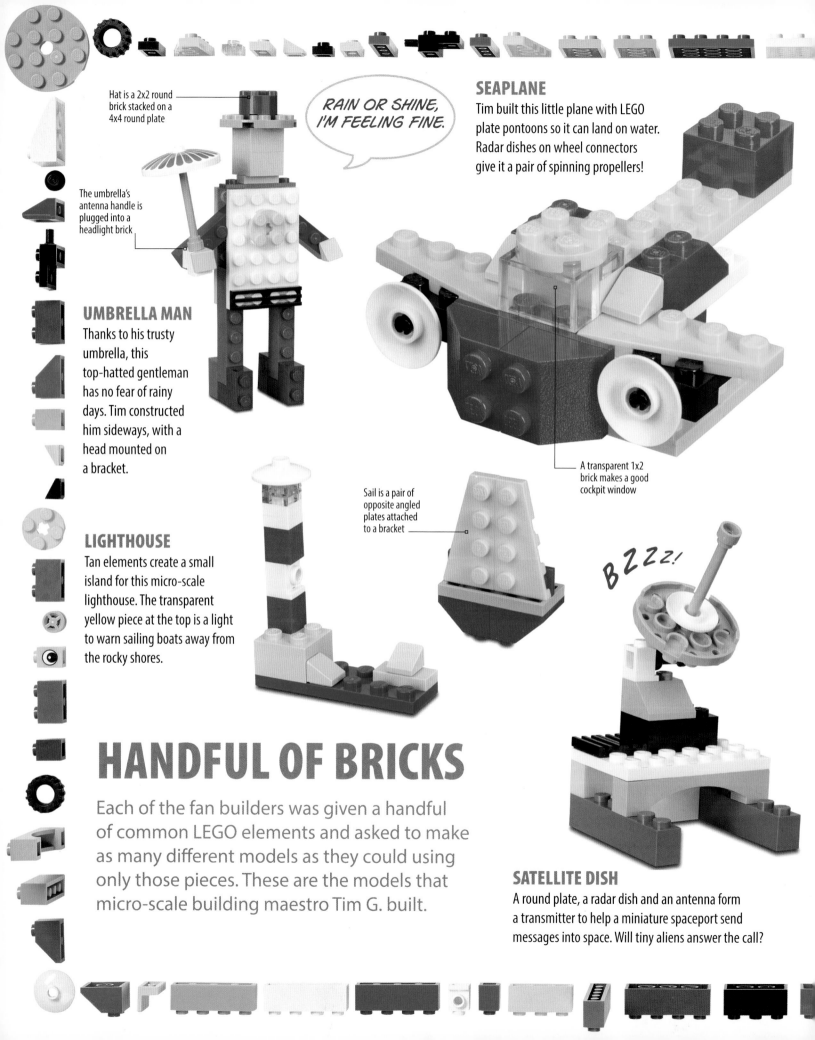

Hat is a 2x2 round
brick stacked on a
4x4 round plate

RAIN OR SHINE,
I'M FEELING FINE.

SEAPLANE

Tim built this little plane with LEGO
plate pontoons so it can land on water.
Radar dishes on wheel connectors
give it a pair of spinning propellers!

The umbrella's
antenna handle is
plugged into a
headlight brick

UMBRELLA MAN

Thanks to his trusty
umbrella, this
top-hatted gentleman
has no fear of rainy
days. Tim constructed
him sideways, with a
head mounted on
a bracket.

A transparent 1x2
brick makes a good
cockpit window

Sail is a pair of
opposite angled
plates attached
to a bracket

LIGHTHOUSE

Tan elements create a small
island for this micro-scale
lighthouse. The transparent
yellow piece at the top is a light
to warn sailing boats away from
the rocky shores.

BZZZ!

HANDFUL OF BRICKS

Each of the fan builders was given a handful
of common LEGO elements and asked to make
as many different models as they could using
only those pieces. These are the models that
micro-scale building maestro Tim G. built.

SATELLITE DISH

A round plate, a radar dish and an antenna form
a transmitter to help a miniature spaceport send
messages into space. Will tiny aliens answer the call?

HORSE PADDOCK

Tim built his horse a set of training jumps to get it in shape for equestrian shows, as well as a water pump and a stack of hay to keep it refreshed.

Just two bricks can add a lot to a scene

A tap for a beaked head

The horse's neck and tail are centred on jumper plates

DUCK

This white duck was built out of just five pieces, including the headlight brick that gives it a turning head. Compare it to the one built by Pete and Yvonne on p.111!

SCORPION CAR

Combine a stinging arachnid with a race car, and what do you get? The fastest thing in the desert, that's what! Tim really got creative with this colourful clawed model.

There's even a hole on top where a minifigure can sit and drive!

ROOSTER

Cock-a-doodle-doo! This mini model captures all the familiar features of a crowing barnyard rooster, from the comb on its head to the plume of tail-feathers on its back.

HMMM... WHAT DOES THIS REMIND ME OF?

HANDFUL OF THOUGHTS

"I looked at the bricks I was given and thought about what they reminded me of. It was fun and challenging to build something with such a small handful!"

ON THE SEA FLOOR

Take a dive beneath the waves and build a scene at the bottom of the ocean! You can find lots of curious things on the sea floor, like a long-forgotten pirate's ship. You might even discover a sunken chest full of treasure with your micro-scale sub. Micro-scale building makes it easy to construct a shipwreck and all of the undersea objects that surround it.

Only one of the ship's masts still stands

BUILDING A WRECK

To make the ship's angled front, build a clip hinge and angle the section of the bow into position. Don't worry if there are gaps in your model – a shipwreck is called a wreck for a reason!

What sank this ship? Maybe you can build a hint into your own version!

Two curved slopes make up the sub's main body

Use binoculars for jet propulsion

The cockpit is 1x1 transparent tiles so aquanauts can see any underwater wrecks clearly

Robot arms for underwater exploration

UNIDENTIFIED MARINE LIFE AHEAD, CAPTAIN.

WATCH WHERE YOU'RE GOING WITH THOSE ROBOT ARMS!

Sea plants have started to grow over the wreck. You could also make barnacles with white round plates

TOP VIEW

Sunken treasure is gold 1x1 round plates, but you could use whatever colourful pieces you have in your collection

Turn to the next page to study this octopus more closely!

Use bricks with side studs to attach the sides of the hull

REAR VIEW

SHIPWRECK

To build a shipwreck, start by constructing the basic shape of a boat – just don't finish it! The parts that have been on the seabed for a long time should suggest what the ship looked like when it was complete. Use plates and tiles to create broken planks and stray pieces of hull.

Fin is a 1x1 slope

Jumper plate

DOLPHINS

It doesn't take many pieces to build a micro-scale dolphin. Use tiny slopes to give your flippered friends distinct features. Jumper plates and a plate with ring at the back will allow you to put the fins in the right positions.

Use transparent pieces to make stands for your extra objects

Pick a base plate colour that looks like a sandy ocean floor

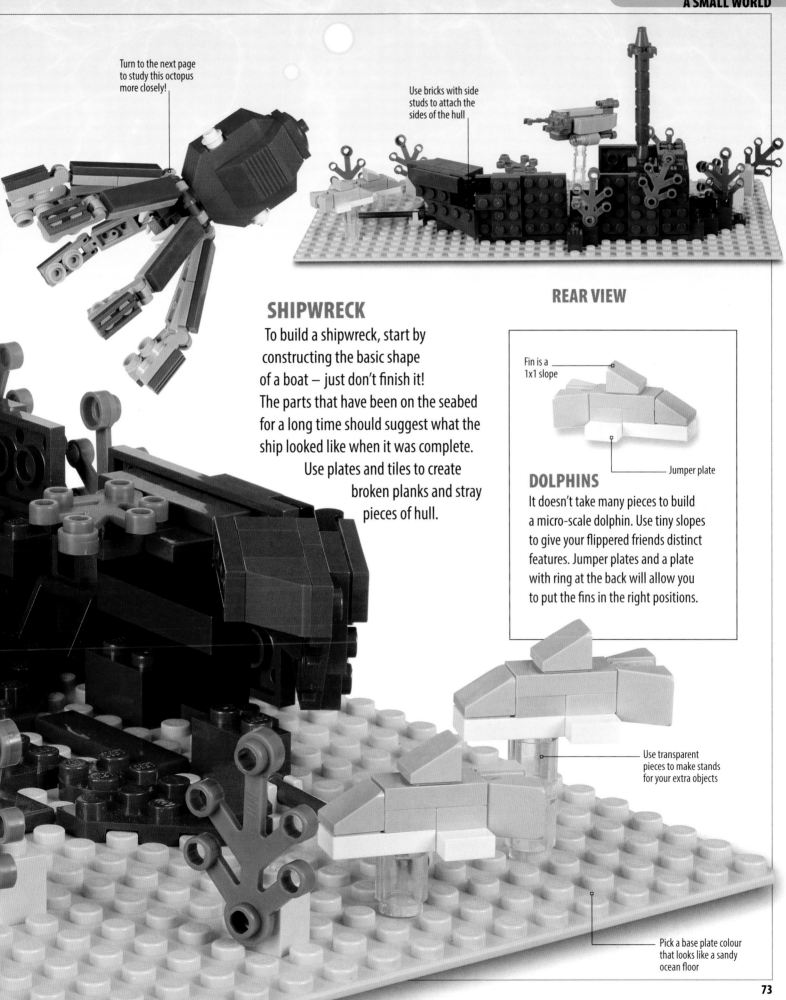

73

MONSTERS OF THE DEEP

The ocean is full of adventure and mystery. You never know what unusual marine life might be swimming around down there in the depths. Use your bricks to build weird and wonderful micro-scale creatures, and a fearless submarine to explore it all.

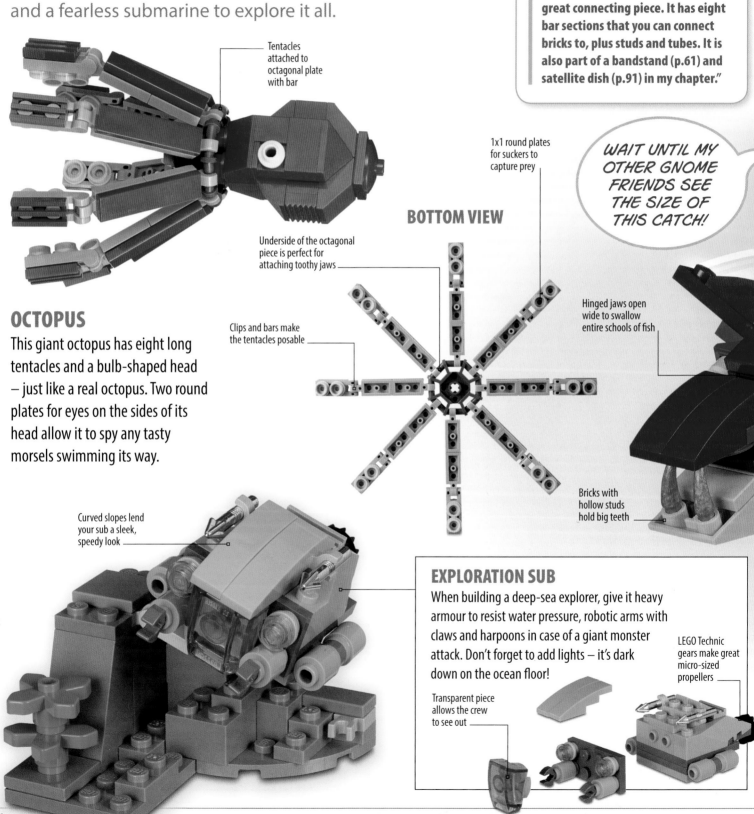

Tentacles attached to octagonal plate with bar

1x1 round plates for suckers to capture prey

BOTTOM VIEW

WAIT UNTIL MY OTHER GNOME FRIENDS SEE THE SIZE OF THIS CATCH!

Underside of the octagonal piece is perfect for attaching toothy jaws

OCTOPUS

This giant octopus has eight long tentacles and a bulb-shaped head – just like a real octopus. Two round plates for eyes on the sides of its head allow it to spy any tasty morsels swimming its way.

Clips and bars make the tentacles posable

Hinged jaws open wide to swallow entire schools of fish

Bricks with hollow studs hold big teeth

Curved slopes lend your sub a sleek, speedy look

EXPLORATION SUB

When building a deep-sea explorer, give it heavy armour to resist water pressure, robotic arms with claws and harpoons in case of a giant monster attack. Don't forget to add lights – it's dark down on the ocean floor!

LEGO Technic gears make great micro-sized propellers

Transparent piece allows the crew to see out

SEA SERPENT

With its snake-like body and three pairs of fins, this reptilian creature is unlike any that you'll find in the oceans of Earth. Or maybe it just hasn't been found yet! The sections of the serpent's body are held together with sturdy click hinges, providing movement for swimming, hunting and battling pesky submarines!

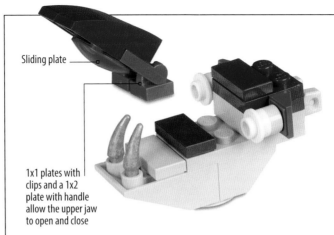

Sliding plate

1x1 plates with clips and a 1x2 plate with handle allow the upper jaw to open and close

MOUTHY MONSTER

To make a jaw strong enough to feast on plenty of fish, lock two curved bricks and a plate with handle together using a 2x2 sliding plate underneath. The lower jaw is made with inverted slope bricks held together by another sliding plate.

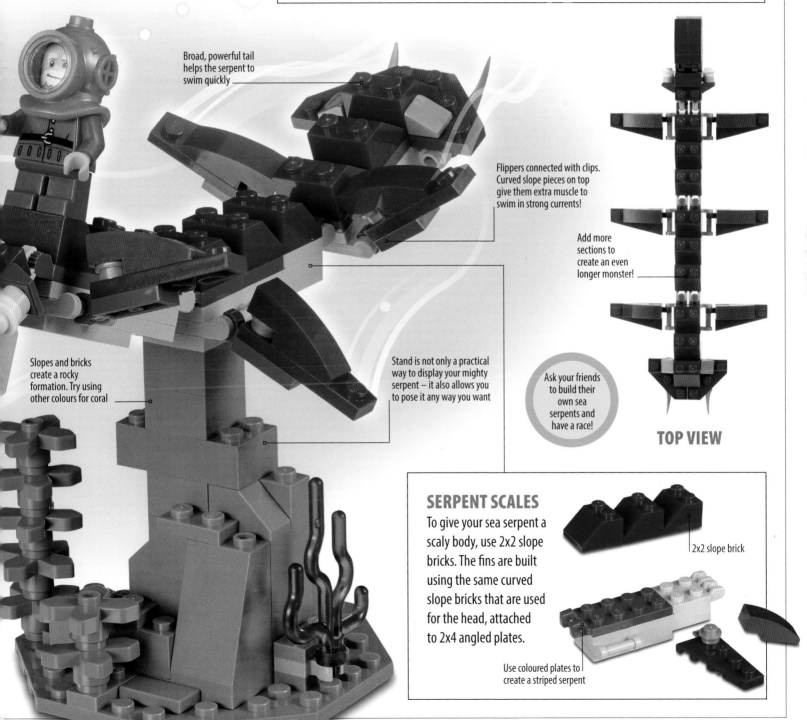

Broad, powerful tail helps the serpent to swim quickly

Flippers connected with clips. Curved slope pieces on top give them extra muscle to swim in strong currents!

Add more sections to create an even longer monster!

Slopes and bricks create a rocky formation. Try using other colours for coral

Stand is not only a practical way to display your mighty serpent – it also allows you to pose it any way you want

Ask your friends to build their own sea serpents and have a race!

TOP VIEW

SERPENT SCALES

To give your sea serpent a scaly body, use 2x2 slope bricks. The fins are built using the same curved slope bricks that are used for the head, attached to 2x4 angled plates.

2x2 slope brick

Use coloured plates to create a striped serpent

OCEAN LIFE

Not all ocean creatures are as scary as the monstrous sea serpent. These sea beasts are a bit more friendly – except perhaps for the pointy-toothed anglerfish! Look through your bricks and see what pieces would work best for animals that live in, and fly above, the sea.

1x1 brick with studs on top and two sides

Front flippers are flag pieces

Back flippers are 1x1 slopes

SEA LION

This playful sea lion gets its shape from 1x1 slopes. The front flippers are LEGO flag pieces attached to 1x2 plates with clips. You could also try buiding a different shape for a swimming pose.

FLIPPER CLIPPER

Each of the blue whale's flippers is made out of a small angled plate and a plate with handle. A piece with a clip attaches it to a sideways-facing stud on the body.

Use clips and bars for the tail too, to allow hinged movements while swimming

Plate with handle attaches underneath the angled plate

Build a waterspout out of transparent round plates and radar dish

Tiles give the top of the head a smooth surface

Tail is built sideways and attached by plates with clips on top

Small eyes are 1x1 round plates built into the model

I MAY BE MICRO-SCALE, BUT I'M STILL THE BIGGEST THING IN THE SEA!

BLUE WHALE

With micro-building, even something as big as a whale can be made portable and pocket-sized. Slope and curved pieces make for a smooth, streamlined body – search for similar shapes in your collection and use them to create your own underwater friends.

QUICK BUILD

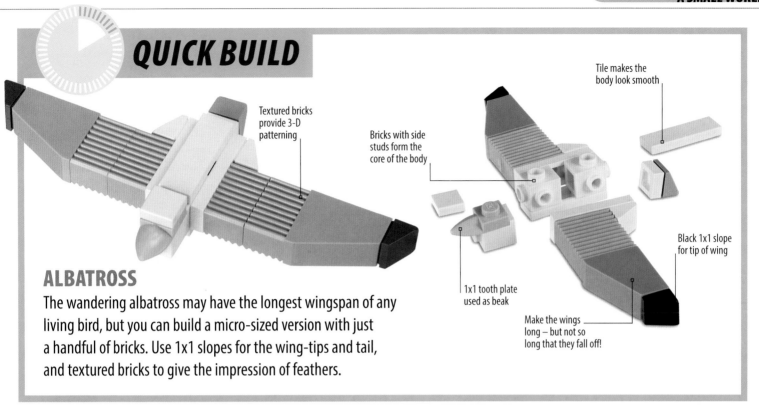

Textured bricks provide 3-D patterning

Tile makes the body look smooth

Bricks with side studs form the core of the body

Black 1x1 slope for tip of wing

1x1 tooth plate used as beak

Make the wings long – but not so long that they fall off!

ALBATROSS

The wandering albatross may have the longest wingspan of any living bird, but you can build a micro-sized version with just a handful of bricks. Use 1x1 slopes for the wing-tips and tail, and textured bricks to give the impression of feathers.

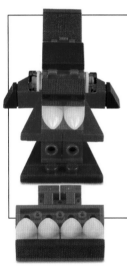

JAWS

Creepy eyes, a glowing lure and sharp teeth create one very frightening fish! Use hinge plates for the upper and lower jaws so that they can open and gobble up tasty morsels.

ANGLERFISH

Deep-sea anglerfish may look like imaginary monsters, but they're very real! This angry angler's lure is a LEGO whip piece with a brightly coloured transparent 1x1 round plate attached to the end.

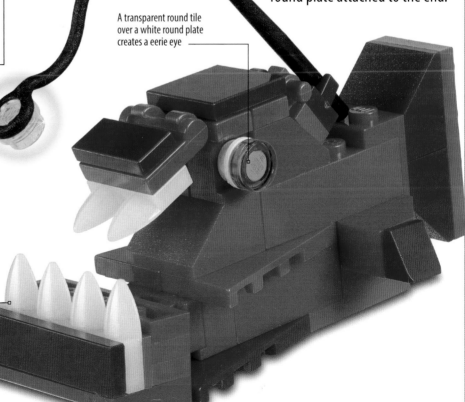

A transparent round tile over a white round plate creates a eerie eye

Glowing lure is used to attract unlucky fish

MUST NOT LOOK AT THE LURE. MUST NOT LOOK AT THE LURE.

Glow-in-the-dark teeth come from a LEGO creature-building set

MICRO-AFRICA

Welcome to Micro-Africa, where miniature animals roam free. Thanks to micro-scale building, you can go wild and turn your bedroom floor into your very own wildlife park! Don't worry about fitting every tiny detail into a micro-model. The main thing is to focus on the big clues – for example, a large brown mane or a trumpeting trunk.

What other micro-animals could you build for your wildlife park? How about a snapping crocodile or a hungry hippo?

"This droid torso is a really useful piece to have because of its many attachment points. Here, it is used for the centre of an elephant's head, but on p.60 it's part of a digger!"

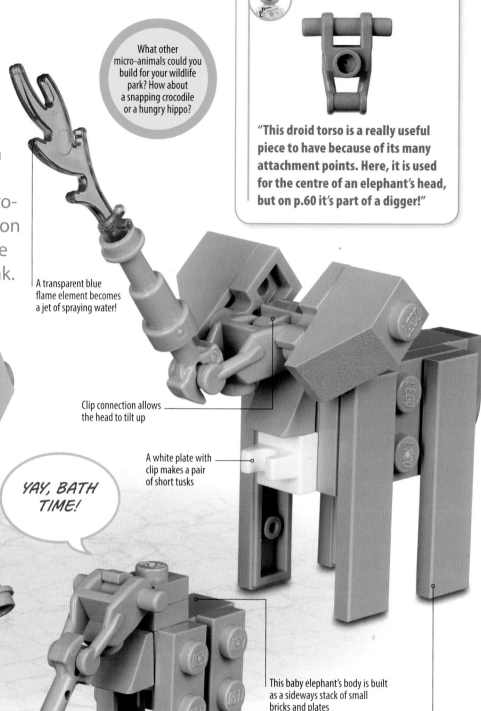

A transparent blue flame element becomes a jet of spraying water!

Clip connection allows the head to tilt up

A white plate with clip makes a pair of short tusks

YAY, BATH TIME!

Legs are 1x4 tiles attached to bricks with side studs

This baby elephant's body is built as a sideways stack of small bricks and plates

ELEPHANT

All you need to make a micro-model look like an elephant is a trunk and two big ears! Why not gather all of your grey bricks together and assemble an entire herd of elephants?

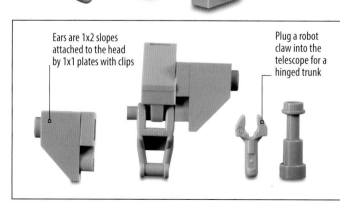

Ears are 1x2 slopes attached to the head by 1x1 plates with clips

Plug a robot claw into the telescope for a hinged trunk

HEAD AND TRUNK

When micro-building, try to find creative uses for unusual pieces. The centre of the adult elephants' heads is the torso from a minifigure-sized robot, and the end of their trunk is a telescope.

GIRAFFE

What do you think of when you picture a giraffe? Long legs, a long neck and a pattern of spots? Then those are the features that you should build into your micro-model.

HEY, THOSE ARE MY LEAVES. TAKE OFF!

Studded plates make the legs look spotted

Two or three leaf pieces are enough for a micro-treetop

This vulture uses tooth plates for its wings and head

Two 1x1 round plates for the neck

Legs are attached to 1x1 bricks with studs on two sides

ZEBRAS

Stripes aren't easy to create at micro-scale, but building your zebras sideways out of alternating black and white plates will help you pull off this difficult-looking feat.

RHINOCEROS

This little grey beast could be a hippo or a warthog... but as soon as you add a horn, everyone will know that it's a rhino.

Like the elephant, the rhino head is a droid torso

SPOT THE GIRAFFE

Scatter a few dark brown pieces around the tan body of your giraffe to create a blotchy hide. Giraffes have long legs, but in micro-scale, you just need short, thin plates.

Plate with vertical clip for horns

Use a cone for a tapering snout

Use a hinge plate for one leg to create a walking pose

A one-stud connection lets the leg move at the shoulder

Horns plug into minifigure binoculars

ANTELOPE

Antelopes need to be quick on their feet to avoid predators. With an animal model this small, it's hard to make four tiny legs — but just two will still give the right visual idea!

LIONS

These lions models are too tiny for eyes and whiskers, but adding little details, like a 2x2 brown plate for mane, makes their identity clear.

Only adult male lions have manes

1x1 plates with vertical clips make good perked-up ears in micro-scale!

A big round nose helps to sniff out prey

Legs are 1x1 slopes for a tired lion having a mid-afternoon nap!

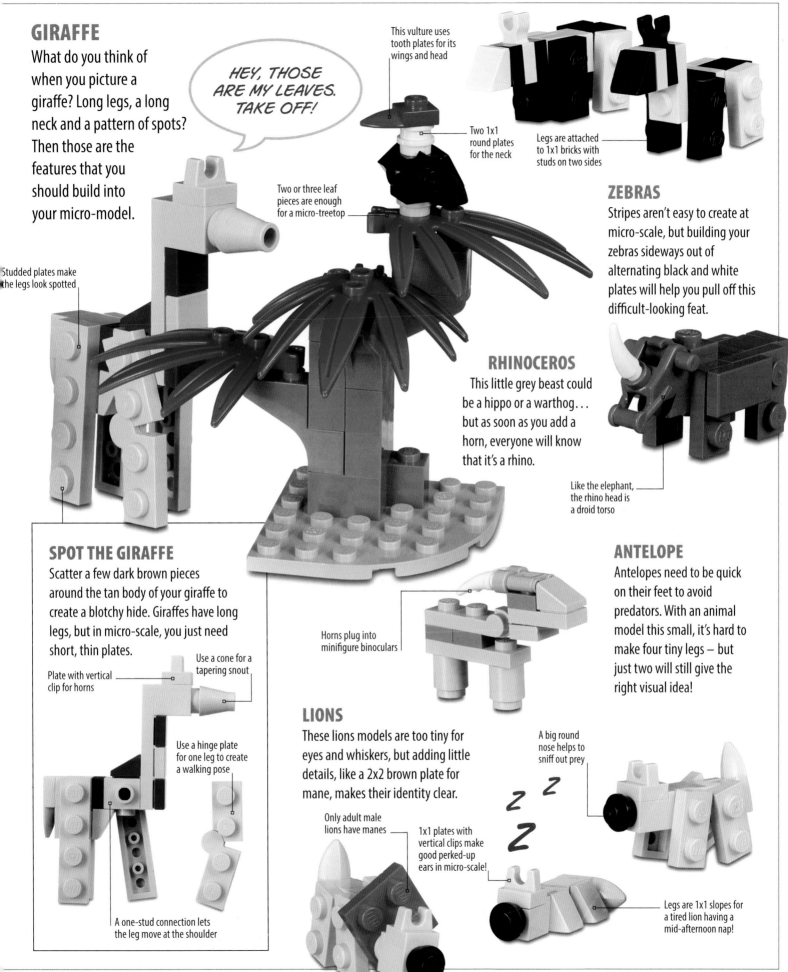

PREHISTORIC BEASTS

Millions of years ago, titanic dinosaurs roamed Earth. Use your LEGO bricks to create a miniature prehistoric scene populated with dinosaurs and their ancient reptilian relatives. Add forests, deserts and other environments so that it feels just like home for your Mesozoic micro-saurs!

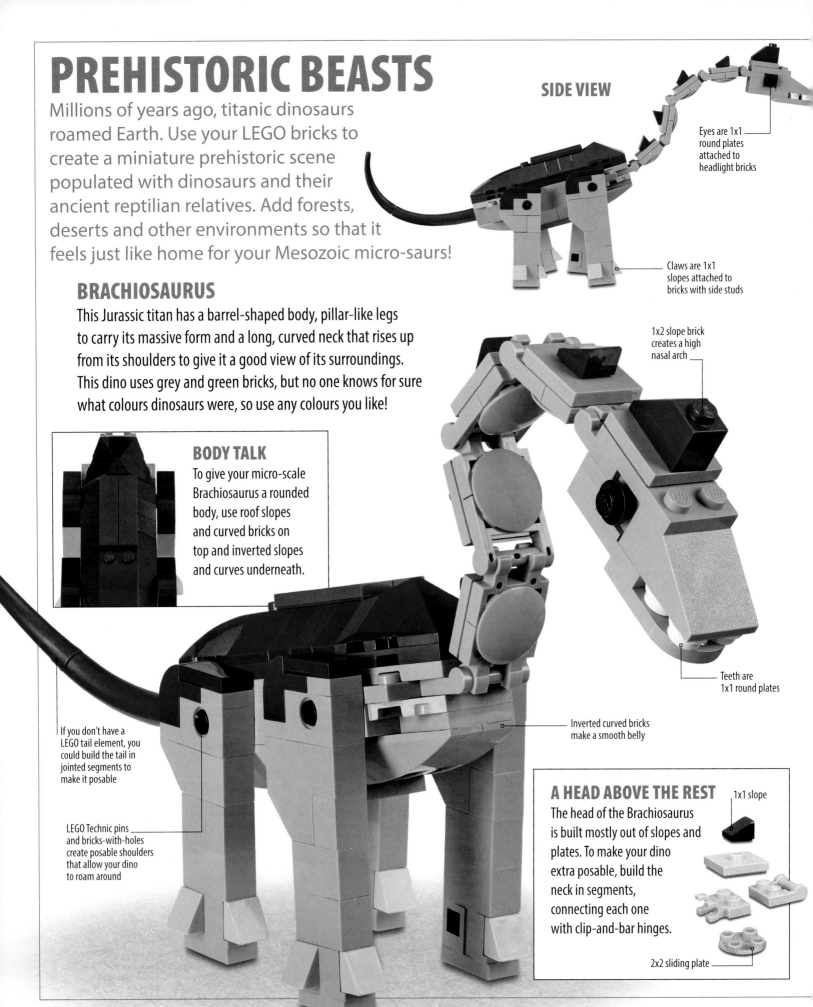

SIDE VIEW

Eyes are 1x1 round plates attached to headlight bricks

Claws are 1x1 slopes attached to bricks with side studs

BRACHIOSAURUS

This Jurassic titan has a barrel-shaped body, pillar-like legs to carry its massive form and a long, curved neck that rises up from its shoulders to give it a good view of its surroundings. This dino uses grey and green bricks, but no one knows for sure what colours dinosaurs were, so use any colours you like!

BODY TALK

To give your micro-scale Brachiosaurus a rounded body, use roof slopes and curved bricks on top and inverted slopes and curves underneath.

1x2 slope brick creates a high nasal arch

Teeth are 1x1 round plates

If you don't have a LEGO tail element, you could build the tail in jointed segments to make it posable

LEGO Technic pins and bricks-with-holes create posable shoulders that allow your dino to roam around

Inverted curved bricks make a smooth belly

A HEAD ABOVE THE REST

1x1 slope

The head of the Brachiosaurus is built mostly out of slopes and plates. To make your dino extra posable, build the neck in segments, connecting each one with clip-and-bar hinges.

2x2 sliding plate

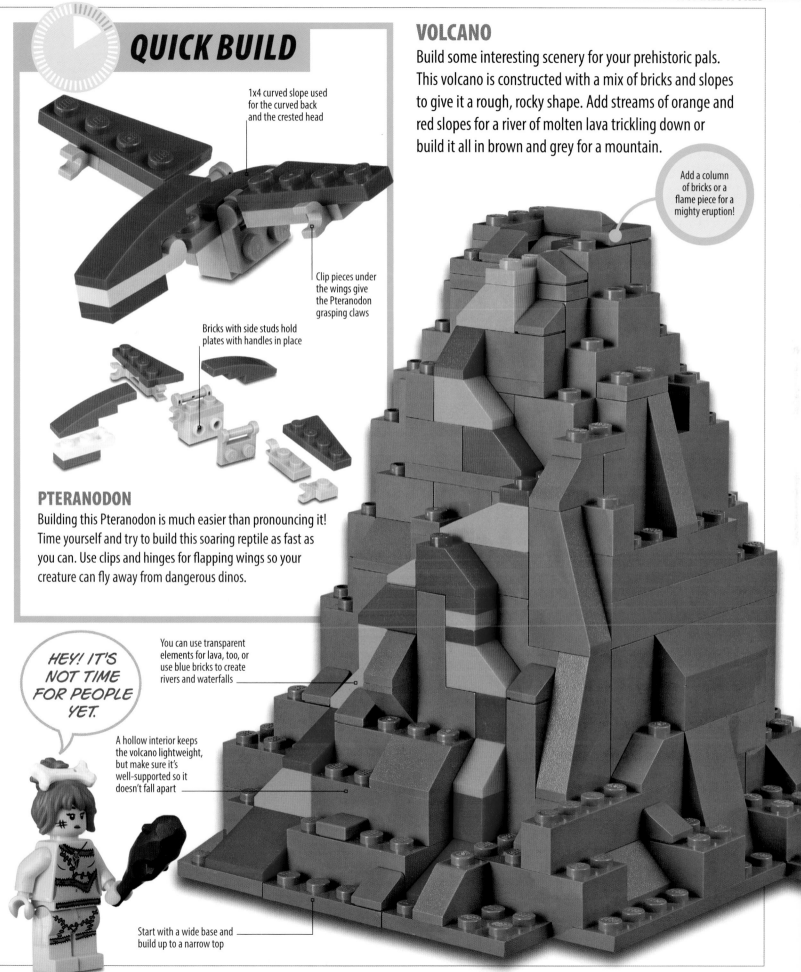

QUICK BUILD

1x4 curved slope used for the curved back and the crested head

Clip pieces under the wings give the Pteranodon grasping claws

Bricks with side studs hold plates with handles in place

PTERANODON

Building this Pteranodon is much easier than pronouncing it! Time yourself and try to build this soaring reptile as fast as you can. Use clips and hinges for flapping wings so your creature can fly away from dangerous dinos.

VOLCANO

Build some interesting scenery for your prehistoric pals. This volcano is constructed with a mix of bricks and slopes to give it a rough, rocky shape. Add streams of orange and red slopes for a river of molten lava trickling down or build it all in brown and grey for a mountain.

Add a column of bricks or a flame piece for a mighty eruption!

You can use transparent elements for lava, too, or use blue bricks to create rivers and waterfalls

A hollow interior keeps the volcano lightweight, but make sure it's well-supported so it doesn't fall apart

HEY! IT'S NOT TIME FOR PEOPLE YET.

Start with a wide base and build up to a narrow top

DANGEROUS DINOSAURS

Watch out! There are even more dangerous dinos about! Fortunately, as the builder, you don't have anything to fear from these micro-scaled menaces…unlike our poor tour guide, who seems to have caught more than he bargained for! What other scary, scaly dinos can you create for your micro-dino display?

GRRr!

The T-rex's sharpest teeth are made from plates with clips

Use hinges for an angled tail and head

TRICERATOPS

Give your Tyrannosaurus a dino to battle with! The Triceratops may be a plant-eater, but it's definitely no prehistoric pushover. Use pointy pieces to make three mighty horns for its head.

These short (but very strong!) legs are round bricks and plates built upside down to turn the studs into toes.

TYRANNOSAURUS REX

No micro-dino display would be complete without the most famous tyrant lizard of them all! This mini T-rex has a big toothy head, powerful legs and a pair of small arms made with robot arm pieces and claws.

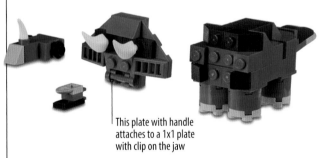

TINY 'TOPS

Use angled plates and slopes to create the Triceratops's bony neck frill. A 1x1 slope gives its head a tough beak. Below, a clip and handle connection makes a chomping jaw.

This plate with handle attaches to a 1x1 plate with clip on the jaw

AWESOME JAWS

Use bricks and slopes to give your Tyrannosaurus a strong skull with jaws that open on a clip hinge. This model uses a combination of normal and sideways building to create its shape.

BAD DINOSAUR! THAT'S MY SUPPER, NOT YOURS!

LEGO fishing rod —made for fish, not dinosaurs

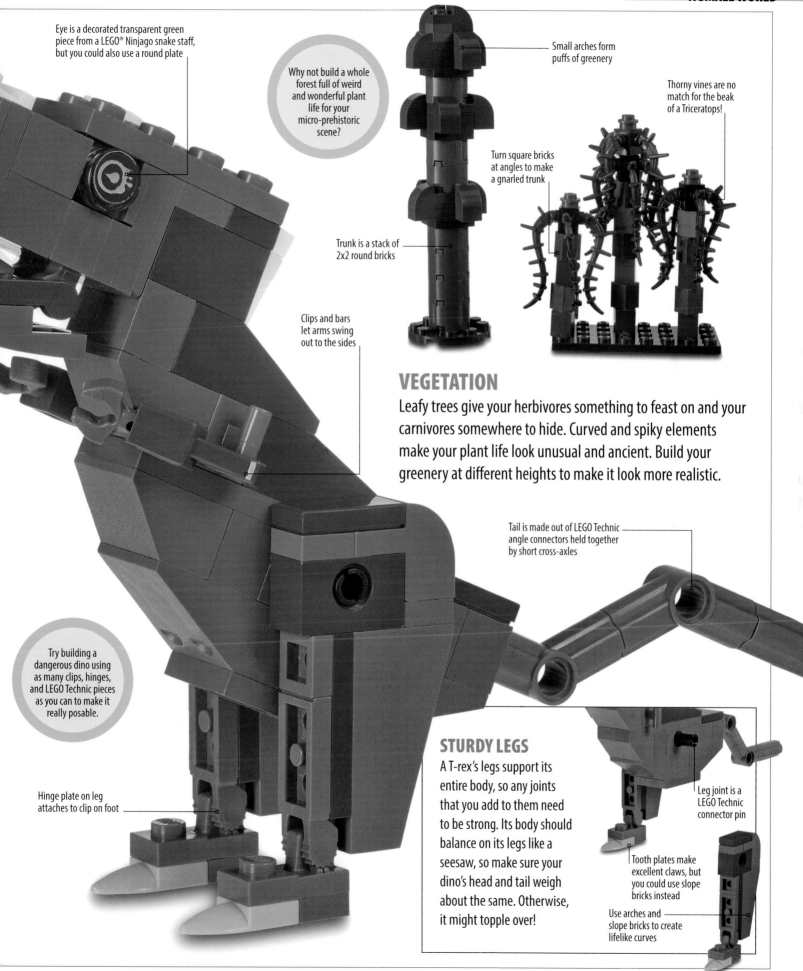

Eye is a decorated transparent green piece from a LEGO® Ninjago snake staff, but you could also use a round plate

Why not build a whole forest full of weird and wonderful plant life for your micro-prehistoric scene?

Small arches form puffs of greenery

Thorny vines are no match for the beak of a Triceratops!

Turn square bricks at angles to make a gnarled trunk

Trunk is a stack of 2x2 round bricks

Clips and bars let arms swing out to the sides

VEGETATION

Leafy trees give your herbivores something to feast on and your carnivores somewhere to hide. Curved and spiky elements make your plant life look unusual and ancient. Build your greenery at different heights to make it look more realistic.

Tail is made out of LEGO Technic angle connectors held together by short cross-axles

Try building a dangerous dino using as many clips, hinges, and LEGO Technic pieces as you can to make it really posable.

STURDY LEGS

A T-rex's legs support its entire body, so any joints that you add to them need to be strong. Its body should balance on its legs like a seesaw, so make sure your dino's head and tail weigh about the same. Otherwise, it might topple over!

Leg joint is a LEGO Technic connector pin

Hinge plate on leg attaches to clip on foot

Tooth plates make excellent claws, but you could use slope bricks instead

Use arches and slope bricks to create lifelike curves

MICRO-CASTLES

Why not become king or queen of your very own micro-castle? With their mighty towers and strong stone walls, castles are a terrific subject for micro-building. As long as you include its most well-known features, even a palm-sized castle model will be instantly familiar to everybody who sees it.

Stack 1x1 round bricks and cones for small towers, and 2x2 pieces for larger ones

Add some foliage to your mountain. These pine trees are green and brown 1x1 cones and round bricks

Use grey bricks, slopes, and tiles to create micro-scale mountains

An inverted 1x2 slope supports the base of the side tower

Transparent 1x1 plate windows are attached to headlight bricks

Think about what else you could add to your mountain. How about mountain goats or colourful plants?

A fortified gatehouse prevents unwelcome guests from crossing the bridge

BUILDING THE CHATEAU

The main building is a basic stack of bricks, with grey plates to represent bare stone. The roof is built using classic LEGO roof slopes.

Bridge is a pair of arches with plate and tile layers on top

A base of jumper plates allows the chateau to be narrower than the mountaintop

MOUNTAIN CHATEAU

This marvellous manor rises from a split mountain peak. Visitors must pass through a gatehouse and cross a bridge high above a flowing river. Yellow walls and a peaked blue roof make it look freshly painted and well-maintained.

Transparent blue tiles form a river. You could try building a waterfall on the mountainside, too!

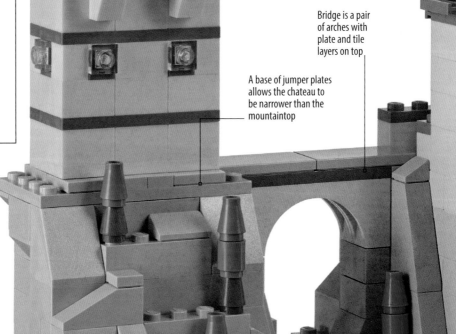

MEDIEVAL CASTLE

This traditional medieval castle has a square stone wall for defence, with a gateway in front and sturdy round towers at the corners. Two loyal knights on horses stand guard, ready to fight off invaders!

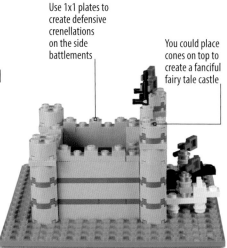

Use 1x1 plates to create defensive crenellations on the side battlements

You could place cones on top to create a fanciful fairy tale castle

SIDE VIEW

Gold 1x1 round plate adds decoration to the grey castle walls

Studs on top look like stone blocks

This 1x1 LEGO Technic brick-with-hole could be a window...or damage from a catapult attack!

Flags are 1x1 plates with clips attached to fire hose handles

Narrow towers are stacked 1x1 round bricks and plates attached to jumper plates, and held in place from behind with clips and bar pieces

I'M ON KNIGHT SHIFT.

KNIGHTS

These mounted knights in shining armour are a little large for the castle's scale, but you can't build them much smaller! They are holding flags, but they could also hold lances for jousting.

Metallic pieces make great armour!

Horse legs are stacks of two 1x1 round plates

CONSTRUCTING THE CASTLE

The castle's corner towers are stacks of 2x2 round bricks, with dark grey round plates to give the appearance of different kinds of stone. The dark grey sides of the castle's entrance are made by attaching tiles to bricks with side studs.

Two dark brown 1x2 tiles lie in front for a wooden drawbridge

HISTORICAL BUILDINGS

Don't just stop at castles – you can build all kinds of micro-scale buildings from the past. Find pictures of a historical building and identify its most recognisable details. Then look through your bricks for pieces that are the right shape and colour to recreate those details in a tiny size.

Συνολικά, είμαι απλώς άλλο ένα τούβλο στον τοίχο.

GREEK TEMPLE

The hardest part of making a micro-scaled version of an ancient Greek temple is creating the columns. Stacks of 1x1 round bricks will work, but for even better accuracy, try barred fence pieces.

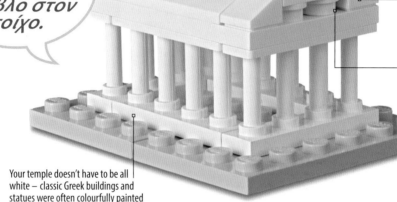

Slopes on the sides give the roof its shape

Round plates imitate sculpted details

Your temple doesn't have to be all white – classic Greek buildings and statues were often colourfully painted

Pick a country, research its historical buildings and then get building!

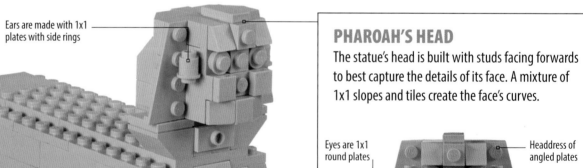

Ears are made with 1x1 plates with side rings

Tan base plate looks like the surrounding desert

PHAROAH'S HEAD

The statue's head is built with studs facing forwards to best capture the details of its face. A mixture of 1x1 slopes and tiles create the face's curves.

Eyes are 1x1 round plates

Headdress of angled plates

DESERT STATUE

This majestic statue has a lion's body and a human head. Build the statue on a base plate to keep it stable. Tan bricks echo limestone blocks, and slopes are used for angled edges.

Plates placed randomly on model create a weathered look

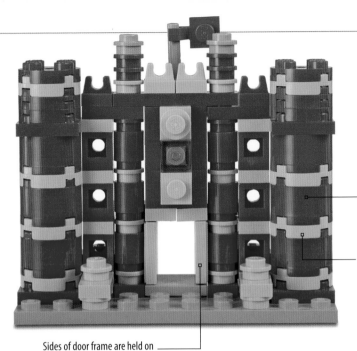

STATELY HOME

You don't always have to build the entire building. Start with an iconic part, like the front of this stately home, and then decide how much of the rest you want to make!

Side towers are made out of 2x2 round bricks and plates

Alternate bricks and plates to make colour patterns

Sides of door frame are held on by 1x1 bricks with side studs

Windmill's sails rotate on a turntable piece attached to a bracket with side studs

2x2 domed brick forms the roof of a storage silo

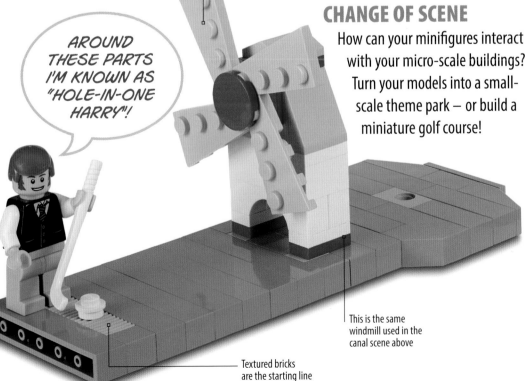

WINDMILL

Why not build different scenes around your micro-models? This old-fashioned windmill sits near a canal with a boat, a wooden jetty and storage silos for the grain produced by the mill.

The boat's windows are transparent 1x1 plates

Sails made from four angled plates held together with a round tile

A second plate layer raises the grass-covered land above the water

You don't have to build the entire boat, just the part that sticks up above the water

CHANGE OF SCENE

How can your minifigures interact with your micro-scale buildings? Turn your models into a small-scale theme park – or build a miniature golf course!

AROUND THESE PARTS I'M KNOWN AS "HOLE-IN-ONE HARRY"!

Aim for the brick with a hole!

Jumper plates are part of the windmill

This is the same windmill used in the canal scene above

Textured bricks are the starting line

CREATING A COURSE

This mini golf course is built like a wall on its side for a smooth surface. Bricks with side studs attach the jumper plates at the base of the windmill.

METRO SKYLINE

You've already seen how to build a modular micro-city, but you can go even smaller than that! By making individual super-micro towers, you can put together an entire metropolis, complete with monuments and skyscrapers, all small enough to display on a dinner plate. Use your pieces to create a variety of architectural wonders for a souvenir-worthy skyline.

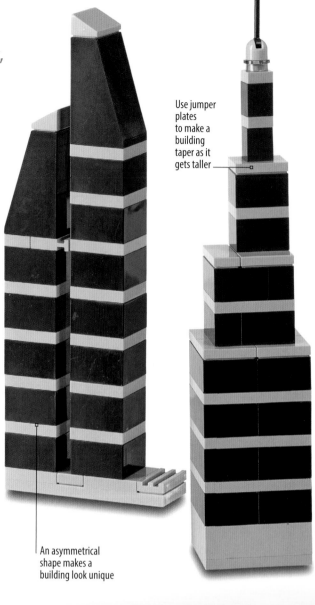

Use jumper plates to make a building taper as it gets taller

I CALL THIS CITY THE LITTLE APPLE!

An asymmetrical shape makes a building look unique

CITY-SCAPE

Super-micro buildings can be as easy or complicated to build as you want them to be. Some are as simple as stacking up bricks and plates. For a more elaborate shape, incorporate slopes and jumper plates.

Here's a custom pedestal for Lady Liberty from the LEGO® Minifigures line. You can create your own statue out of bricks, too!

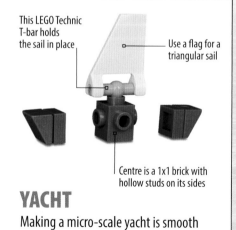

This LEGO Technic T-bar holds the sail in place

Use a flag for a triangular sail

Centre is a 1x1 brick with hollow studs on its sides

YACHT

Making a micro-scale yacht is smooth sailing if you've got the right pieces. If you don't have all of these parts, make up your own design!

Black bricks make the best shiny glass windows

Bricks with sideways studs will help you create vertical lines with plates

STRIKING SKYLINE

Think of ways to make your city buildings look interesting. Adding little details, such as antennas and exposed studs, helps create a spectacular skyline.

Antenna is a minifigure lance

The notches on the bottom of the pieces mimic little windows!

A hidden core of bricks with side studs holds this building together

Alternate stacks of bricks in one colour, and plates in another to build a basic tower

A blue tile creates a rooftop swimming pool

Smokestacks are LEGO® Alien Conquest ray guns clipped on by their handles, but you could stack round plates instead

OCEAN LINER

An ocean liner is a great way to view the city skyline from the water. With its high deck and multiple floors, it gives passengers plenty of opportunities for snapping photos of all their favourite buildings.

Cabin levels are made by alternating black and white plates

OUTER SPACE

Are you ready to boldly go where few have built before? Then blast off for outer space and start constucting and exploring your very own micro-scale galaxy! To begin your cosmic journey you'll need a powerful rocket, and a space station to be your first port of call.

Enlarged section for carrying satellites and other payloads

Textured bricks add extra surface detail

3...2...1 LAUNCH

Your rocket will need removable boosters if it's going to launch into orbit. The boosters are attached to the sides of the rocket by sideways-building.

ROCKET

The body of this rocket is built with 2x2 round bricks and plates, and holds two large cones base-to-base to create the bulge near the top. To make the body of the rocket more solid, and to connect the two cones, build a long LEGO Technic axle through its centre.

Plug in a flame piece for a launching effect

Bracket piece holds the rocket to the gantry during countdown

LAUNCH PAD

Before it can blast off, your rocket needs a launch pad. This gantry is built with C-shaped wall elements, but you could also use 1x2 bricks and 2x4 plates.

Use tiles for a heat-resistant platform under the rocket

A transparent red round plate acts as a warning light – when it flashes, stand clear of the launch pad!

SPACE STATION

The core of this space station is made of six half-cylinder pieces, with sturdy pylons supporting the large solar-panel "wings". The attached modules are round and domed bricks. Each one has its own function, such as astronaut quarters and labs for scientific experiments.

Tail is a 1x3 slope attached to jumper plates, topped with a 1x1 slope

A transparent grey piece provides a curved cockpit window

SPACE SHUTTLE

A micro-scale space station needs a micro-scale spaceship! This simple ship is built in a streamlined, studs-free style, which gives it a sleek and futuristic look. Its wings include slopes attached to bricks with side studs.

Shuttle attaches to a docking tube made from 2x2 textured round bricks

Blue and white colour scheme matches the rocket

Solar panels are stands from LEGO Minifigures collectible characters

Four brackets at the centre hold everything together

Create viewports with transparent 1x1 round tiles or plates

I'VE ALWAYS WANTED TO BE AN ASTROGNOME!

ALL IN THE DETAIL

You could make a communications dish with just a dish piece, but this detailed one is built with eight robot arm pieces, clipped to a plate with octagonal ring.

1x1 round plate

GREETINGS, EARTHLINGS

Build a communications dish so that our astronauts (or astrognomes) can keep in touch with Earth during their outer-space travels.

Include a computer bank and control panel, too

A 2x2 tile with one stud and a 1x1 plate with clip allow the dish to be aimed towards the sky

FUTURE WORLDS

Meet the micro-city of tomorrow! In the distant future, humanity has reached and colonized Mars. Here on the Red Planet, needle-like towers rise high into the sky and robotic machines dig for precious energy crystals. Use your smallest bricks to create your own alien landscapes and futuristic worlds – micro-scale style!

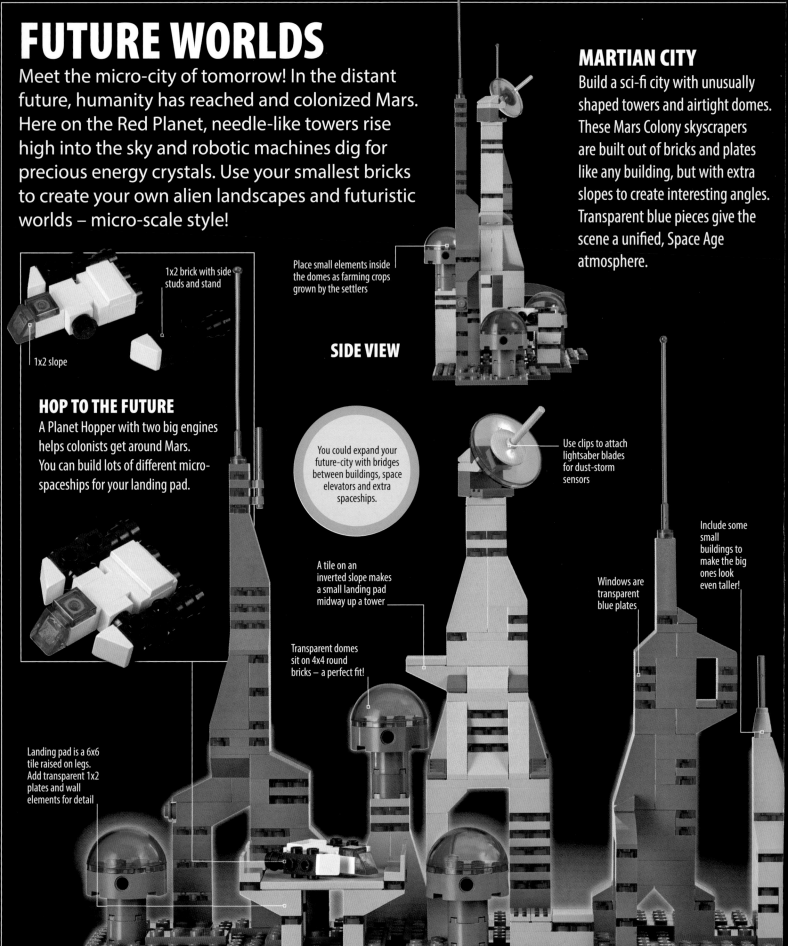

1x2 brick with side studs and stand

1x2 slope

MARTIAN CITY

Build a sci-fi city with unusually shaped towers and airtight domes. These Mars Colony skyscrapers are built out of bricks and plates like any building, but with extra slopes to create interesting angles. Transparent blue pieces give the scene a unified, Space Age atmosphere.

Place small elements inside the domes as farming crops grown by the settlers

SIDE VIEW

HOP TO THE FUTURE

A Planet Hopper with two big engines helps colonists get around Mars. You can build lots of different micro-spaceships for your landing pad.

You could expand your future-city with bridges between buildings, space elevators and extra spaceships.

Use clips to attach lightsaber blades for dust-storm sensors

A tile on an inverted slope makes a small landing pad midway up a tower

Transparent domes sit on 4x4 round bricks – a perfect fit!

Windows are transparent blue plates

Include some small buildings to make the big ones look even taller!

Landing pad is a 6x6 tile raised on legs. Add transparent 1x2 plates and wall elements for detail

SPACE CRUISER

In the future, rockets and space shuttles might be a thing of the past. Build a super-fast space cruiser that can dodge asteroids, outrace comets and fly between worlds in the blink of an interstellar eye!

Wings attach at two points for a solid connection

Each wing uses two plate-with-bar pieces to attach to the clips on the body

Cones can be boosters or blasters!

CRUISER CONSTRUCTION

The space cruiser is built around a core of bricks with side studs. Clips on the body attach a pair of sleek, flared-out wings, which are the same long, curved shape as the spaceship's top.

A LEGO Technic pin helps the saws to spin

A tall 1x1 column supports the saw arm

MINING ROVER

This Martian mining machine is out of this world! It grinds up rock with its saws, pipes the rubble through its central section for refinement, and deposits ores and crystals into the hover-truck at the other end.

Grey colour scheme looks strong and industrial

Rover wheels are mounted on 1x6 LEGO Technic bricks

Dark orange and brown plates create an uneven Martian surface. Use slopes for alien rocks

Hover-truck's jets are 1x1 plates with side rings

FUTURE TECH

The mining rover's saws are propellers from a LEGO submarine set. The pipes at the front and back are column pieces, and the heavy-treaded wheels are LEGO Technic gears.

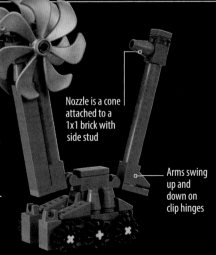

Nozzle is a cone attached to a 1x1 brick with side stud

Arms swing up and down on clip hinges

COOL BRICK

"This blade propeller makes a powerful saw for Martian mining equipment here, but it could be used as helicopter blades, a fan in a house, or as part of a set of wheels on a futuristic car!"

Go Wild!

The world is full of animals. They run, swim, fly and crawl. They can be as small as an insect or as big as a whale. They may be covered in fur, feathers or scales, with dozens of legs or none at all. But there's one thing that every animal has in common: you can build it with your LEGO® bricks. It's a wild world out there – so explore it!

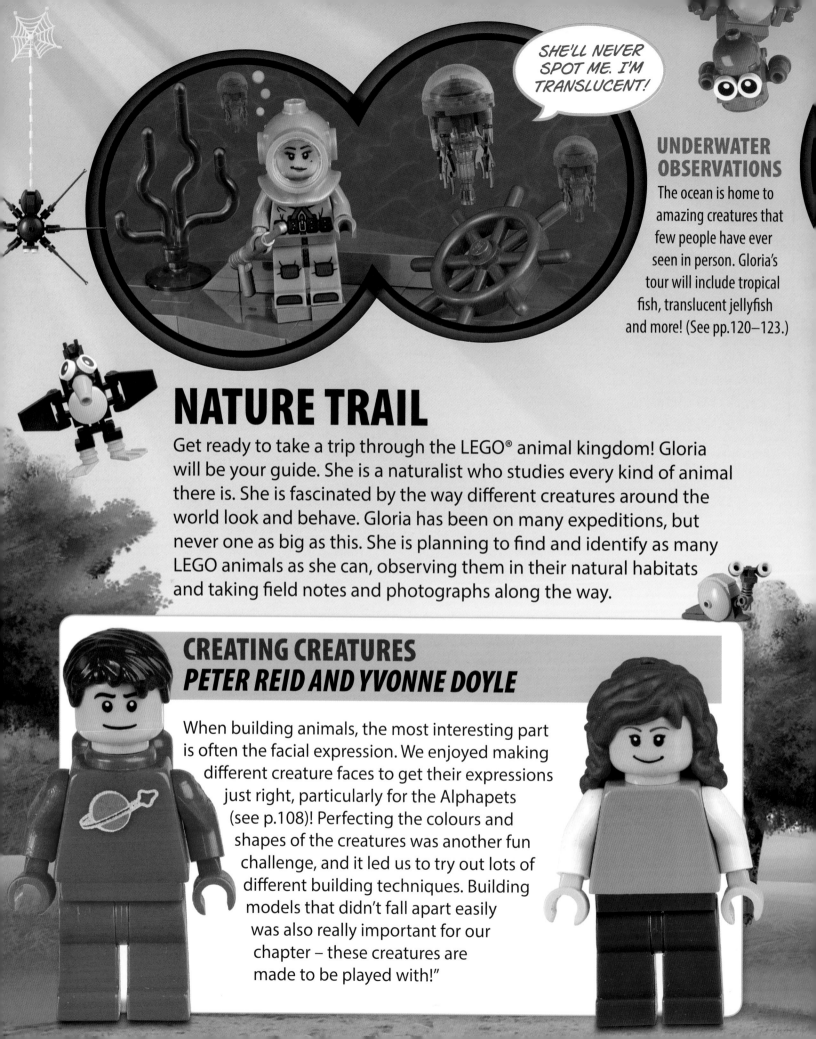

SHE'LL NEVER SPOT ME. I'M TRANSLUCENT!

UNDERWATER OBSERVATIONS

The ocean is home to amazing creatures that few people have ever seen in person. Gloria's tour will include tropical fish, translucent jellyfish and more! (See pp.120–123.)

NATURE TRAIL

Get ready to take a trip through the LEGO® animal kingdom! Gloria will be your guide. She is a naturalist who studies every kind of animal there is. She is fascinated by the way different creatures around the world look and behave. Gloria has been on many expeditions, but never one as big as this. She is planning to find and identify as many LEGO animals as she can, observing them in their natural habitats and taking field notes and photographs along the way.

CREATING CREATURES
PETER REID AND YVONNE DOYLE

When building animals, the most interesting part is often the facial expression. We enjoyed making different creature faces to get their expressions just right, particularly for the Alphapets (see p.108)! Perfecting the colours and shapes of the creatures was another fun challenge, and it led us to try out lots of different building techniques. Building models that didn't fall apart easily was also really important for our chapter – these creatures are made to be played with!"

POLAR EXPLORATION

No location is too remote and no environment too extreme for this naturalist! Gloria will travel from the frozen Antarctic to the North Pole, meeting penguins, polar bears and everything in between. (See pp.124–127.)

...AND BEYOND!

Not content to study only the animals she can find on Earth, Gloria will peer through a telescope to study strange creatures from other planets!

ON SAFARI

Kick off your animal adventure by going on an African safari! Put together a camouflaged lookout and keep watch to see what creatures wander past. Be very quiet and hold still – you don't want to scare the animals!

SAFARI... SO GOOD!

You could also build window covers to hide the lookout – or to give your minifigures some shade!

Place plants on a tan or yellow base to create a natural landscape

Use a step element or build a ladder to access the lookout

SIDE VIEW

1x2 log bricks look like side-by-side tree trunks

CAN YOU STAY ON THE STEPS, GLORIA? IT HELPS ATTRACT THE LIONS.

TREE-TOP HIDEAWAY

Palm leaves disguise the lookout's square plate roof so that the people inside won't be noticed by nearby animals. Flat and smooth shapes look artificial, so add some lumpy bits on top!

Use brown pieces so the structure blends in with the environment

Stilts can be 2x2 bricks or pairs of 1x2 bricks

LOOKOUT

On a safari you can go looking for animals, or you can wait for the animals to come to you. By building a lookout designed to blend in with the trees, your minifigures can observe the wildlife undetected.

Stilts keep the viewing platform out of reach of ground creatures

GIRAFFE

It's hard to overlook a giraffe out there on the savanna! With their long necks and legs, these towering titans really stand out in a crowd. Use 1x1 pieces to make the skinniest sections, and regular and inverted slopes for realistic angles.

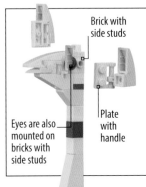

Brick with side studs

Plate with handle

Eyes are also mounted on bricks with side studs

EAR, EAR

The giraffe's ears are 1x3 curved slope pieces attached to clips. To make them move, connect the clips to plates with handles before attaching them to the bricks with side studs on the giraffe's head.

Nose is made from the same piece as the ears: a 1x3 curved slope

Use a tooth plate for a protruding lower lip

A steep slope piece adds height and strength to the base of the neck

Studs on the back are hidden by tiles

Assemble the legs and neck separately before attaching them to the body

Tail is a yellow harpoon gun with its handle plugged into a LEGO® Technic half-pin

Build even more trees and plants to add to your safari scene.

Start the body with a large plate in the middle

This sculpted head makes an interesting lion face

Feet are 1x2 slopes

Build a scene for your giraffe, with a tall, leafy tree and sand or grass for a base

Legs are LEGO Technic pieces, but you could use 1x1 round bricks and plates instead

S-shaped tail is attached to a brick-with-hole with a LEGO Technic pin

THE MANE EVENT

Most of this powerful hunter's mane is built out of angled plates. A pair of brackets on each side attaches them to the head and shoulders of the lion. The central parts of the mane are built directly into the body.

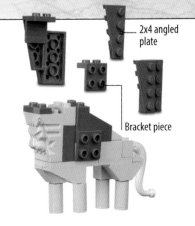

2x4 angled plate

Bracket piece

LION

No safari would be complete without a lion sighting. Use tan pieces to build the body of this fearsome feline, and brown or black for its shaggy mane. A clever use of special pieces will give you a unique model design.

SAFARI GIANTS

What giant-sized beasts will you see on your safari? You might spot a trumpeting elephant at the watering hole, an ostrich sprinting across the plains or a herd of horned buffalo keeping an eye out for danger. Build them all for a grand wildlife adventure!

ELEPHANT

Elephants are the biggest animals you'll encounter on your expedition, so make sure you have plenty of grey bricks in your collection! Try starting your build with a six-stud-wide plate and building the body up from there.

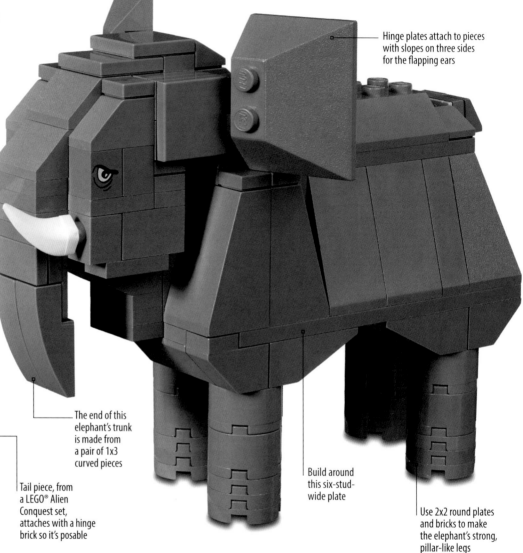

Hinge plates attach to pieces with slopes on three sides for the flapping ears

Use slope bricks to create the shape of the elephant's angled forehead

The end of this elephant's trunk is made from a pair of 1x3 curved pieces

Build around this six-stud-wide plate

Use 2x2 round plates and bricks to make the elephant's strong, pillar-like legs

SIDE VIEW

Attaching the legs last will make the rest of the body easier to build

Tail piece, from a LEGO® Alien Conquest set, attaches with a hinge brick so it's posable

⭐ CHALLENGE

ELEPHANT STAMPEDE

Challenge your friends to an elephant race! Put five bricks of different colours into a bag and take turns picking a brick from it. The colour of the brick you pick determines which body part you can build for that turn. The winner is the first player to build a complete elephant.

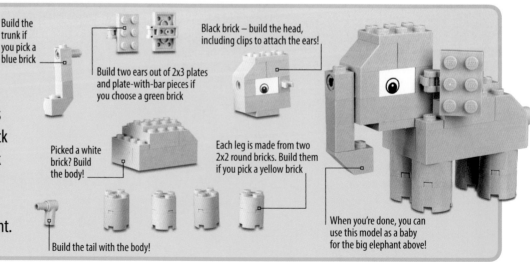

Build the trunk if you pick a blue brick

Build two ears out of 2x3 plates and plate-with-bar pieces if you choose a green brick

Black brick – build the head, including clips to attach the ears!

Picked a white brick? Build the body!

Each leg is made from two 2x2 round bricks. Build them if you pick a yellow brick

Build the tail with the body!

When you're done, you can use this model as a baby for the big elephant above!

Beak is a skeleton leg from a LEGO® Ninjago set

YOU CAN'T RUFFLE MY FEATHERS – THEY'RE PLASTIC!

OSTRICH

These large, flightless birds are extremely fast runners, so give your model a pair of long, straight legs. Make sure your ostrich's body is well balanced so it doesn't fall over. Female ostriches are brown or grey – why not use your pieces in those colours to build a female version?

Centre of the head is a 1x1 brick with studs on four sides

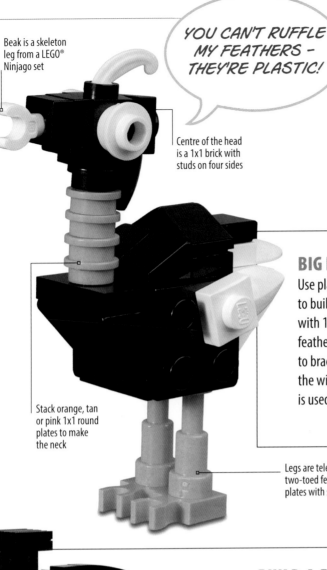

BIG BIRD BODY

Use plates and inverted slopes to build the ostrich's lower body, with 1x1 slopes for its raised, feathery back. Attach tooth plates to brackets on both sides to create the wings. Another tooth plate is used for the tail feathers.

Tooth plate

1x1 slope piece

Stack orange, tan or pink 1x1 round plates to make the neck

Legs are telescopes, and two-toed feet are 1x1 plates with side clips

What other safari animals can you build to add to your safari scene?

BUILD-A-BUFFALO

A pair of bricks with two side studs holds the whole model together on the inside. Angled plates attach to them sideways to create the buffalo's thick hide, and grilles make the hair of its shaggy coat.

2x3 angled plate

Long curved bricks create a true-to-nature humpbacked shape

Bricks with side studs

1x2 grille

The buffalo's eyes are headlight bricks

BUFFALO

Don't be tricked by its cow-like appearance – the buffalo is as short-tempered and tough as they come! Build as many as you can and create a whole herd of these majestic, but grumpy, beasts to populate your safari scenes.

Horns from a LEGO cow plug into headlight bricks with hollow side studs

Plates with click hinges let the head hang at an angle

Use tooth plates to create short, sharp hooves peeking out from under the hair

SAFARI TRUCK

Fallen trees, bumpy roads and rivers are just a few of the hazards that you will come across on your safari. You need a rugged vehicle that won't get stuck in the mud or break down in the path of a charging elephant. Build a truck that will get you everywhere you want to go – and let you make a speedy exit if you need to!

BOTTOM VIEW

A plate with inverted slopes on its sides supports the centre of the truck

A long plate locks together the truck's underside

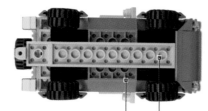

BUILDER TALK

"Sometimes it helps to make the most difficult area of a model first – like the body on this safari truck – then build the rest around it."

If your roof piece isn't long enough, extend it with plates, slopes, and tiles

The roof can be removed if it's not too sunny...and there aren't any monkeys around!

Build a trailer to attach to your truck. You could fill it with banana pieces to keep the monkeys happy!

THOSE LIONS SEEM TO BE GETTING CLOSE, GLORIA.

Use multiple grilles for an impact-resistant front end. You could build up a reinforced bumper, too!

Use plates to add decorative stripes and details

Transparent slopes make bright headlights

Use tyres with big treads for traction on dust, dirt and mud

A 1x2 tile mounted on a plate with side ring makes a handy side mirror

Attach a tile to headlight bricks to create a thick door in case of an angry rhino attack!

TRUCK POWER

Your safari truck needs to be built for adventure.
Include a rugged chassis to resist bumps and thumps,
big tyres to drive over any obstacles, headlights to
light the way in the dark and open windows so your
minifigures can photograph the wildlife with ease.

GLORIA?

A blank
minifigure
head with a
round tile on
the end holds
the spare tyre
onto the back
of the truck

A curved bar with
studs keeps the
photographer from
falling out of the truck!

This socket piece can
be used to tow other
vehicles or supplies

Use grey or
silver pieces
to give the
impression of
strong metal

REAR VIEW

Small windows
support the
sides of the roof

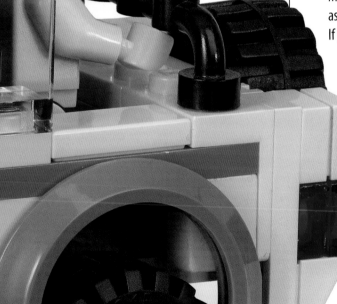

Make sure the bottom of your
truck is raised up high to clear
rocks, roots and ruts

UNDER THE HOOD

Most of the safari truck is built with basic LEGO bricks, but a few parts – such
as the wheels, mudguards and windshield – are specific to automobile sets.
If you don't have these pieces, then improvise with what you do have!

A tall roll bar
holds up the
back of the roof

Punctured tyres
are a real problem
out in the wild, so
always pack a spare!

This piece can be used as
a vehicle's hood or roof

A hollow space
beneath the hood
will keep your
model lightweight
and fast, but you
could build an
engine inside

Install mudguards
over the wheels

BARNYARD BEASTS

Expand your farm and build animals that baa, bray, moo, or neigh! They will all need their own place to live and food to eat, so do a bit of research before you build. How else will you know how to take proper care of them all?

COUNTING THESE SHEEP MAKES ME FEEL SLEEPY... YAWN!

Sheep like to munch on low-growing plants

Make a fence out of bar or antenna pieces attached to 1x1 bricks with side studs

SHEEP PEN

When building a sheep pen, use a green base plate so your sheep have plenty of fresh grass for grazing. If you have enough pieces, build the fence all the way around and add a gate so that the farmer can get inside.

Build smaller, simpler versions of your sheep to make lambs – or skinny pink versions for shearing season!

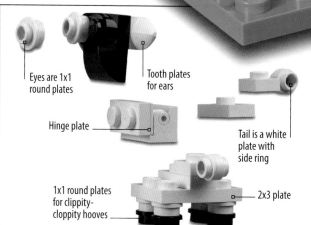

Eyes are 1x1 round plates

Tooth plates for ears

Hinge plate

Tail is a white plate with side ring

1x1 round plates for clippity-cloppity hooves

2x3 plate

SHEEP

Want to make a woolly sheep? Start with a 2x3 plate and attach a hinge for the neck. Plates with side rings sticking out create a thick and curly coat.

COWS

Add a couple of cows to your farm scene. Use contrasting black and white pieces to create their patchy hides. A cow's wide back can be made with a curved 2x4 brick and a droid torso piece is just the right shape for its head!

MOO.

A sheep-herding dog safeguards the pen

Legs are LEGO Technic pins

Using black and white pieces together creates a good contrast

Curved 2x4 brick

Droid torso piece is clipped onto a hinged plate so that it can moo-ve up and down

DONKEY

The bodies of big farm animals like donkeys and horses can all be built in a similar way. All they need are different heads and details! Start with a two-stud-wide plate and add more plates, slopes and arches to fill out the shape.

Ears are armour pieces from a LEGO® Ben 10™ set, but you could use plates or tiles instead

HEE-HAW!

Two-stud-wide plate

Inverted slopes

Clip-and-hinge connection

DONKEY DIAGRAM

Once you have built the base of your donkey, you can add pieces to create the shape. Use inverted slopes to create tapered shoulders, and a clip-and-hinge connection when constructing the head so that your donkey can hee-haw to its heart's content!

This 1x2 textured brick makes the nose look furry

If you don't have a carrot, you can make one with an orange LEGO cone

1x1 cones or round bricks make good hooves for larger beasts

FARM FOWL

You don't have to travel too far afield to discover interesting animals. Take a trip to the farm and you will find cows, pigs, horses and much more – not to mention the different kinds of birds that live there. Let's meet a few of our most familiar and favourite feathered friends.

DUCK POND

Ducks love water, so build a pond on your farm where they can quack and splash to their hearts' content. Ponds can be found anywhere, surrounded by grass or in the dirt. You could also add some frogs or fishy friends to your pond!

Use colourless transparent tiles for a frozen winter pond!

QUICK BUILD

Tile for a smooth body

1x1 brick with studs on four sides

1x1 cone for a tail

Wings are tooth plates

Head is a fire hose nozzle

DUCKS

These little ducks are made with just seven pieces. Start with a 1x1 brick with studs on four sides, and attach a tail, wings and a clip to hold the head.

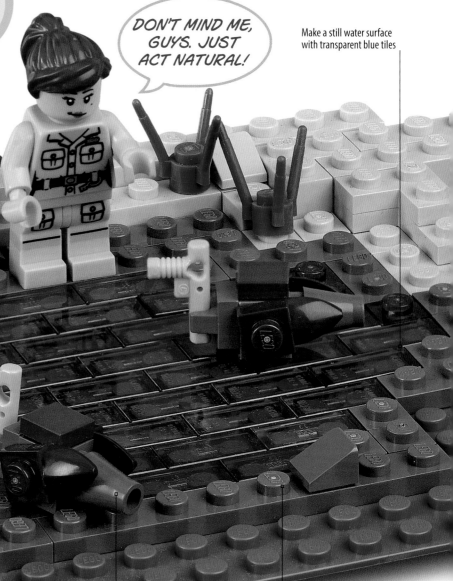

DON'T MIND ME, GUYS. JUST ACT NATURAL!

Make a still water surface with transparent blue tiles

Place plants at the edge of the pond or sticking out of the water

Ducks can perch on the side or go for a swim

Build a ring of grey plates for stone, or brown for mud, around the pond

CHICKEN COOP

Your chickens will need to be protected from foxes and other predators, so build a coop to keep them (and their precious eggs) safe.

I'M FEELING COOPED UP IN HERE.

Ice cream cone tops or 1x1 round plates make egg-cellent eggs!

Grilles give the impression of a feathery back

Use small plates to make straw bedding

If you don't have these latticed fences, any fence pieces will do

You could build a fence all the way around so your chickens don't get out, and nothing else gets in!

The comb is a plume from a minifigure hat, plugged into a hollow stud on top

A plate with side clip hangs down to create a wattle

Inverted slope bricks make good tails and chests for your poultry pals

Beak is a 1x1 plate with a vertical clip

Eyes are 1x1 round plates with hollow studs from LEGO® Games

Use tooth plates for feathers and wings

TURKEY

What's like a chicken but a whole lot bigger? No, not a dinosaur – a turkey! They may not be the prettiest birds, but turkeys are a familiar sight (and sound) on many farms.

Legs are 1x1 round bricks

Neck is centred on a jumper plate

Bracket piece

GOBBLE, GOBBLE

Turkeys are larger than most farm birds, so you will need more bricks to build them. Use bracket pieces to make a wide body and provide attachment points for feathers on the sides and back.

WHY DID THE CHICKEN CROSS THE ROAD?

OH, NOT THAT OLD JOKE AGAIN, BERNARD!

CHICKEN

How many ways can you build a chicken? As many ways as you can think of! These chickens' heads are 1x2 bricks with two holes. The one on the right's lower body is made with two downward-facing headlight bricks.

Tooth plate for a beak

A flower from a LEGO® Friends set attached to a jumper plate makes a nice crest

Chest and feet are grilles

1x1 round plates for little legs

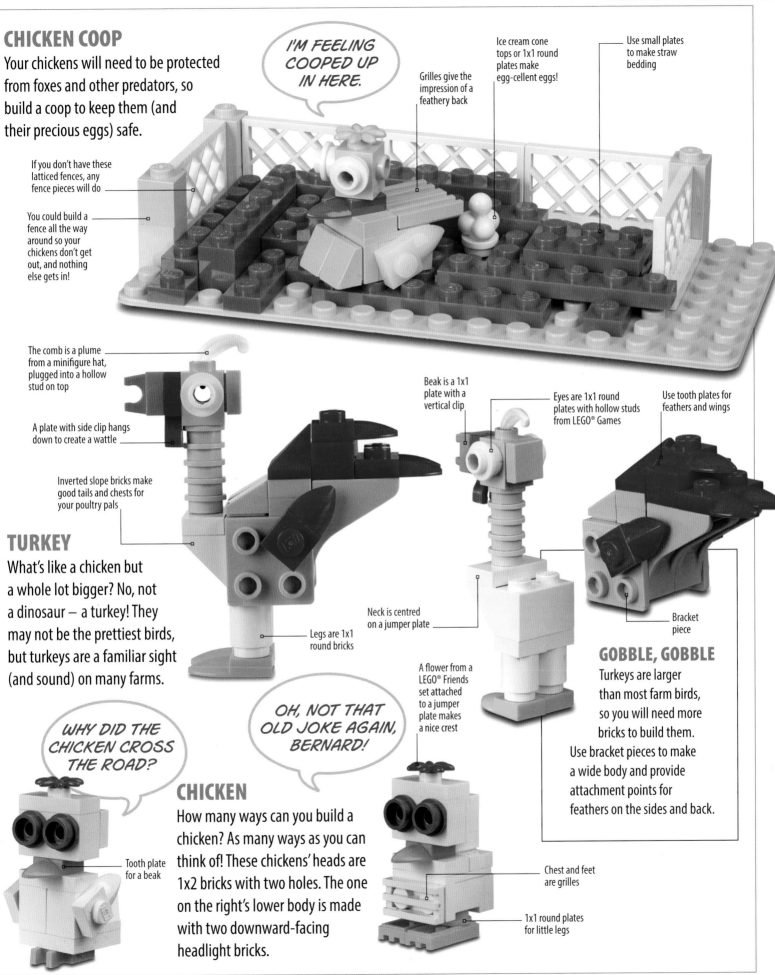

ALPHAPETS

Building these peculiar little creatures is as easy as A-B-C! You can make all sorts of strange, silly and unusual animal faces by using LEGO tiles with printed numbers and letters. If you don't have these decorated tiles, then try other ones with interesting patterns and colours from your collection.

With two Q tiles and an upside-down Y, this cat looks curious and hopeful

Use tooth plates for pointy, triangular ears

Two V tiles and a P tile create scrunched up eyes and a tongue sticking out!

Back can be a slope or a curved brick

Red hinge plate creates a cat's collar

Four tooth plates make the front and hind feet

Base of body is a 2x3 plate

What other animals could you add to your Alphapet collection?

HERE, BIRDIE! TWEET, TWEET!

CATS

Use different letters to give your crouching kitty a new expression! Even without letter tiles, you can use pieces with printed grilles or dials to change your creation's face and mood.

A hinge base lets the head tilt up and down

PET PIECES

Think about how to use your pieces in different ways, like tilting a tooth plate to create a floppy ear. Experiment with your pieces and you'll discover lots of ways to fill your creations with heaps of fun.

Use pieces with side studs to build in different directions

Use sideways tooth plates for stubby little legs

Angle the ears back to make the pup look like it's running

A grille creates a fuzzy white chest

BIRD

Sometimes you find the perfect piece to make an animal part. This bird's wings are a pair of LEGO minifigure fan accessories, plugged into 1x1 plates with side rings.

Letter Ö tiles give this bird a wide-eyed look

Fluttering wings can twist in their rings and rotate on the body's side studs

1x1 brick with side studs

Neck is a 1x2 plate. Use a longer plate for a longer neck

BIRD BODY

Birds come in many shapes. The head and body of this bird is built around a pair of 1x1 bricks with studs on four sides.

Plate with side ring

Beak is a horn plugged into a hollow stud

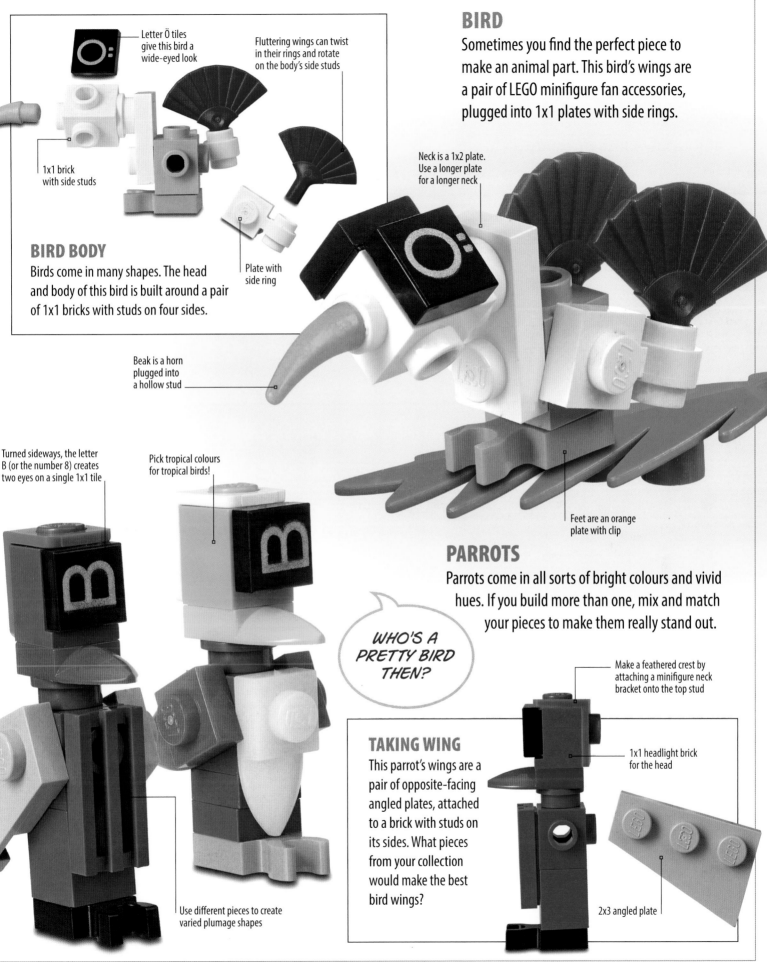

Turned sideways, the letter B (or the number 8) creates two eyes on a single 1x1 tile

Pick tropical colours for tropical birds!

Feet are an orange plate with clip

PARROTS

Parrots come in all sorts of bright colours and vivid hues. If you build more than one, mix and match your pieces to make them really stand out.

WHO'S A PRETTY BIRD THEN?

Make a feathered crest by attaching a minifigure neck bracket onto the top stud

TAKING WING

This parrot's wings are a pair of opposite-facing angled plates, attached to a brick with studs on its sides. What pieces from your collection would make the best bird wings?

1x1 headlight brick for the head

Use different pieces to create varied plumage shapes

2x3 angled plate

HANDFUL OF BRICKS

Each of our fan builders was given a handful of common LEGO elements and asked to make as many different models as they could using only those pieces. Check out the custom creations that creature-makers Pete and Yvonne built.

Eyes are radar dishes with black 1x1 round plates in the centre

PLANT

This dancing flower was born to boogie! Pete and Yvonne used one shade of green to make the stem, another for the leaves and an orange plate for a colourful blossom on top.

A sturdy base of bricks is key for a tall, thin model

CHIRP!

BIRD

Eyes, a beak, and wings are all this little bird needs to be recognisable. Placing one slope-brick foot in front of the other makes it look like it's taking a step.

Angled plate wings are attached with sideways building

It's no surprise that an antenna piece makes a great antenna!

Leave some room in the middle for your minifigure to sit in

RACE CAR

For a fast-looking auto, build a long body that's low to the ground with a raised spoiler. Turn a racer into a remote-controlled car by attaching an antenna on top.

4X4 CAR

To make a simple LEGO brick car, just include four spinning wheels and a transparent piece for a windshield. Headlights, a rear spoiler and a front grille are optional extras!

Two grilles make an extra-wide bumper

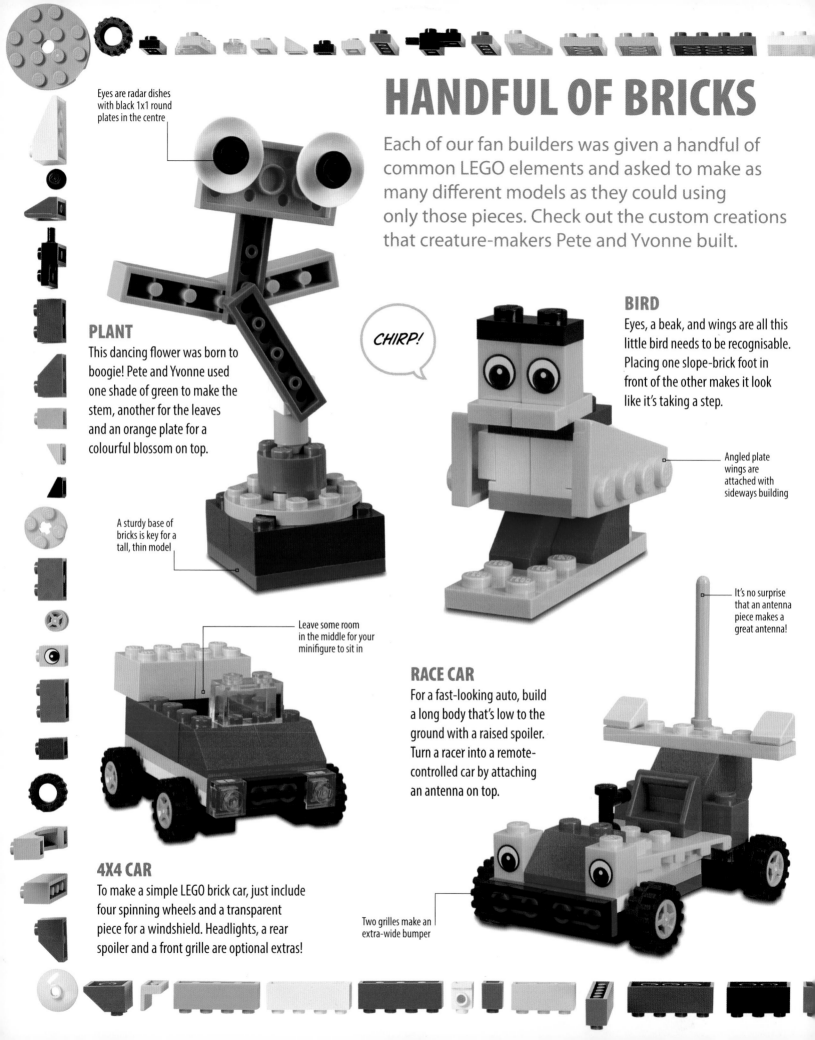

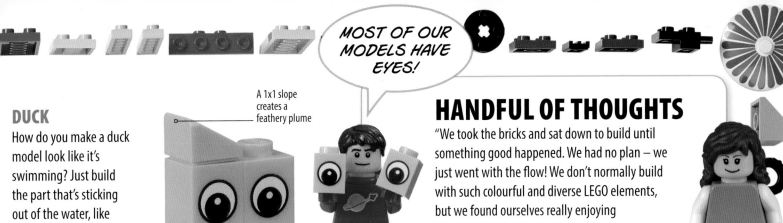

DUCK

How do you make a duck model look like it's swimming? Just build the part that's sticking out of the water, like Pete and Yvonne did here!

A 1x1 slope creates a feathery plume

Angled plates can be tail feathers, too

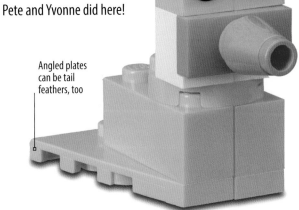

With four wheels, this creation spins around and around and around!

WHIRLIGIG

Not every model has to be something specific. Try combining pieces in random or silly ways to make equally random or silly models!

Floppy ears are brown 1x2 bricks

DOG

What kinds of animals can you build out of a handful of bricks? Here's a peculiar pooch with a tap for a nose and a cone for a panting tongue!

MOST OF OUR MODELS HAVE EYES!

HANDFUL OF THOUGHTS

"We took the bricks and sat down to build until something good happened. We had no plan — we just went with the flow! We don't normally build with such colourful and diverse LEGO elements, but we found ourselves really enjoying the challenge."

Pop a radar dish on top of an antenna for a shady umbrella

BEACH SCENE

An umbrella, a comfy reclining chair and a bottle of sunblock will help you enjoy a day at the sandy beach. Watch out for the ocean tickling your toes!

Bottle is a 1x1 round brick with a tap on top for the dispenser

I LOVE MY LEDERHOSEN!

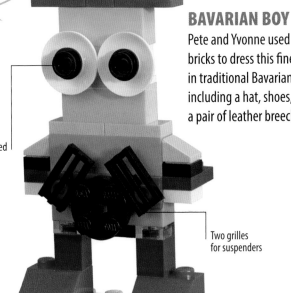

BAVARIAN BOY

Pete and Yvonne used colorful bricks to dress this fine fellow in traditional Bavarian clothing, including a hat, shoes, and a pair of leather breeches.

Innocent, wide-eyed expression

Two grilles for suspenders

CREEPING CRITTERS

Just look at these darlings, with all of their legs and eyes and mandibles and antennae. Build some bugs and grubs, and spiders and centipedes – these little critters can be cute, too! Show how much you love them by building the creepiest crawlies you can imagine.

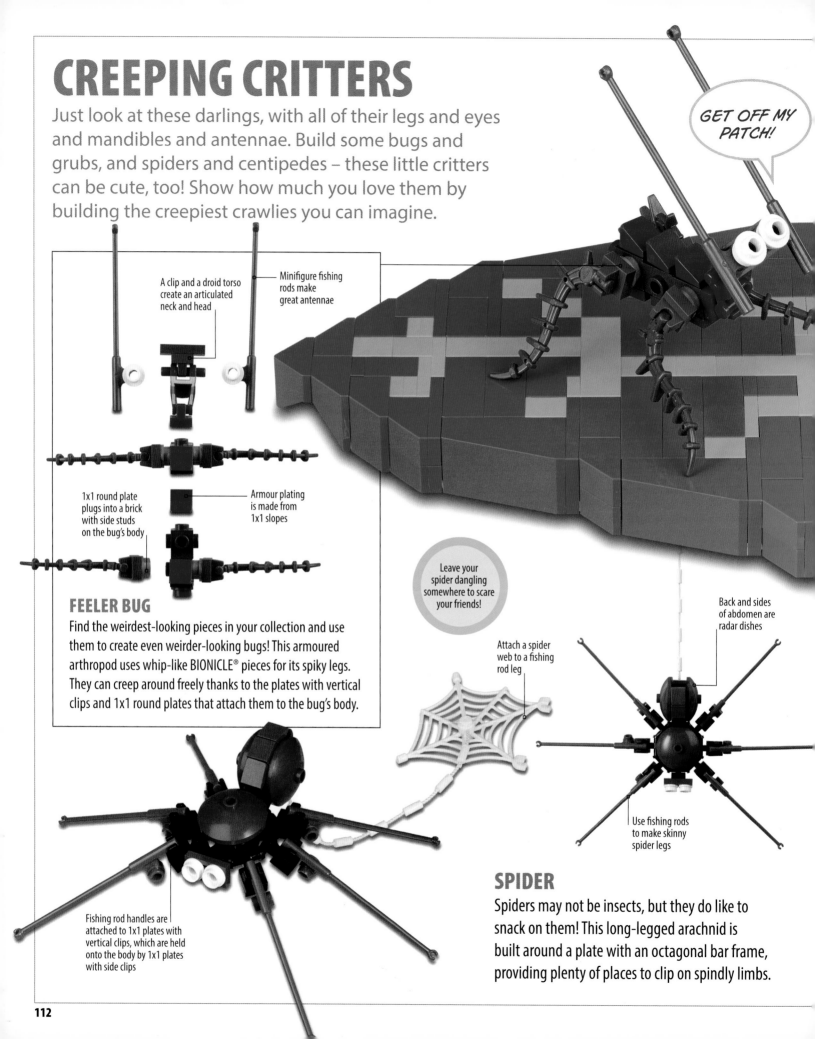

GET OFF MY PATCH!

A clip and a droid torso create an articulated neck and head

Minifigure fishing rods make great antennae

1x1 round plate plugs into a brick with side studs on the bug's body

Armour plating is made from 1x1 slopes

FEELER BUG

Find the weirdest-looking pieces in your collection and use them to create even weirder-looking bugs! This armoured arthropod uses whip-like BIONICLE® pieces for its spiky legs. They can creep around freely thanks to the plates with vertical clips and 1x1 round plates that attach them to the bug's body.

Leave your spider dangling somewhere to scare your friends!

Attach a spider web to a fishing rod leg

Back and sides of abdomen are radar dishes

Use fishing rods to make skinny spider legs

Fishing rod handles are attached to 1x1 plates with vertical clips, which are held onto the body by 1x1 plates with side clips

SPIDER

Spiders may not be insects, but they do like to snack on them! This long-legged arachnid is built around a plate with an octagonal bar frame, providing plenty of places to clip on spindly limbs.

CENTIPEDE

When constructing a long critter like this centipede, build a chain of identical body sections — as many as you want! Give each section a pair of legs so it can stand up and scurry.

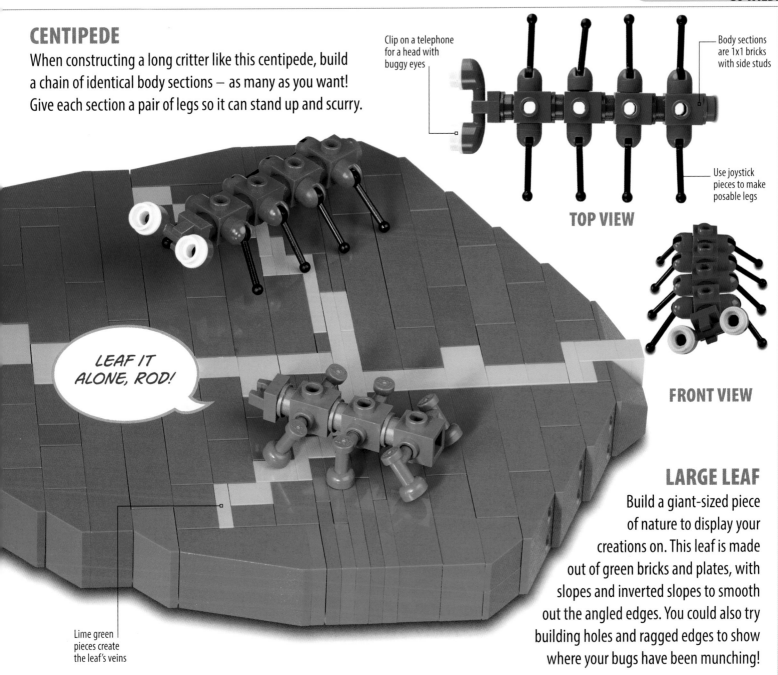

Clip on a telephone for a head with buggy eyes

Body sections are 1x1 bricks with side studs

Use joystick pieces to make posable legs

TOP VIEW

FRONT VIEW

LEAF IT ALONE, ROD!

Lime green pieces create the leaf's veins

LARGE LEAF

Build a giant-sized piece of nature to display your creations on. This leaf is made out of green bricks and plates, with slopes and inverted slopes to smooth out the angled edges. You could also try building holes and ragged edges to show where your bugs have been munching!

GREEN BUG

This skittering critter is built entirely out of small LEGO pieces. Its segments are made from 1x1 bricks with side studs, and 1x1 round plates in between.

Head is a 1x1 plate with vertical clip

Plug in tap pieces or other small elements for legs

TOP VIEW

COOL BRICK

"This 1x1 brick with studs on top and four sides allows you to build outwards in lots of directions. It's a great brick for an animal head or the centre of a body."

MORE CREEPING CRITTERS

There are lots of other invertebrates out there that you can build! Just look under a rock, up a tree or in a garden and you're sure to find all sorts of creeping, crawling, slithering and slimy creatures to inspire your creativity.

SNAILS

Snails may not be the fastest critters around, but these ones are quick builds if you have the right parts. You could also make a slug by leaving off the shell part!

WAIT UP! YOU'RE GOING TOO FAST!

SNAIL SHELL

A snail's shell is its home, so take care when building this part! The centre of the snail's shell is a 1x1 brick with side studs. Radar dishes attach to the 1x1 brick's side studs.

You could use radar dish pieces in any color

Small radar dish fits under the larger radar dish

1x1 brick with side studs

Eyestalks are a telephone handset on a clip

A minifigure ray gun creates a detailed, angled neck

A grille slope and a tooth plate make a tapering tail

QUICK BUILD

LADYBIRDS

You can build a little ladybird out of just seven pieces. For a bigger challenge, try to change the design so that your ladybird is flying!

Body is two dome bricks held together by a small LEGO Technic axle

Head is a black 1x1 brick with four side studs

Use a plate with a vertical clip for mandibles

Gaps in shell look like a ladybird's black spots!

SLICED BREAD

Start the construction of your bread slice with a big white wall in the middle. Use tan or brown bricks for the crust. 1x1 slopes and arch bricks create the distinctive "bread" shape at the top. You could also add some green bricks for a touch of mould!

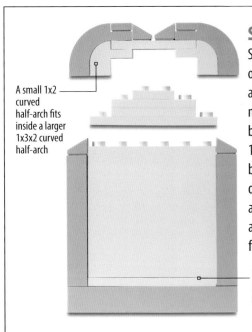

A small 1x2 curved half-arch fits inside a larger 1x3x2 curved half-arch

Use one big wall element or stack lots of white bricks to form the white part of the bread slice

SHOO, FLY!

To make the body of this fly, use three 1x1 bricks with studs on four sides. For the head, use another 1x1 brick with side studs, but in a different colour.

Use contrasting coloured angled plates for the wings

1x1 plates attach the wings to the body

Eyes are decorated 1x1 round tiles from a LEGO Ninjago set

Robot-claw legs plug into hollow studs

Why stop at one fly? Build a whole swarm!

A FEAST FIT FOR A FLY!

FLY AND BREAD

If you leave food out long enough, you are sure to attract some buzzing company. A slice of bread makes an inviting landing pad for a hungry fly – and it might even bring some friends!

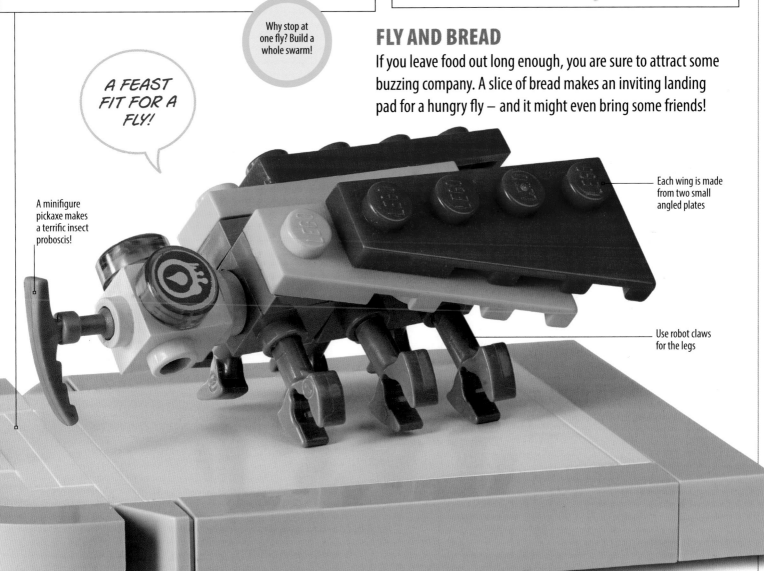

A minifigure pickaxe makes a terrific insect proboscis!

Each wing is made from two small angled plates

Use robot claws for the legs

Legs are robot arms, clipped onto an octagonal plate with bar

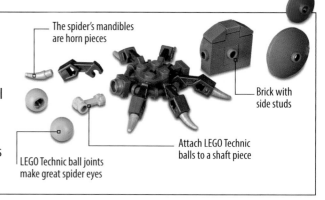

SPIDER HOUSE

Many zoos are home to different species of spiders and other invertebrates. Build some creepy-crawler creations for your zoo.

Use transparent 1x1 round tiles for eyes that look like they're glowing

This bug variation uses a second octagonal plate with bar for its abdomen

CHECK OUT MY "WEB" SITE!

A 1x1 round stud supports the radar dish on top

AT THE ZOO

A zoo is a marvellous place to see creatures from all over the word in one location. Think about what will keep your zoo animals happy, like an enclosure with climbing bars to monkey around on and trees to climb.

Body and head are both 1x1 bricks with studs on four sides

A minifigure pistol plugs into a cone to create a slender tail

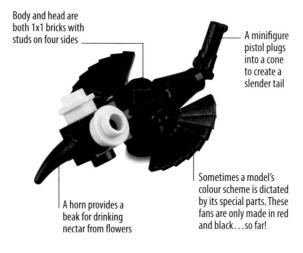

A horn provides a beak for drinking nectar from flowers

Sometimes a model's colour scheme is dictated by its special parts. These fans are only made in red and black...so far!

HUMMINGBIRD

A hummingbird is small and light, so you don't have to use a lot of bricks to build its body. LEGO minifigure fans make perfect rapidly beating wings.

SNAKE

The joints of this super-posable snake are made from droid torsos (see the Cool Brick on p.78), with segments assembled from side-stud bricks, small plates and plates with vertical clips. If you don't have enough parts to build a snake this long, build a shorter one!

1x1 plates create brightly coloured stripes

HISSING SNAKE

The snake's head is a 1x1 brick with four side studs. A round brick is used for a nose and its hissing tongue is a unicorn's horn!

Round brick

A droid torso connects the head to the first segment of the body

Tip of tail is a robot claw

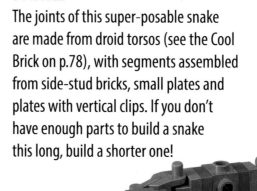

MONKEY

Monkeys are always up to something, so let them play by giving them different head and limb positions. This one is designed to sit on the ground. Its head is built upside down to give it a cheeky and whimsical expression!

Hinge plates allow its legs to swing out to the sides

One 2x2 dome gives the monkey's snout a little round mouth, and another gives it a bellybutton!

Climbing bars built out of LEGO Technic bricks and long bar elements

Arms are LEGO Minifigure® ray guns

Top of head is a 2x2 slide plate from underneath a boat

Use plates with side rings to make the monkey's ears

Eyes are attached to headlight bricks

MONKEY BUSINESS

To make this cheeky monkey's head, use a 2x2 dome connected to bricks with side studs. If you don't have plates with printed eyes, any 1x1 round pieces will do!

MONKEY PEN

You can build an animal enclosure out of bricks, fence pieces, or even a ring of clipped-together ladders. Fill your zoo displays with objects that will keep the animals inside exercised and entertained.

This monkey's legs are 1x2 curved half-arches, and its feet are tooth plates

A rubber auto tyre can provide hours of interaction for a curious primate

This small tree is built with bricks, small plant leaves and regular and inverted slopes

WHAT'S THAT, GLORIA? WHY OF COURSE YOU CAN HAVE A BANANA!

Plates with vertical clips make hands that can hold onto objects

OOO! OO!

MADE-UP CREATURES

Imagine discovering a creature that no one has ever seen before. What would it look like? Maybe it's something totally alien that could never possibly exist on our planet. What kinds of made-up creatures can you build with your bricks?

"The ray gun is a space weapon, but it's used here as part of the dancing alien's leg! You will also see it used as part of a snail's head (p.114) and a monkey's elbow (p.117)."

Head is one giant eyeball made from two radar dishes, held together by a pulley wheel

I'VE GOT MY EYE ON YOU!

Lower arms are 2x2 domes connected with a short LEGO Technic cross-axle

Fire hose nozzles attached to clips give the shoulders and hips plenty of movement

Build the arms and legs first before attaching them to the main body

A droid torso and a clip create a posable neck to attach the head to the body

ALIEN OBSERVER

Play with shapes and proportions. This creature may have two arms, two legs and a head, just like humans do, but the way those body parts are built makes it very different indeed.

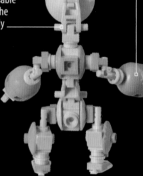

REAR VIEW

Top and bottom body sections are built around 1x1 bricks with studs on four sides, with a droid torso in between

A small transparent radar dish over a larger white one creates a wide, staring eye

DANCING GOOFBALL

Here's another creature with a big eye, but that's where the similarities end. With its strong legs and suction-cup feet, it must come from a world with really low gravity!

Brown radar dishes make alien shoes that are built for dancing!

Multi-jointed neck is built out of plates with clips and handles

Body is an octagonal plate with bar, covered by a radar dish

LASER LEGS

Two ray guns with a tap element in the middle make up each leg. The ray guns' handles plug into hollow studs on the body and feet.

Tap piece

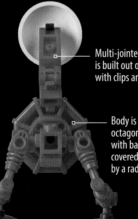

REAR VIEW

BLUE BOUNCER

This alien creature loves to hop around on its frog-like feet. Everything it meets is a delightful surprise – that's why its eyes and mouth are so round!

Eyes are made with transparent round tiles, white radar dishes and paddles

Use tiles for mouth and hat body details

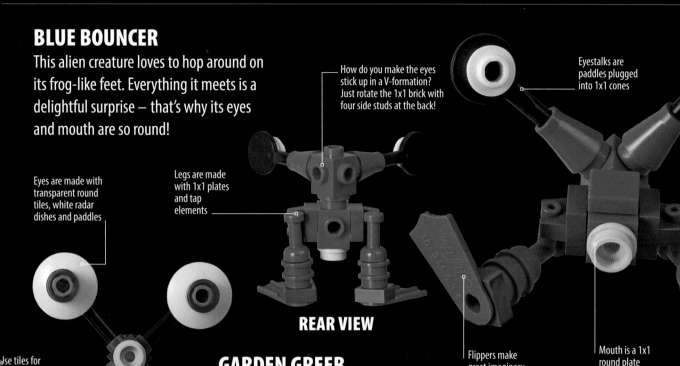

How do you make the eyes stick up in a V-formation? Just rotate the 1x1 brick with four side studs at the back!

Legs are made with 1x1 plates and tap elements

REAR VIEW

Eyestalks are paddles plugged into 1x1 cones

Flippers make great imaginary creature feet

Mouth is a 1x1 round plate

GARDEN GREEB

Nobody knows where this creature came from, but it sure hates it when you forget to water the garden. Make sure it gets plenty of sunlight to help it grow!

1x3 plates make feet that are perfectly camouflaged for standing near carrots!

Yellow socks made from pairs of 1x1 round plates

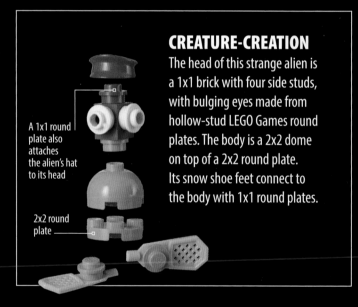

CREATURE-CREATION

The head of this strange alien is a 1x1 brick with four side studs, with bulging eyes made from hollow-stud LEGO Games round plates. The body is a 2x2 dome on top of a 2x2 round plate. Its snow shoe feet connect to the body with 1x1 round plates.

A 1x1 round plate also attaches the alien's hat to its head

2x2 round plate

UNDERCOVER ALIENS

Even if you only have a few pieces, you can still make a wild and wacky alien creature. Build a whole crew and give them different hats to help them blend in on Earth. Use a minifigure hat, or simply a small cone or round brick.

Use minifigure flippers or snow shoes for flapping feet

Cap from a lumberjack in the LEGO Minifigure series

A small cone makes a great fez!

I HAVE A UNIQUE STYLE.

Clown bowler hat from the LEGO Minifigures series

TROPICAL FISH

Strap on a snorkel and check out these eye-catching underwater fish! Some sea creatures are patterned to blend in with their environments, but not these flashy fellows. Their vivid colourations stand out from the crowd. Use your most colourful bricks to make some tropical fish friends of your own.

A 1x1 plate with a vertical clip makes a pair of fishy lips

Use different slope shapes and colours to build different types of fish

AXLE-EYED FISH

Here's a novel way to make fish eyes! Build a 1x2 LEGO Technic brick with a cross-shaped hole into the head, then slide a short cross-axle through and add a half-bush on each side.

Put slopes together with their matching inverted slopes to give your fish a diamond-shaped body

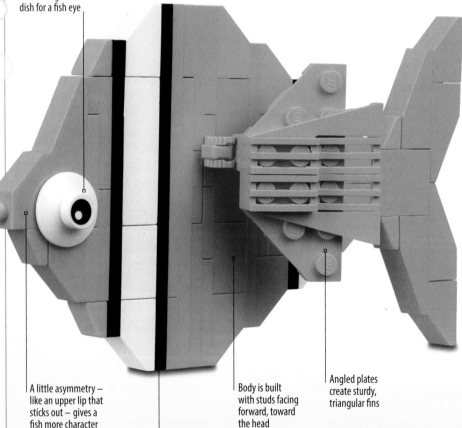

Attach a 1x1 round plate or tile to a big radar dish for a fish eye

A little asymmetry – like an upper lip that sticks out – gives a fish more character

Create thin black stripes with plates and thick white stripes with bricks

Body is built with studs facing forward, toward the head

Angled plates create sturdy, triangular fins

CLOWNFISH

Do you have a lot of orange bricks and slopes? Then build a cheerful clownfish! Except for the eyes and fins, its brightly hued body is built like a wall and entirely flat. Its body is very narrow, so attach its left fin higher than the one on its right. By putting the left fin's own click hinge plate lower than the right fin's, you will even both sides out.

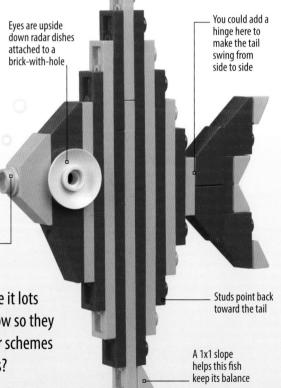

Eyes are upside down radar dishes attached to a brick-with-hole

You could add a hinge here to make the tail swing from side to side

Mouth is a 1x1 round plate plugged into the bottom of an inverted slope

Studs point back toward the tail

STRIPY FISH

Build a fish's body entirely out of plates to give it lots of skinny stripes. Stagger the plates in each row so they all stay locked together. What other wild color schemes can you come up with for your marine models?

A 1x1 slope helps this fish keep its balance

Build top fins out of slopes, plates and tiles

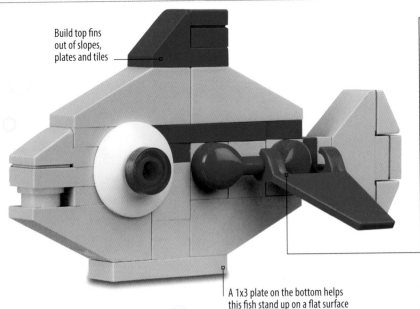

Radar-dish eye also attaches to a brick with side studs

Telephone handset

Brick with side studs

Flag piece

FISH FIN

To make this fish's fin, attach a telephone handset to bricks with side studs that are built into the fish's body. Clip a flag onto the telephone's handle to make a fin that can move up and down as the fish swims.

A 1x3 plate on the bottom helps this fish stand up on a flat surface

GRINNING FISH

A 1x1 plate inside its mouth gives this odd fish a round-toothed smile. A transparent red tile attached to a radar dish for an eye adds to its strange appearance!

Eye is a 1x1 round plate plugged into a 1x1 brick-with-hole

SMALL FISH

Use little slopes to build a little fish. Small slopes give your model all kinds of interesting angled shapes and patterns.

WHY ARE FISH SO SMART?

Side fins are held on by brackets

Use two 1x3 slopes to make the tail

BECAUSE WE ARE ALWAYS IN A SCHOOL!

Radar dish eyes are held in place by a 1x1 brick with studs on two sides

BIG-HEADED FISH

Not every fish has to be made out of straight lines and angles. Use curved bricks to add smooth, rounded features to your aquatic creations. Curved pieces also make a fish look graceful and streamlined.

The body is built from the bottom up, starting with a 1x6 plate

Create a layered effect by nesting clear pieces inside each other

MARINE LIFE

Fish aren't the only creatures that you'll find beneath the waves. The oceans are teeming with life, from the tiniest shrimp to the largest whale. Some of them swim, some of them float and some scuttle along the bottom. Look through your pieces for something that reminds you of an animal that lives underwater – then start building!

UMBRELLA JELLYFISH

Do you have a lot of transparent elements in your collection? Then build a jellyfish! Start with an umbrella-shaped dome on top, and add trailing tentacles below.

DOME JELLYFISH

Some jellyfish can grow quite large. Mix white or light-coloured pieces with your transparent elements to make the biggest jellyfish you can assemble!

Top is a stack of clear and transparent blue radar dishes in different sizes

If you use a dome for the top, add a round plate or brick underneath it

Fill out the centre with a stack of transparent blue round pieces

I HAVE THE STRANGEST CRAVING FOR PEANUT BUTTER.

A sliding plate makes the top rounded and smooth

Clip on transparent seaweed pieces for tentacles

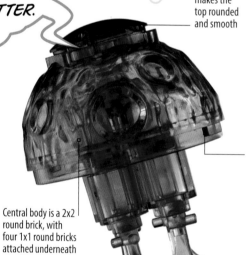

JELLY BELLY

The innermost part of this jellyfish's floating body is a white 1x1 brick with side studs. Transparent purple flames are plugged into 1x1 plates with side rings on the four sides.

Dome is the bottom half of a crater-pocked rock sphere

A transparent blue grille looks like three short tentacles

1x1 round plates link the plates with side rings to the centre brick

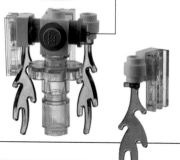

Central body is a 2x2 round brick, with four 1x1 round bricks attached underneath

Tentacles are transparent flame pieces

CRATER JELLYFISH

This jellyfish is constructed entirely out of transparent blue pieces. Build a stand to make it "float" and place it near a light source for an otherworldly glow.

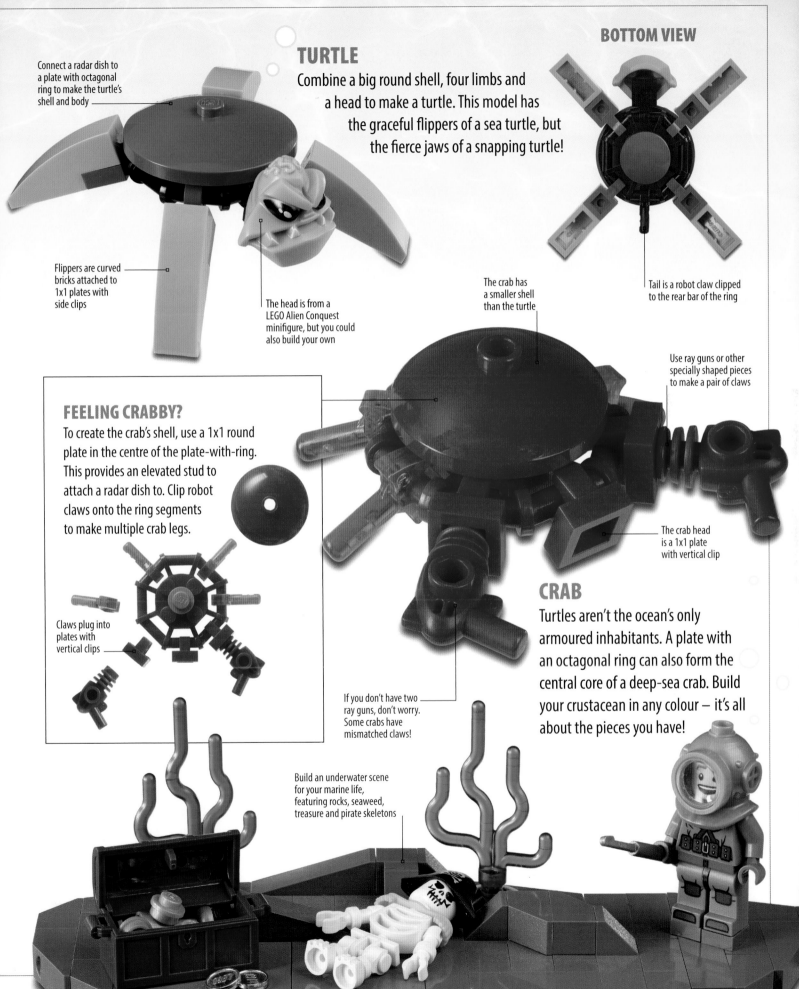

Connect a radar dish to a plate with octagonal ring to make the turtle's shell and body

TURTLE

Combine a big round shell, four limbs and a head to make a turtle. This model has the graceful flippers of a sea turtle, but the fierce jaws of a snapping turtle!

BOTTOM VIEW

Flippers are curved bricks attached to 1x1 plates with side clips

The head is from a LEGO Alien Conquest minifigure, but you could also build your own

The crab has a smaller shell than the turtle

Tail is a robot claw clipped to the rear bar of the ring

Use ray guns or other specially shaped pieces to make a pair of claws

FEELING CRABBY?

To create the crab's shell, use a 1x1 round plate in the centre of the plate-with-ring. This provides an elevated stud to attach a radar dish to. Clip robot claws onto the ring segments to make multiple crab legs.

Claws plug into plates with vertical clips

The crab head is a 1x1 plate with vertical clip

CRAB

Turtles aren't the ocean's only armoured inhabitants. A plate with an octagonal ring can also form the central core of a deep-sea crab. Build your crustacean in any colour — it's all about the pieces you have!

If you don't have two ray guns, don't worry. Some crabs have mismatched claws!

Build an underwater scene for your marine life, featuring rocks, seaweed, treasure and pirate skeletons

AT THE POLES

If you think winter is tough where you live, try living in the Arctic or the Antarctic! The animals there have to be tough, hardy and well-insulated against the cold. Build an icy polar scene and some creatures to fill it, but be warned – you may need to use all of your white bricks!

When building a background, add higher ridges to create far-off hills and snow banks

POLAR PEAKS

Use your micro-scale building skills to make a miniature background for your icy scene. A mixture of white and grey pieces creates a stark and atmospheric snow-capped mountain vista.

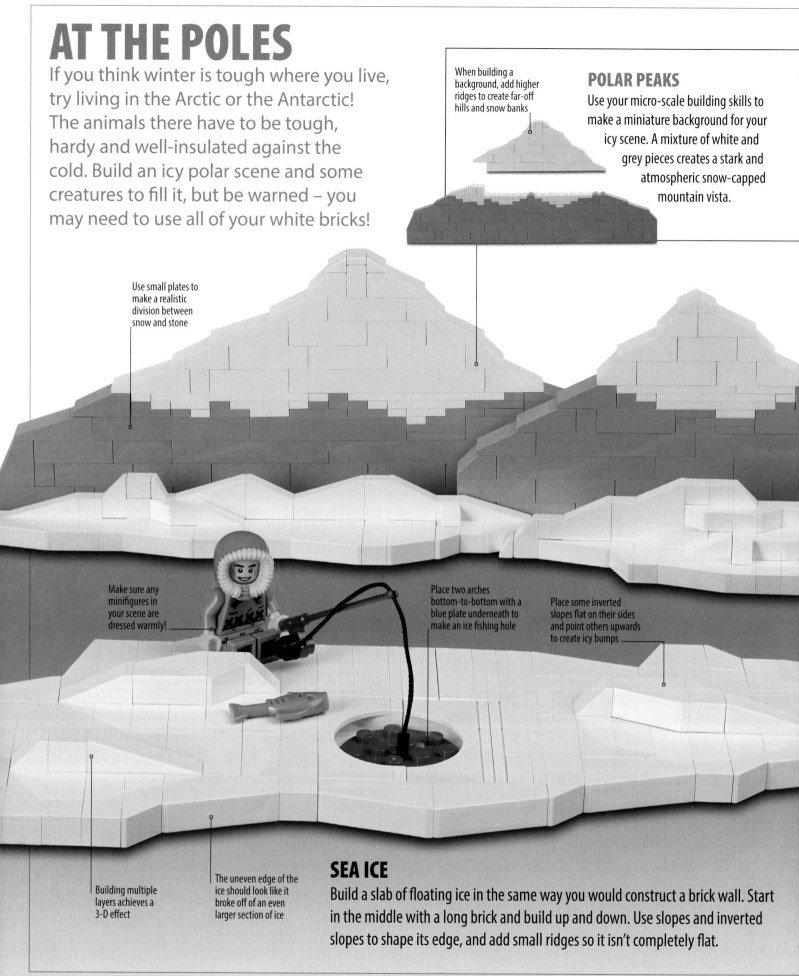

Use small plates to make a realistic division between snow and stone

Make sure any minifigures in your scene are dressed warmly!

Place two arches bottom-to-bottom with a blue plate underneath to make an ice fishing hole

Place some inverted slopes flat on their sides and point others upwards to create icy bumps

Building multiple layers achieves a 3-D effect

The uneven edge of the ice should look like it broke off of an even larger section of ice

SEA ICE

Build a slab of floating ice in the same way you would construct a brick wall. Start in the middle with a long brick and build up and down. Use slopes and inverted slopes to shape its edge, and add small ridges so it isn't completely flat.

COOL BRICK

"This 1x1 tooth plate makes great feet, beaks and teeth! It can also be used to create feathers, as seen on the ducks and chickens on pp.106–107."

PENGUINS

Start your penguin with a 1x1 brick with studs on all four sides. Add a round plate for a neck, black tooth plates for wings and 1x2 tiles in front and back.

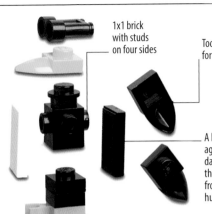

1x1 brick with studs on four sides

Tooth plate for wings

A black back against deep, dark water hides the penguin from predators hunting above

Why not add an igloo to keep your minifigures warm on cold polar nights?

By including bricks with side studs in your ice slab wall, you can attach the mountains as vertical walls

Binoculars make keen eyes for spotting fish

Baby penguins are covered in fuzzy down to keep them warm until they are grown-up

One-stud connections let you swivel and pose the head and wings

Use a tooth plate for a pointy beak

MUSH, DOGGIES! WE'VE GOT TO GET HOME BEFORE RUSH HOUR!

Feet are a single 1x1 plate with side clip

Use a1x1 round tile for a penguin chick's belly

DOG SLED

Move over, snowmobile – out here on the polar ice, canine power is the way to travel! Start your dog sled with a 2x4 plate and attach a pair of runners for smooth movement over snow.

If you don't have hockey sticks for runners, use poles or bars instead

You could add a longer section at the back for carrying important supplies

An angled front cuts down on wind resistance for faster speed

Round plates on the end of string elements attach to studs on the backs of LEGO dogs

ARCTIC ANIMALS

To see the wildest animals on the planet, you've got to travel to the ends of the Earth. Here at the North Pole, it's eat or be eaten…and few creatures are as good at eating as these ones! Build some ferocious predators to fill your polar scene. What other cold-weather animals could you build?

KILLER WHALE

To build this mighty killer whale's streamlined body, start in the middle with a long, two-stud-wide black brick or plate. Use white pieces for its stomach and a patch on its body.

CHILLY CHOMPERS

The killer whale's mouth is full of 1x1 round plate teeth, surrounding a pink tile tongue. Its upper jaw is attached with a hinge so it can open and close for a great big chomp.

Add 1x1 round plates for the top teeth, too

Hinge plate

If you build a bigger killer whale model, you could use cones as pointy teeth!

Attach the white section under the jaws with jumper plates

Use jumper plates to center a dorsal fin, built from slope and curved bricks

Use arches to build the rounded snout

The whale's eyes are transparent 1x1 round plates attached to headlight bricks

WHY CAN'T THERE BE PENGUINS ON MY PAGE?

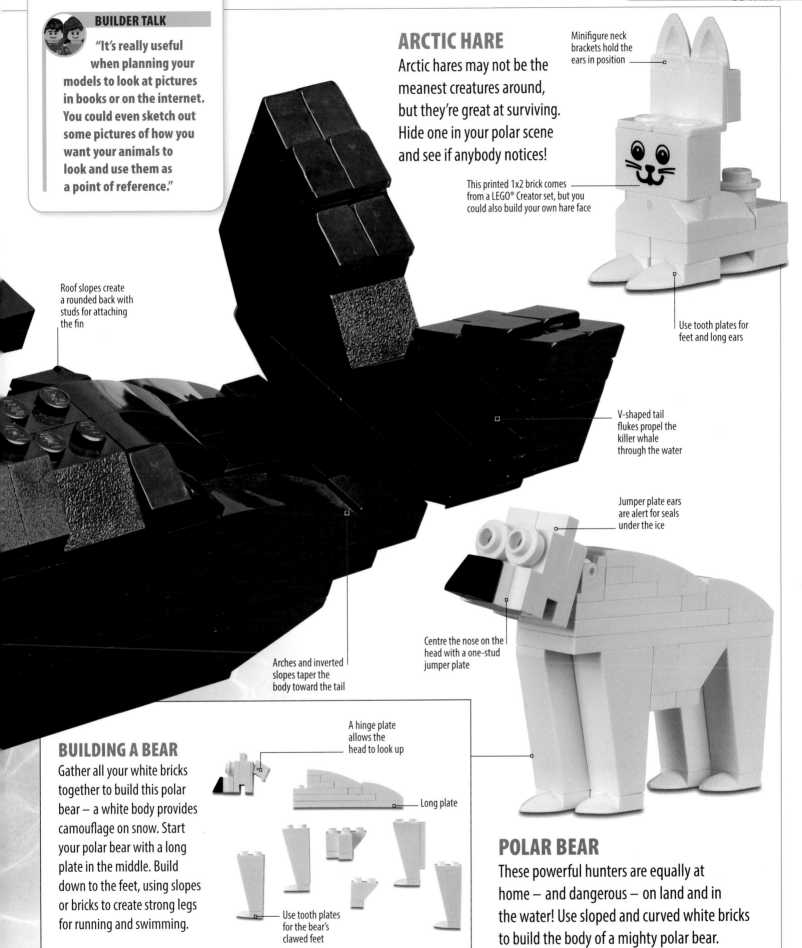

ARCTIC HARE

Arctic hares may not be the meanest creatures around, but they're great at surviving. Hide one in your polar scene and see if anybody notices!

Minifigure neck brackets hold the ears in position

This printed 1x2 brick comes from a LEGO® Creator set, but you could also build your own hare face

Use tooth plates for feet and long ears

Roof slopes create a rounded back with studs for attaching the fin

V-shaped tail flukes propel the killer whale through the water

Jumper plate ears are alert for seals under the ice

Centre the nose on the head with a one-stud jumper plate

Arches and inverted slopes taper the body toward the tail

BUILDING A BEAR

Gather all your white bricks together to build this polar bear – a white body provides camouflage on snow. Start your polar bear with a long plate in the middle. Build down to the feet, using slopes or bricks to create strong legs for running and swimming.

A hinge plate allows the head to look up

Long plate

Use tooth plates for the bear's clawed feet

POLAR BEAR

These powerful hunters are equally at home – and dangerous – on land and in the water! Use sloped and curved white bricks to build the body of a mighty polar bear.

THINGS THAT GO BUMP IN THE NIGHT

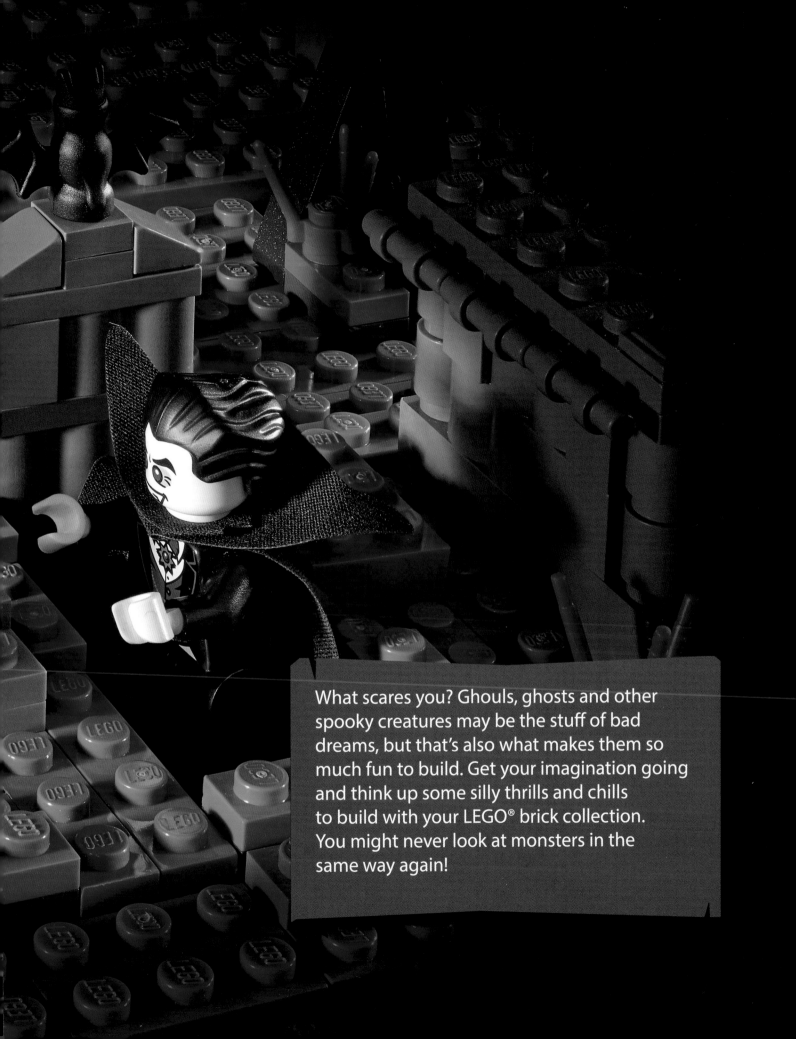

What scares you? Ghouls, ghosts and other spooky creatures may be the stuff of bad dreams, but that's also what makes them so much fun to build. Get your imagination going and think up some silly thrills and chills to build with your LEGO® brick collection. You might never look at monsters in the same way again!

I'M TIMMY AND I'M NOT FRIGHTENED OF ANYTHING.

...BUT I AM!

FRIGHT NIGHT

Meet Timmy. He's an ordinary boy who adores scary things. He thinks that bad dreams are the best! Timmy has spent all day reading scary books, watching scary movies and thinking up scary stories. He even ate a big piece of cheese right before bedtime! Now Timmy is about to go on a wild ride through the realm of nightmares. Time to see if Timmy is as brave as he thinks he is.

I've got a BONE to pick with you, Timmy!

SKELETON CHASE

Yikes – pursued by a giant skeleton! But that's the least of Timmy's worries… because he is about to meet a whole graveyard full of them! (See p.162.)

To ensure a nightmare night, Timmy eats small "cheese" slopes just before he goes to bed

BUILDING BAD DREAMS
ROD GILLIES

"For my theme, I wanted to tackle some of the classic scares we're all familiar with from movies and books – but with a comic twist, since they're all LEGO® creations! I also wanted to make my own creations different in style to the official LEGO® Monster Fighter sets. For most of the bigger models, I sketched out rough drawings in advance, but for the details or for smaller creations I tended to get inspired by just picking up bricks and seeing what happened!"

BZZZ! WHRRR! Sweet dreams do not compute!

Find out how to make Timmy's bed on p.144

ROBOT ATTACK

Look out! An army of rampaging robots is just one of the frights that Timmy will be encountering tonight. (See p.152.)

HOW NICE, A VISITOR!

WE HAVEN'T HAD ONE OF THOSE IN CENTURIES!

HOUSE OF VAMPIRES

Have you ever wanted to tour a vampire's haunted castle? It looks like Timmy's nightmare is taking him there, whether he likes it or not! (See p.136.)

SPOOKY CIRCUS TRAIN

"Whoooooo wants to see the greatest show in Nightmare Land?" Timmy's nightmare starts with a circus train – but it isn't for any ordinary circus. The engine is decorated with bones, and the clowns and ringmaster are all skeletons! The circus is usually a place for laughs and cheers, but in the realm of bad dreams, it can be very spooky indeed.

ALL ABOARD!

If you have some LEGO train wheel bases, use them to build a circus train for a nightmare carnival. Make an engine in front and a car for it to pull. Inside could be snakes, spiders, or something even scarier!

COME ONE, COME ALL, TO THE NIGHTMARE CARNIVAL!

Build a hollow box for the freight car

Turn plates sideways to build letters. Pick a colour that will stand out against the background

If you don't have this "cow catcher" piece, build one out of slope bricks

WE ONLY RUN A SKELETON SERVICE.

White robot arms create ribcage-like decorations on the engine's sides

Smokestack connects to 2x2 plate

Bone elements are held on by clips

A set of wheels at each end means you can make the freight car as long or as short as you want

Train connector to link cars together

EERIE ENGINE

The locomotive is based on an old-style steam engine. Use roof slopes to build the tube-like shape of the front boiler, and include a small cabin in back for the ectoplasmic engineer.

Even the jolliest jester looks creepy with a skeleton head

Blue LEGO Technic half-pins provide detail

The skull has LEGO Technic bricks-with-holes for eye sockets and a brick with a cross-axle hole for its nose

FRONT VIEW

FORTUNE TELLER

In the land of nightmares, fortune tellers never warn you about tomorrow's surprise math test. Mix and match minifigure parts and accessories to populate your carnival with colourful performers and other odd characters.

I SEE NICE THINGS IN YOUR FUTURE.

NO! I LIKE HORRIBLE THINGS!

Crystal ball is a transparent minifigure head piece under a transparent 2x2 hollow dome

Bell is a 1x1 round plate and a 2x2 round brick attached to a radar dish with a printed swirl

GAME OF STRENGTH

You don't have to add bone details to this test-your-strength game to make it spooky. Just build it out of clashing colours and give it a scary attendant – it will fit right in with your nightmare carnival!

Use a tooth plate to mark the strongest swing

Build the game as a long, thin base with a short wall at one end, and then flip it up

Hammer is a long bar, a brick with a hollow side stud, two 1x1 plates and a 1x1 tile

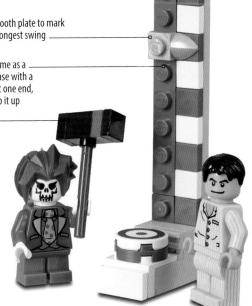

NIGHTMARE CARNIVAL

"Last stop! Everybody off!" The carnival is a maze of games, rides, and snack booths, each with its own scary twist. Timmy likes cotton candy, but he is pretty sure he doesn't want to try the rotten candy that they're selling here! Build fiendishly fun rides and attractions to give visitors to your nightmare carnival a good scare.

Make sure the tunnel arches are high enough for the car and passengers to roll through

A spider in a web makes any scene look extra-spooky!

ENTRANCE VIEW

GHOSTLY RIDE

You don't have to build the entire carnival ride — just a stretch of track and a haunted interior. Build spooky details into the wall that will make the riders jump in their seats!

Sign is a sideways wall of stacked green and black bricks and plates

Add plants, cats, bats and frogs to bring your scary ride to life

Use textured bricks in the back wall to make it look old and decrepit

Old-fashioned lamps are four-forked palm tree tops with transparent 1x1 round plates inside and a small radar dish as a lid

Lock pieces together well so the arches don't fall apart

I WANT MY MUMMY!

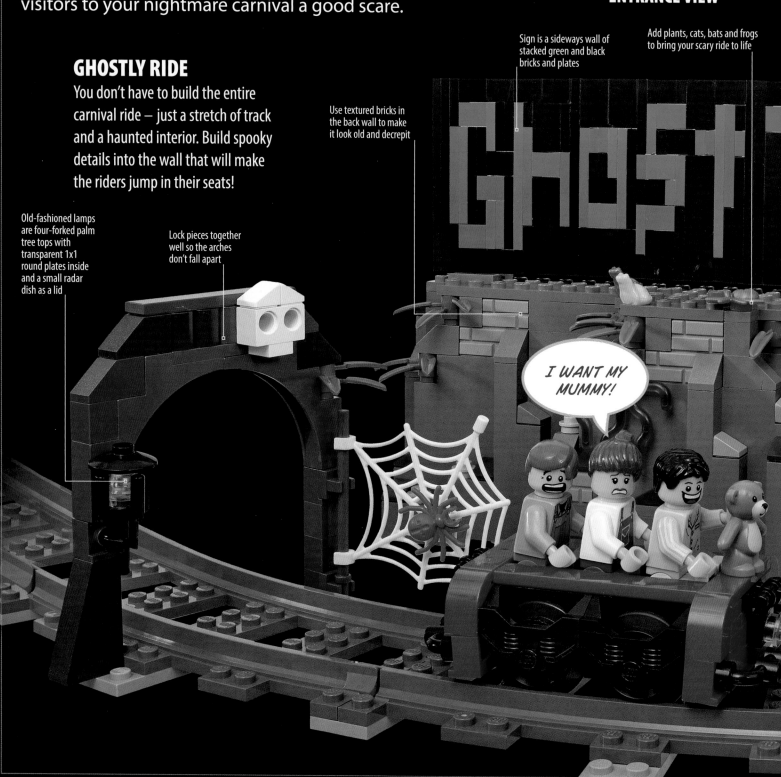

ON TARGET

Use printed tiles and microfigures from LEGO® Games as targets for a carnival shooting game. Hit one and you will get a prize... but are you sure you want whatever it is that you'll win?

IF YOU MISS, YOU HAVE TO SIT ON THE SHELF.

Crossbow handles are plugged into jumper plates

Make a striped awning with arch pieces in alternating colours

Use stacked-up log bricks or 1x2 brown bricks to make the stall's wooden sides

CRAZY CAR

Use a pair of train wheel bases to make a small ride car. A 2x6 hollow space on top is just the right size for three frightened minifigures to sit inside. Build your car in a colour that stands out against the wall's dark background.

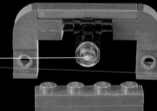

Car is symmetrical front-to-back so it can roll either way

Headlight is a 1x1 transparent yellow round plate

Bumpers are sideways-built curved bars with studs attached to headlight bricks

Where will your ghost train go next? Will there be more track, or a sheer drop?

HAUNTED HOUSE

Next, Timmy dreams about a house where monsters live. It has all kinds of creepy rooms and an attic full of specters! A haunted house is more than just a brick building with creatures placed inside. Think about what kinds of rooms your monsters would like, and don't forget the most important part of the model: the ghosts!

Black fence pieces look like a foreboding iron railing

Mix round and square plates in different colours to make a low stone wall

FRONT VIEW

Sprinkle in some dark grey bricks for an old stone building

Build bricks with side studs into the walls to attach vines and ivy to the outside

Get your teeth into this Vampire Car build on p.142!

SIDE VIEW

A LEGO Technic brick creates a hole for bats to fly in and out!

Spider web attaches to a bar mounted on clips in the wall

Blood-red rooftops add to the haunted ambience

UP-SCARES, DOWN-SCARES

This model is half house and half castle, full of musty old history. Inside are cavernous chambers with arches and alcoves that could hide all manner of scary things. It is built in two halves — each half is connected by 1x2 hinge bricks so it can swing open, revealing the shadowy, haunted interior.

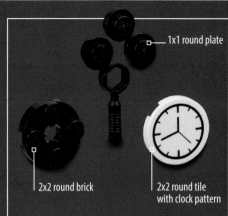

1x1 round plate

2x2 round brick

2x2 round tile with clock pattern

TIME PIECE

It won't take a long time to build this clock! A printed round tile is used for the clock face and a minifigure wrench for the pendulum.

A pair of plates with handles becomes a gothic carved windowsill

Use an arch or build a column in the middle of the open side to support the roof bricks overhead

Why not extend your haunted house? Fill it with more rooms full of spooky stuff to scare visitors!

Upper storey lifts off, making it easier to access the study

BOO!

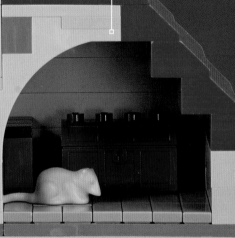

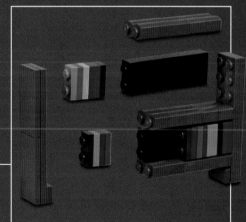

HELLO! IT MUST BE TIME FOR SUPPER!

THE MASTER'S LAIR

The cultured Count has his own library and study in the main downstairs chamber. His prized bookcase is built sideways, with stacks of coloured 1x2 plates as books on the shelves.

Jumper plates in the tile floorboards connect animals and objects

WITCH'S HOVEL

The witch seemed nice enough until she asked Timmy to sweep the floor. No matter how hard he tries to hold on, the broom just keeps flying around and making an even bigger mess! The witch who lives in this small shack could be good or bad. Fill it with potions, knick-knacks, and other components for casting magic spells!

THIS JOB REALLY SWEEPS YOU OFF YOUR FEET!

Stack up varied grey bricks to build a stone chimney

Use jumper plates to hold potions in place

SHELF OF SPELLS

Shelves help the witch keep her magical potions and lotions well-organised. For bottles and jars, use different coloured transparent round pieces and put 1x1 round plates or tiles on top as lids.

WHILE YOU'RE UP THERE, CAN YOU DUST THE CHIMNEY?

Stone doorway is built on jumper plates so it sticks a little way out of the wall

The interior door frame is built with inverted slopes

MAGIC SHACK

The witch's hovel has hinge bricks built into the chimney so it can open up to show off the interior. Inside are shelves full of everything a witch could need for brewing up hexes, curses and strange elixirs.

Use jumper plates in the floor to keep furniture and accessories from sliding around when the model is moved

The table legs are telescopes

If your shack is too small for a bubbling cauldron, use a barrel instead!

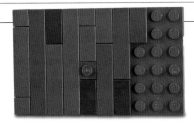

Attach a tile at an angle to the stud on a 1x1 plate to patch a hole in the worn-out roof

RAMSHACKLE ROOF

Build a layer of tiles onto a large plate for a roof made of wooden planks. Different shades of brown will make it look like some of the boards have been repaired and replaced.

Table legs are 1x1 round bricks on top of 1x1 round tiles

TOP TABLE

Assemble a table to lay out all the ingredients for your next spell. This one uses brown plates, tiles, clips and jumper plates.

Use slope bricks at the top of the frame to support the angle of the roof

White walls with black outlines resemble old, timber-framed construction

Place wild plants around the outside of the hovel

REAR SIDE VIEW

Window is attached to jumper plates

Door is attached with clip-hinges

Every witch should have a broom

Rat is safe from the witch's cauldron...for now!

Talking goblin head keeps the witch company

Cobblestone path is made with 1x1 tiles

FRONT VIEW

MONSTER MOTORS

What is that terrifying growling sound? Is it a werewolf? A dinosaur? No – it's a crazy custom car with a monster at the wheel! Build a pint-sized auto to fit your favourite LEGO monster minifigure. Give it a design and colour scheme that reflects what kind of creature drives it, and roll it around to wreak some havoc!

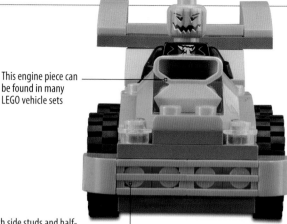

This engine piece can be found in many LEGO vehicle sets

Bricks with side studs and half-arch bricks at the front of the car allow you to attach a sideways-built bumper

FRONT VIEW

IF I GET A FLAT TYRE, I USE A PUMPKIN PATCH!

Curved elements mimic a pumpkin's shape

PUMPKIN CAR

What could be a better ride for a pumpkin-headed monster than a pumpkin-themed car? With its bright orange colour scheme and rounded curves, this model definitely shows its jack-o'-lantern influence.

FRONT VIEW

CAR NO WORK. FRANKIE USE HIS BOLTS.

Big exposed wheels and engine capture the look of a classic hot rod racer

MONSTER CAR

Use pieces that resemble wood, aluminum and brass to build a chugging, puffing steampunk roadster fit for a makeshift monster assembled by mad science! Try combining your more unusual pieces to create even more unusual shapes.

Stack two plates with handles for a double bumper

Ray guns attach to silver telescopes held on by clips

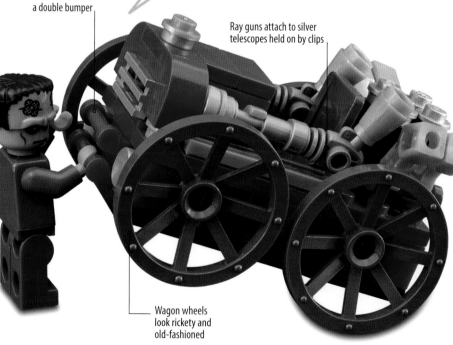

STEAM POWER

The engine is built with a mix of metallic-coloured elements. Gold robot arms and cones plugged onto silver ray gun handles give it six smokestacks for venting heat and steam.

Gold robot arms

Wagon wheels look rickety and old-fashioned

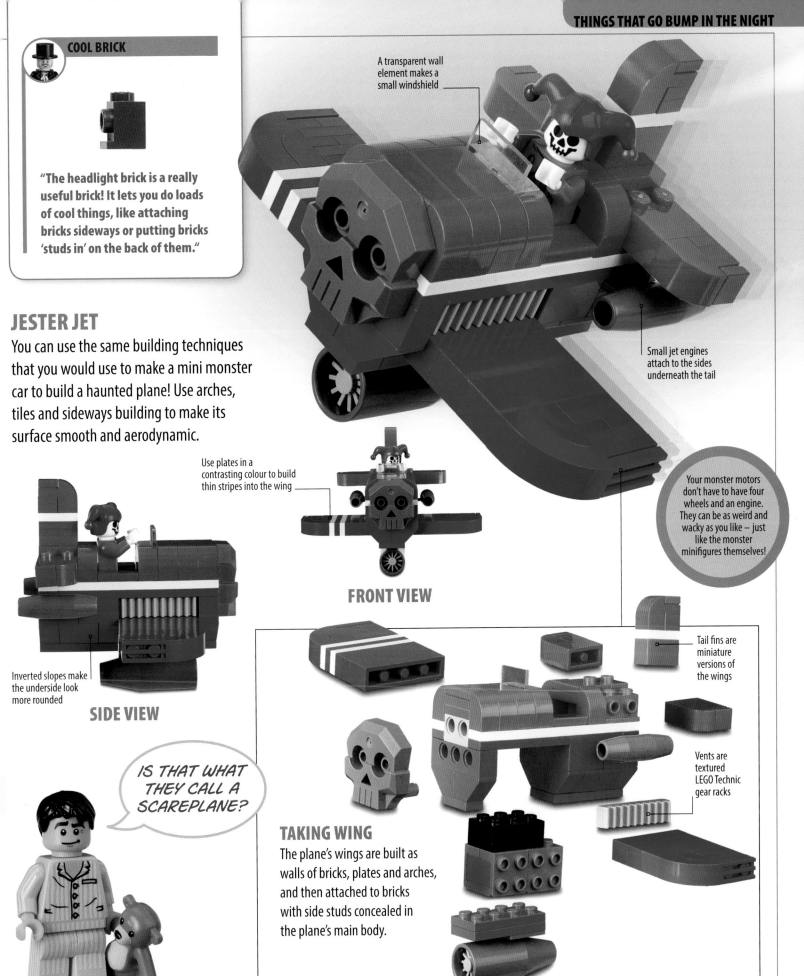

A transparent wall element makes a small windshield

Small jet engines attach to the sides underneath the tail

JESTER JET

You can use the same building techniques that you would use to make a mini monster car to build a haunted plane! Use arches, tiles and sideways building to make its surface smooth and aerodynamic.

Use plates in a contrasting colour to build thin stripes into the wing

Your monster motors don't have to have four wheels and an engine. They can be as weird and wacky as you like – just like the monster minifigures themselves!

Inverted slopes make the underside look more rounded

SIDE VIEW

FRONT VIEW

Tail fins are miniature versions of the wings

Vents are textured LEGO Technic gear racks

IS THAT WHAT THEY CALL A SCAREPLANE?

TAKING WING

The plane's wings are built as walls of bricks, plates and arches, and then attached to bricks with side studs concealed in the plane's main body.

141

MONSTER RACE

Scary racers, start your engines! Timmy has no idea how he hs ended up as a referee for this race – as the racers career down the track, he realises that he has no idea what the rules are, either! Build more monster cars to add to your monster collection – which one do you think would win in a monster race?

Headlights are unnecessary when the driver can see in the dark!

A 2x3 curved plate with hole creates a tombstone-like decoration

FRONT VIEW

GETTING STUCK IN TRAFFIC DRIVES ME BATTY!

Use a grille and two grille slopes to make a ribbed bumper

VAMPIRE CAR

Vampires are associated with the colour black, bats and coffins. That's why this model reflects all three! Roof slopes give the car the long, angular shape of a coffin and the curved fins on the back are reminiscent of a bat's sweeping wings.

Close-fitting mudguards around the wheels provide a sleek silhouette

Plates with handles add side details

Neon green bulbs make the engine look like it's powered by swamp water!

Use slope bricks to make angled surfaces

A textured brick makes a good small car grille

FRONT VIEW

Big tyres for traction on marshy terrain

SWAMP MONSTER CAR

Create a complementary colour scheme by matching your car to the look of its driver. Can you tell that the swamp monster's favourite colour is green? Transparent and bubble-like elements add to the auto's aquatic appearance.

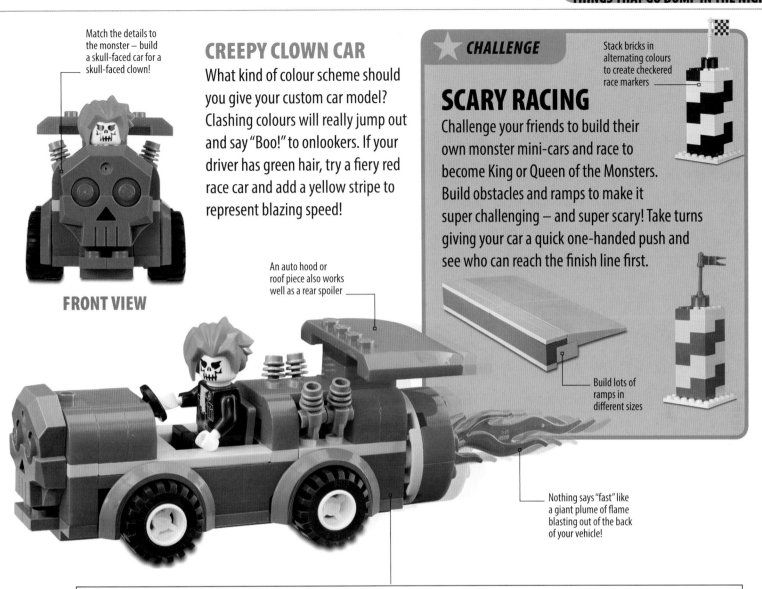

Match the details to the monster – build a skull-faced car for a skull-faced clown!

CREEPY CLOWN CAR

What kind of colour scheme should you give your custom car model? Clashing colours will really jump out and say "Boo!" to onlookers. If your driver has green hair, try a fiery red race car and add a yellow stripe to represent blazing speed!

FRONT VIEW

An auto hood or roof piece also works well as a rear spoiler

⭐ **CHALLENGE**

Stack bricks in alternating colours to create checkered race markers

SCARY RACING

Challenge your friends to build their own monster mini-cars and race to become King or Queen of the Monsters. Build obstacles and ramps to make it super challenging – and super scary! Take turns giving your car a quick one-handed push and see who can reach the finish line first.

Build lots of ramps in different sizes

Nothing says "fast" like a giant plume of flame blasting out of the back of your vehicle!

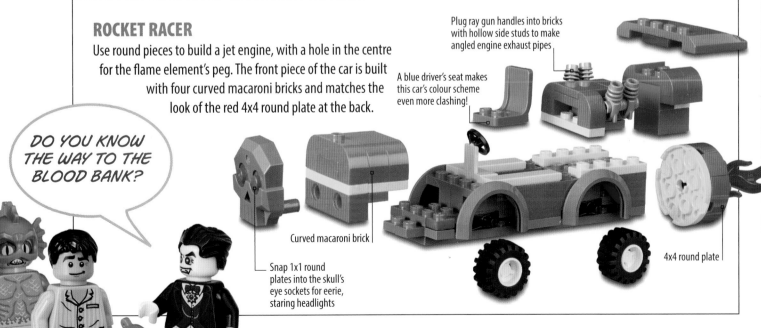

ROCKET RACER

Use round pieces to build a jet engine, with a hole in the centre for the flame element's peg. The front piece of the car is built with four curved macaroni bricks and matches the look of the red 4x4 round plate at the back.

Plug ray gun handles into bricks with hollow side studs to make angled engine exhaust pipes

A blue driver's seat makes this car's colour scheme even more clashing!

DO YOU KNOW THE WAY TO THE BLOOD BANK?

Curved macaroni brick

Snap 1x1 round plates into the skull's eye sockets for eerie, staring headlights

4x4 round plate

SWEET DREAMS

"Phew, thank goodness that's over," Timmy says as he opens his eyes. But a sudden rattling tells him that he is still stuck in the nightmare! A bedroom is a place of safety and comfort...so where better to hide a spooky scare? Whether you build a skeleton in the closet or a monster under the bed, there won't be any sweet dreams here tonight!

Use printed or stickered tiles for wall decorations

A treasure chest can double as a trunk for storing clothes and toys

YIKES!

Attach decorations to brackets or bricks with side studs in the walls

Inverted slopes form braces for the bookshelf

A black section of wall behind the wardrobe makes it look dark and shadowy when the door is opened

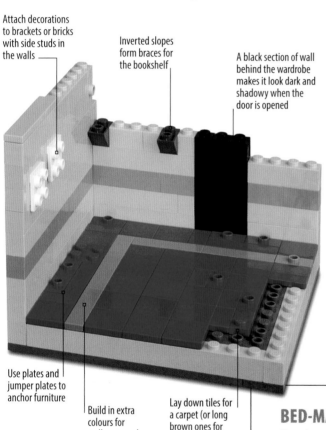

Use plates and jumper plates to anchor furniture

Build in extra colours for wallpaper and rug designs

Lay down tiles for a carpet (or long brown ones for a wooden floor)

ROOM DESIGN

You can use this basic design to make lots of different kinds of rooms. It's just a floor and two walls, built up the normal way. The details and contents are up to you!

There's some space under the bed, so why not add a creature there?

BED-MAKING

Use plates to build the bed's frame and legs. Place small arches over the edges and fill in the centre with tiles to make a patterned blanket or bed cover.

Lay a white tile across some jumper plates for the pillow

Include a plate to attach a sleeping minifigure or give a frightened one somewhere to stand

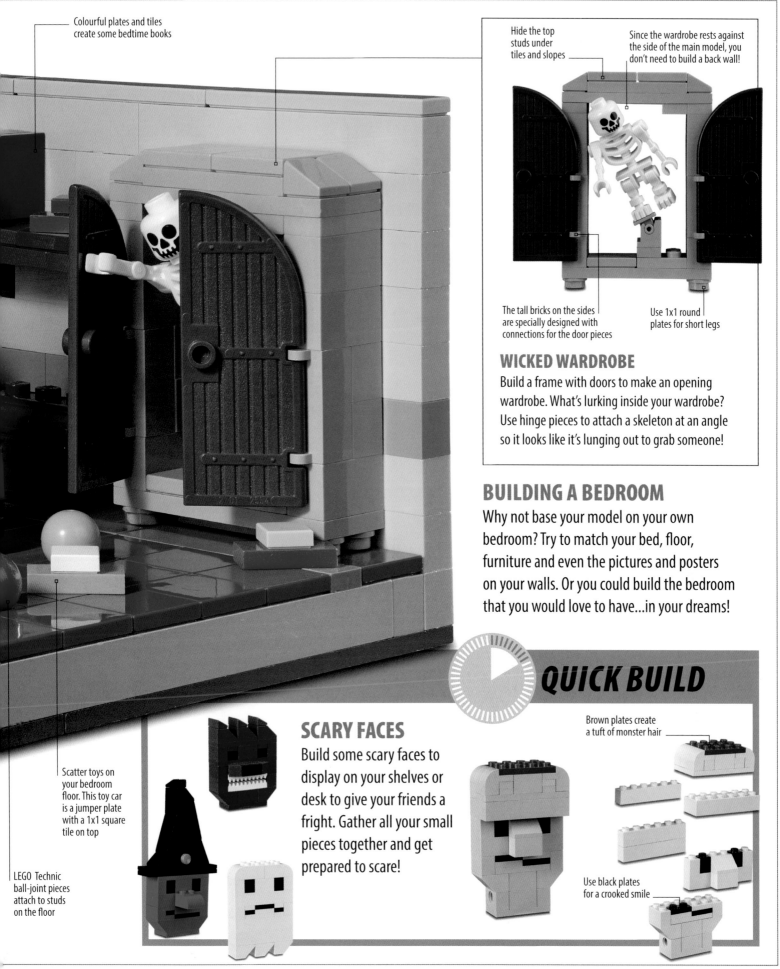

Colourful plates and tiles create some bedtime books

Hide the top studs under tiles and slopes

Since the wardrobe rests against the side of the main model, you don't need to build a back wall!

The tall bricks on the sides are specially designed with connections for the door pieces

Use 1x1 round plates for short legs

WICKED WARDROBE

Build a frame with doors to make an opening wardrobe. What's lurking inside your wardrobe? Use hinge pieces to attach a skeleton at an angle so it looks like it's lunging out to grab someone!

BUILDING A BEDROOM

Why not base your model on your own bedroom? Try to match your bed, floor, furniture and even the pictures and posters on your walls. Or you could build the bedroom that you would love to have...in your dreams!

QUICK BUILD

Scatter toys on your bedroom floor. This toy car is a jumper plate with a 1x1 square tile on top

LEGO Technic ball-joint pieces attach to studs on the floor

SCARY FACES

Build some scary faces to display on your shelves or desk to give your friends a fright. Gather all your small pieces together and get prepared to scare!

Brown plates create a tuft of monster hair

Use black plates for a crooked smile

SOMETHING IN THE BATH

Fleeing into the bathroom doesn't help Timmy. There are all kinds of strange noises in the plumbing…and what just made that splash?! An ordinary home can become an extraordinary one in the world of bad dreams. Bathrooms are just the start – think about what you can do to transform a kitchen or living room scene into some silly, scary fun!

Red and blue round plates on top of faucets show which is for hot water and which is for cold

Sink and bathtub are attached to the wall using bricks with side studs

A black nighttime background establishes the time and makes the monster stand out even more

LEGO® Alien Conquest head

BATHROOM NIGHTMARE

This bathroom is built in much the same way as the bedroom on p.144, but with different fixtures and furnishings. The familiar tub, sink and toilet make it clear where in the house this particular scare is taking place!

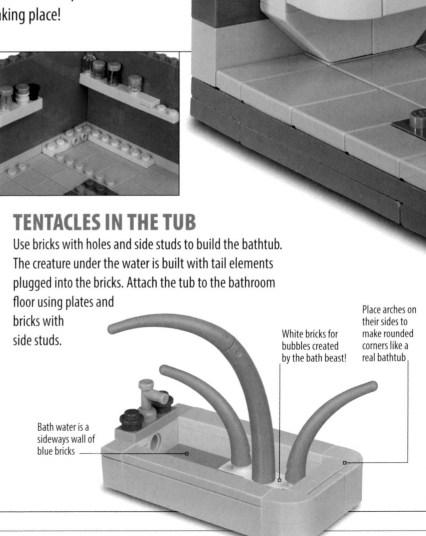

BOO!

BOO HOO!

TENTACLES IN THE TUB

Use bricks with holes and side studs to build the bathtub. The creature under the water is built with tail elements plugged into the bricks. Attach the tub to the bathroom floor using plates and bricks with side studs.

Exposed studs make the red floor look like a deep-pile carpet

Place arches on their sides to make rounded corners like a real bathtub

White bricks for bubbles created by the bath beast!

Bath water is a sideways wall of blue bricks

KNOCK KNOCK!

Mum, there's a monster outside! A spooky face in the window turns a simple home-life scene into the start of an alien invasion. Building it in a slightly larger scale makes the minifigure look like a small (and very scared) child.

Attach two-stud-wide plates into the wall to create shelves

BUILDER TALK

"Sometimes it's worth starting with the hardest bit of a model and then working your way back. I built the curved ends of the tub and sink first and finished with the bits against the wall, and then attached them to the rest of the bathroom."

EEK! WHAT WAS IN THAT BOTTLE OF BUBBLE BATH?

Instead of using tentacle pieces, you could create your own creature underneath the water!

It's no surprise that LEGO tiles make ideal bathroom floor tiles!

A brick-with-hole acts as a drain to keep the tub from over-filling

SIDE VIEW

For a bath mat, use tiles with exposed studs to create the impression of deep, fuzzy material — and to attach a fleeing minifigure

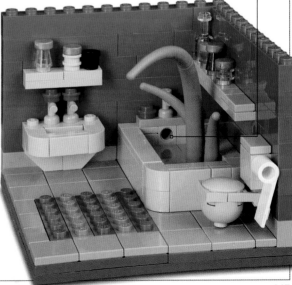

PERILOUS POTTY

This looks like a perfectly normal toilet, but who knows what could be lurking in there? The bowl is an upside-down 2x2 dome, clipped to the wall by the plate with handle above it.

A sliding plate works well as the toilet lid

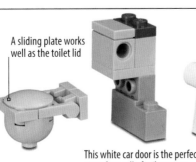

This white car door is the perfect piece for a roll of toilet paper

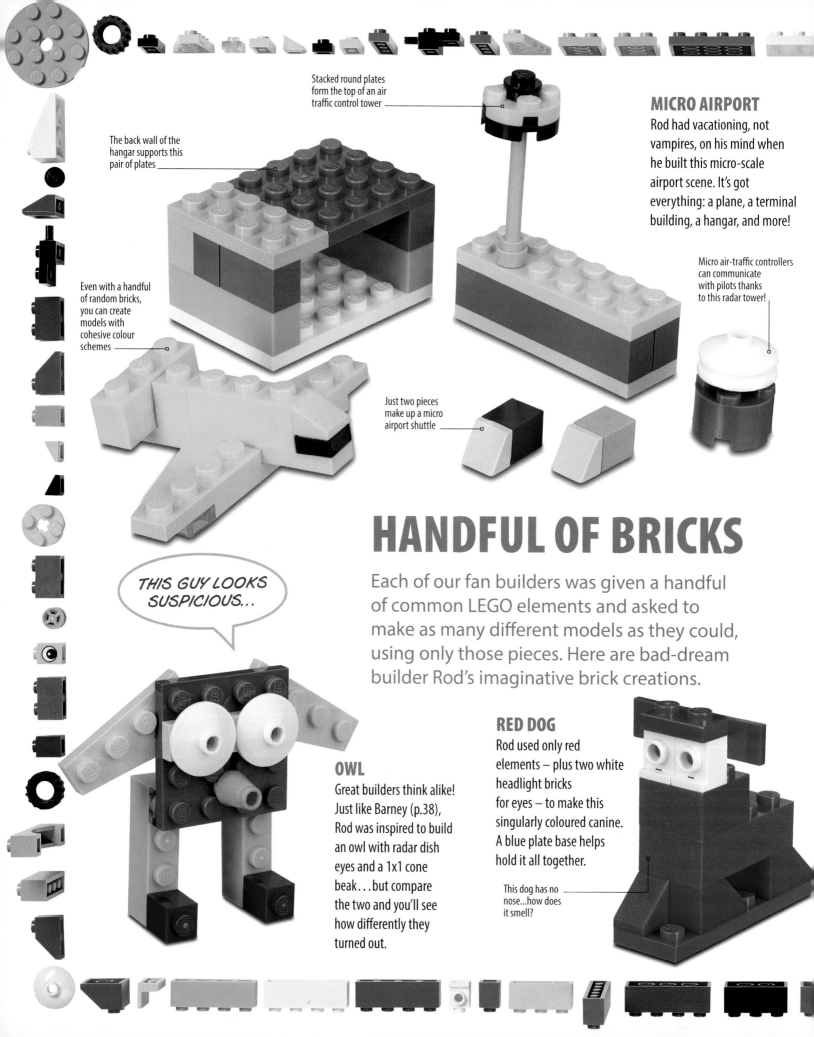

Stacked round plates form the top of an air traffic control tower

The back wall of the hangar supports this pair of plates

Even with a handful of random bricks, you can create models with cohesive colour schemes

MICRO AIRPORT

Rod had vacationing, not vampires, on his mind when he built this micro-scale airport scene. It's got everything: a plane, a terminal building, a hangar, and more!

Micro air-traffic controllers can communicate with pilots thanks to this radar tower!

Just two pieces make up a micro airport shuttle

HANDFUL OF BRICKS

Each of our fan builders was given a handful of common LEGO elements and asked to make as many different models as they could, using only those pieces. Here are bad-dream builder Rod's imaginative brick creations.

THIS GUY LOOKS SUSPICIOUS...

OWL

Great builders think alike! Just like Barney (p.38), Rod was inspired to build an owl with radar dish eyes and a 1x1 cone beak...but compare the two and you'll see how differently they turned out.

RED DOG

Rod used only red elements – plus two white headlight bricks for eyes – to make this singularly coloured canine. A blue plate base helps hold it all together.

This dog has no nose...how does it smell?

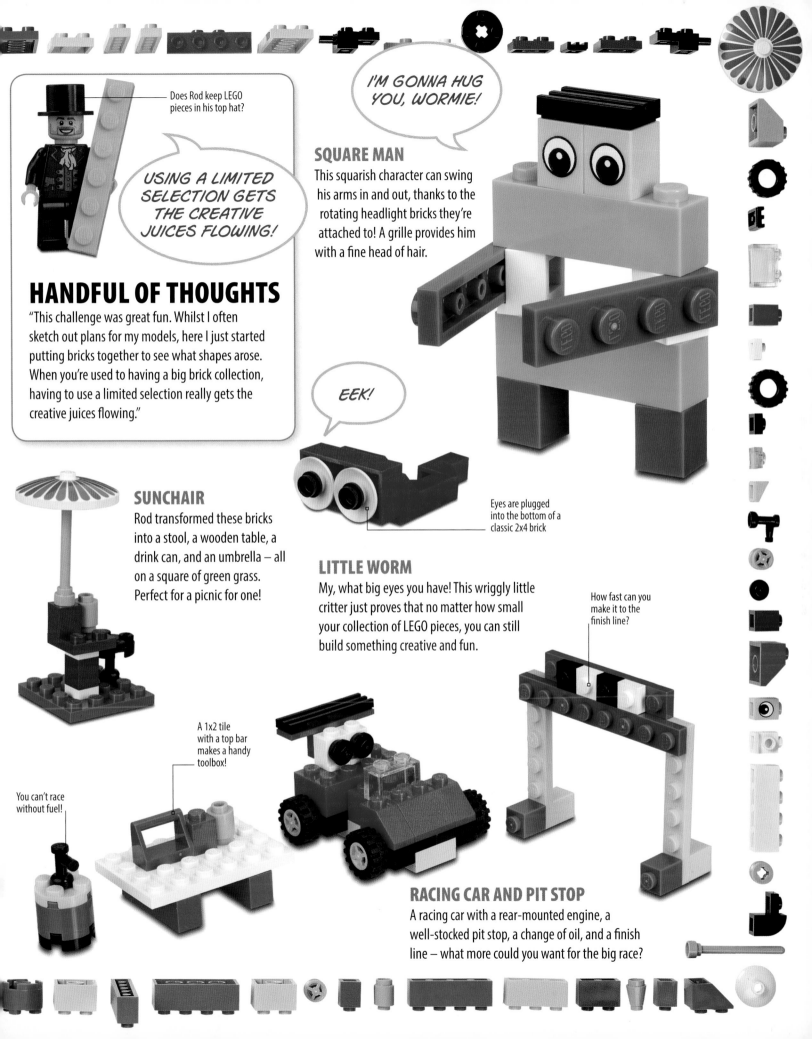

Does Rod keep LEGO pieces in his top hat?

I'M GONNA HUG YOU, WORMIE!

USING A LIMITED SELECTION GETS THE CREATIVE JUICES FLOWING!

SQUARE MAN

This squarish character can swing his arms in and out, thanks to the rotating headlight bricks they're attached to! A grille provides him with a fine head of hair.

HANDFUL OF THOUGHTS

"This challenge was great fun. Whilst I often sketch out plans for my models, here I just started putting bricks together to see what shapes arose. When you're used to having a big brick collection, having to use a limited selection really gets the creative juices flowing."

EEK!

SUNCHAIR

Rod transformed these bricks into a stool, a wooden table, a drink can, and an umbrella — all on a square of green grass. Perfect for a picnic for one!

Eyes are plugged into the bottom of a classic 2x4 brick

LITTLE WORM

My, what big eyes you have! This wriggly little critter just proves that no matter how small your collection of LEGO pieces, you can still build something creative and fun.

How fast can you make it to the finish line?

A 1x2 tile with a top bar makes a handy toolbox!

You can't race without fuel!

RACING CAR AND PIT STOP

A racing car with a rear-mounted engine, a well-stocked pit stop, a change of oil, and a finish line — what more could you want for the big race?

MAD SCIENTIST'S LAB

Timmy should have heeded the warning on the sign outside, but when he sees the flashing lights and hears the weird noises from inside the lab, he can't resist taking a peek! Build a mad scientist's laboratory to conduct strange experiments in and fill it with machines, devices and mysterious chemicals.

Two 1x1 slopes make a cradle for the monster's head

ON THE SLAB
Use a 2x6 plate as the base for a monster-building operating table. A hinge placed underneath allows it to lie flat or be raised up at an angle.

The studs of a 1x2 plate attach to the holes in the minifigure's legs to hold it in place

Lab playset is easily portable when folded up

FRONT SIDE VIEW

Windows let in light so the details on your model can be seen clearly

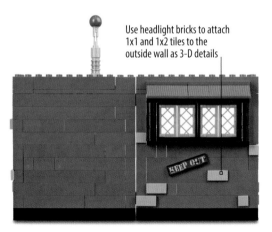

Use headlight bricks to attach 1x1 and 1x2 tiles to the outside wall as 3-D details

OPEN FRONT VIEW

MAKING SCIENCE

The mad scientist's laboratory is built as a small box that opens up to reveal a larger space for playing and storytelling. Inside are the scientist's latest projects: a pair of mechanical robots and a monster that he's bringing to life!

To find out how to build your own robots, turn to p.152

A red LEGO Technic ball at the top of a spire collects electricity from lightning storms to power the mad scientist's work

LAB EQUIPMENT

Your lab will need equipment to concoct all sorts of weird and wonderful distillations. Build pipes and tubes out of faucets, lightsaber handles, round bricks, LEGO Technic T-bars and other interestingly shaped elements.

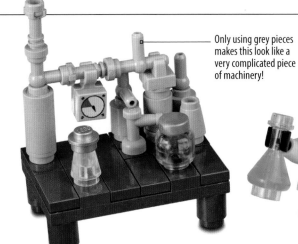

Only using grey pieces makes this look like a very complicated piece of machinery!

FRESHLY BREWED!

To prevent the halves from wobbling, place one hinge near the bottom and one near the top

What else could you add to your lab? Fill the empty space with even more wacky equipment!

NEXT SUBJECT!

The scientist's assistant rolls in his next experimental subject. The trolley is a simpler version of the operating table, with a pair of wheels at the bottom so it can be pushed around.

THESE TEST SUBJECTS SURE ARE BONE IDLE.

A plate with handle lets a minifigure hold on at the top

Tiles with printed gauges and dials are very helpful for building machinery

Grille locks the headlight bricks together

Skeleton's feet plug into headlight bricks

151

'BOTS ON THE LOOSE

Oh no! When Timmy opened the door to the lab, something got out. In fact, a whole lot of somethings did! Now his dream is full of clanking, stomping, beeping robots. When you build your own LEGO brick robots, you can make them big, small, round, square, or anything in between. Give them lots of metallic pieces and mechanical detail.

Stack a 2x2 round tile on a 2x2 round plate to make the classic stud on top of the head

MEGA 'BOT

Do you have a favourite minifigure? Then blow it up – in scale, that is! This one is based on the Clockwork Robot. Use your bricks to construct a giant-sized version with as many of the same colours and details as possible.

Eyes are 1x1 square plates mounted on radar dishes

The head is built just like the body, only smaller

Use a large turntable for your mega 'bot's neck

Posable robotic claws are built from clips, plates with handles, sliding plates and 1x1 slopes

Tiles, grilles, radar dishes and round plates recreate the original printed details on the minifigure in 3-D

Attach tiles to side studs for smooth surfaces

SIDE VIEW

TITANIUM TORSO

The giant robot's torso has a core of bricks with side studs. Plates and tiles are attached to create the look of a smooth body with bolts around the chest, just like on the minifigure!

It doesn't matter what colour bricks you use on the inside – they'll be hidden from view!

Feet are tipped with grille slopes

IT REALLY CAPTURES MY WINNING SMILE!

Clockwork Robot

Why not extend your 'bot family? Baby Bot might like an older brother and sister!

'BOT HEAD

To allow Mrs. Bot to turn her head, use a jumper plate with a tile on each side. Her wide jaw is made from a 2x3 curved plate with hole. Give Mrs. Bot a cute bow by attaching two 1x1 slopes.

1x1 slope

2x3 curved plate with hole

Jumper plate

Eyes are silver 1x1 round plates attached to headlight bricks

Shoulders are ray guns with their handles plugged into headlight bricks

MRS. BOT

Dark red pieces, silver accents and lots of round elements give this robot a stylish art deco design. Her skirt is a Technic wheel element from a LEGO® *Star Wars*™ set.

FAMILY PHOTO TIME, EVERYBODY!

Each foot is made from a 1x2 plate and a 1x2 tile flipped upside down

Use 1x1 round bricks for the legs, lower arms and parts of the torso

A free-rotating LEGO Technic pin allows the arm to swing back and forth

Elbow is a 1x1 round tile attached to a half-pin

SIDE VIEW

Grille-slope mouth creates a quirky expression

A plate with handle built into the body adds a projecting decoration

Arm built out of LEGO Technic cross-axle connectors

Upper legs are barrel-shaped droid body elements linked by a LEGO Technic pin

Feet are inverted slopes attached to corrugated tubes by a LEGO Technic axle-with-stud

Grilles become treads on the bottom of the feet

BABY BOT

What's the smallest robot you can build? This miniature marvel is made out of just eight pieces, starting with a brick with two side studs for its body!

Wide eyes are a binocular piece attached to a 1x1 round plate

1x1 plates with side clips make tiny arms

Legs are 1x1 cones plugged into a 1x2 jumper plate

MR. BOT

This retro, industrial-looking robot is built mostly out of grey pieces to imitate metal. His arms swivel at the shoulders, and an unusual upside-down construction gives his feet treads.

ROBOT RAMPAGE

"You dare to unleash robots in MY city?" says the Inventor. "Let's see how they do against my own mechanical minions!" Suddenly there are two armies of robots battling it out in Timmy's dream. Build some 'bots that are designed for demolition and destruction! Give them claws, spikes and any other tools they'll need to mash, smash, crunch and munch their rivals.

Golden eyes plug into the bases of headlight bricks that are turned on their backs

A plate with a handle creates a bar to protect the robot's head

Tiles printed with dials make great robotic features

Antenna picks up commands from its inventor

One-stud connections let the head and shoulders be posed

SIDE VIEW

TORNADO-TRON

This riotous red robot can spin its body around to send enemies toppling to the ground. Its boxy construction shows that it's tough and ready to rumble.

2x2 turntable

SPIN CYCLE

A 2x2 turntable in the middle of the model lets its upper body rotate freely with a flick of your finger. Or hold it by the shoulders and make its legs spin around!

Big feet keep this 'bot from toppling over

A plate with side bars creates an antenna on each side of the head

ROBOTS: ATTACK! OOPS, DID I FORGET TO BUILD AN OFF BUTTON?

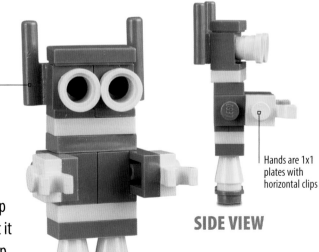

Hands are 1x1 plates with horizontal clips

ZOOM-BOT

What this robot lacks in size, it makes up for with speed. Its legs are jets to rocket it around and its claws pack an electric zap that sends bigger 'bots packing!

SIDE VIEW

Legs are 1x1 cones with round plates at the base

CHOMP CHOMP

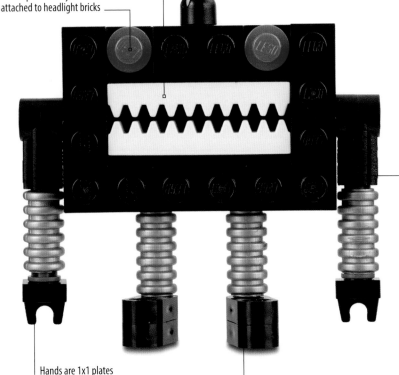

Teeth are 1x4 LEGO Technic gear racks

Round plates for eyes are attached to headlight bricks

Hands are 1x1 plates with vertical clips

Feet are made from small LEGO Technic liftarms

BIT-OR

It can be fun to build a robot model around one particular feature – such as a giant set of teeth! This fellow's chompers can reduce its rivals to scrap in seconds.

HEAVY METAL

The toothy robot's limbs are sheathed in silver corrugated tubes. Thread LEGO Technic cross-axles with studs on the ends through the tubes to connect LEGO Technic pieces to regular bricks.

Use LEGO Technic pins to connect the arms to the body

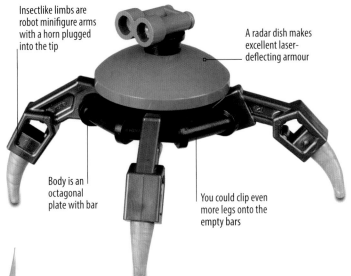

Insectlike limbs are robot minifigure arms with a horn plugged into the tip

A radar dish makes excellent laser-deflecting armour

Body is an octagonal plate with bar

You could clip even more legs onto the empty bars

SPI-DRONE

Not all robots have to be humanoid—let their missions determine their form. With its stealthy shape and dark colour scheme, this automated arachnoid is designed to scramble across walls and ceilings as it snoops on its unwitting foes.

MINIFIGURE MEMORY

Gather a heap of your scariest minifigures and challenge your friends to a minifigure memory test! Give your friends some time to look over the minifigures, then hide them all behind a blanket and remove one. The winner is the first friend to correctly guess which minifigure is missing.

THE MUMMY'S TOMB

When Timmy calls for his mummy, this isn't what he meant. Archaeological sites are a great place to discover the past, but in the world of nightmares, they are also home to venomous snakes, moving statues, hidden traps and pharaohs' curses!

ANCIENT RUINS

When constructing a building that is thousands of years old, don't just make clean, smooth walls. Include pieces that are rounded or textured to show its age. Off-colour bricks will make it look like bits of the original stone have fallen away.

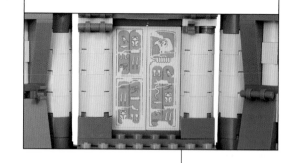

Hinges make the side walls angle in, or you could build one straight long wall

WHO DARES TO ENTER MY TOMB?

Plates with handles resemble decorative carvings

The addition of some leaves shows how nature has crept into the ruin

Scattered tan tiles on the ground give the impression of an old temple taken over by the desert

156

MUMMY ATTACK!

When the hidden stand behind the door bricks is pushed, the door bricks topple forward, making the lurking mummy smash through the wall!

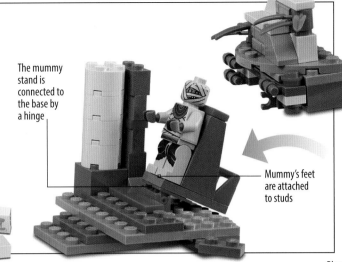

The mummy stand is connected to the base by a hinge

Mummy's feet are attached to studs

What other nightmarish creatures could be hiding in your ancient ruins?

STONE PROTECTOR

Use a rotating turntable base to create a special action function: a wall that spins around to reveal one of the tomb's guardian statues. . .or a secret treasure!

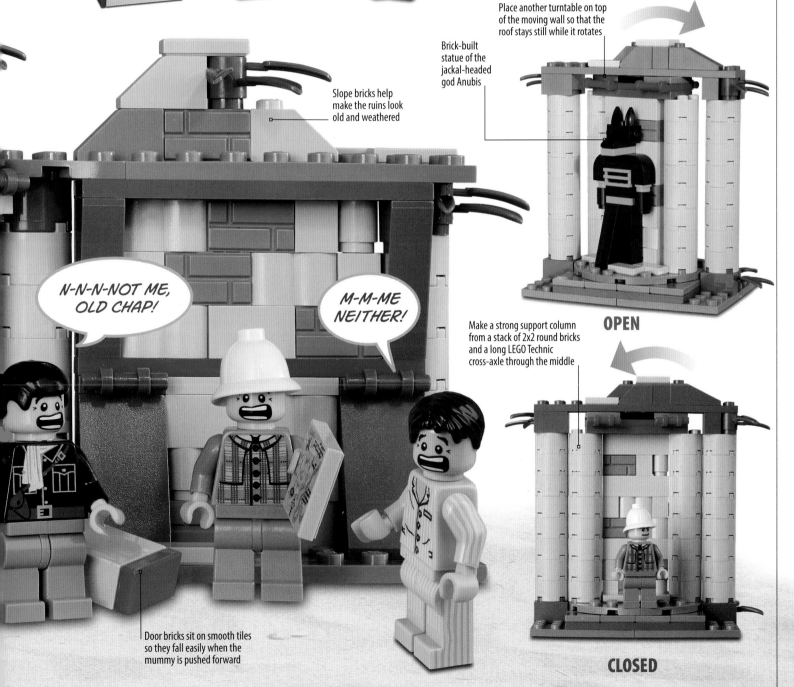

Place another turntable on top of the moving wall so that the roof stays still while it rotates

Brick-built statue of the jackal-headed god Anubis

Slope bricks help make the ruins look old and weathered

N-N-N-NOT ME, OLD CHAP!

M-M-ME NEITHER!

OPEN

Make a strong support column from a stack of 2x2 round bricks and a long LEGO Technic cross-axle through the middle

Door bricks sit on smooth tiles so they fall easily when the mummy is pushed forward

CLOSED

SKELETON

Well, that was some gratitude! As soon as Timmy finished putting the skeleton together, it started chasing him and threatening to gobble him up. It is certainly a good thing that it is all bones and no tummy. Look through your collection for long bars, curved elements and oddly shaped pieces, and use them to build a big, scary skeleton!

SKELETAL SPECIES

Who says this has to be a human skeleton? Make it a monster by adding horns, claws and oversized hands and feet. Now it looks both grim and a little bit goofy – just right for a LEGO brick nightmare!

BOO!

2x2 round tile for a skullcap

Brick with two holes

Horns plug into headlight bricks

Neck is a 1x1 cone

NO BRAINS HERE!

The skull's eyes are a brick with two holes. For its mouth, use a transparent 1x2 plate so that the studs on the piece beneath show through as teeth.

The centre of the collarbone is a 1x1 brick with four hollow side studs

The hands are built just like the feet, but tipped with claws

A 1x2 plate with handle creates the back of the pelvis

Top of the legs are round bricks

1x1 plates with vertical clips let the arms move at the shoulder

Skeleton's ribs are minifigure skeleton arms!

The spine is a long rod piece

Hips are headlight bricks attached sideways to a brick with four side studs

Shoulder blades are 1x1 plates with side rings

Position big feet at an angle to help the skeleton keep its balance

HOW'D MY PAL GET TO BE SO BIG? LOTS OF MILK!

SKINNY BONES

Each of the skeleton's leg bones is an antenna, with cones for knees. For the feet, attach a jumper plate onto a 1x2 plate with handle, and clip on three robot arms for the toes.

Robot arm

Antenna

The box's sides are square wall elements

Top edge is lined with tiles

If you don't have these tall bricks for the corners, then stack up regular 1x1 bricks

MONSTER BOX

Here's a monstrous box that you could use to hide your secret treasures. A sinister skeleton guardian will scare off anyone who tries to sneek a peek! What will you store inside?

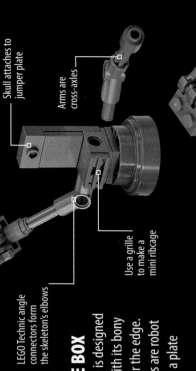

Skull is a sculpted piece, but you could build your own

Skull attaches to jumper plate

Arms are cross-axles

Use a grille to make a mini ribcage

LEGO Technic angle connectors form the skeleton's elbows

SCARE IN THE BOX

This scary skeleton is designed to sit in the box, with its bony fingers draped over the edge. The posable fingers are robot claws clipped onto a plate with handles.

VAMPIRE'S CASTLE

Timmy runs away from the skeleton as fast as his little legs will carry him, until he reaches the steps of a big stone castle. "Velcome, child," he hears as the door slowly creaks open. "Von't you come in for a bite?" Vampires like to hide in castles during the day, and the older the better. Give your castle lots of classic furnishings and décor!

CRYPT SWEET CRYPT

Look at pictures of old castles and mansions to get ideas for your vampire's lair. For colours, use grey to resemble stone, with black and red accents. Avoid open windows – vampires aren't too fond of sunlight!

Moon (a printed glow-in-the-dark radar dish) is attached to the black rear wall using a brick with side stud

A couple of slopes can make an entire peaked rooftop

Use the backs of headlight bricks for dark, square windows

PLEASED TO EAT—I MEAN MEET YOU!

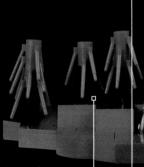

Trees are brown telescopes with upside-down flower stems on top

Pillars are plates with handles built sideways

Alternate 2x2 tiles to make a checkerboard floor pattern

MICRO-TRANSYLVANIA

If you don't have enough pieces to make an entire vampire castle, create a micro-scale façade with your smallest LEGO pieces! Give it classic monster story details, such as a rocky mountain peak, a spooky forest and a big full moon outside.

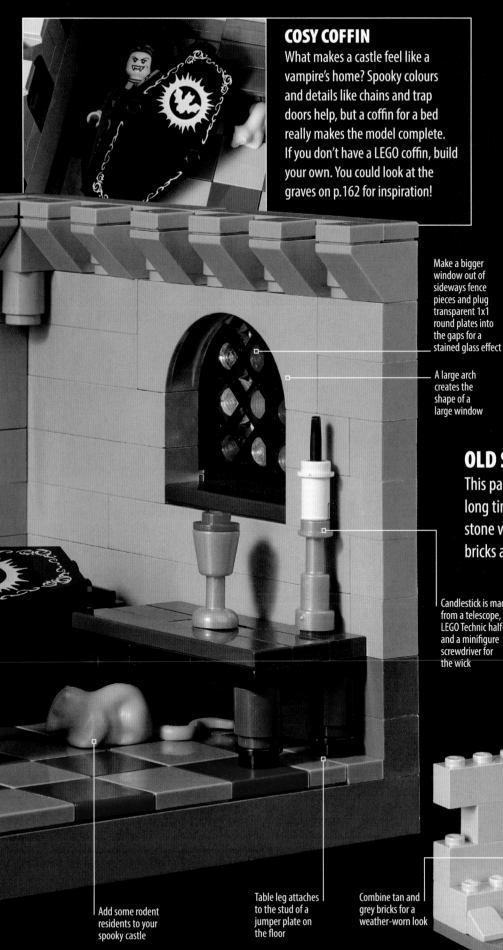

COSY COFFIN

What makes a castle feel like a vampire's home? Spooky colours and details like chains and trap doors help, but a coffin for a bed really makes the model complete. If you don't have a LEGO coffin, build your own. You could look at the graves on p.162 for inspiration!

Make a bigger window out of sideways fence pieces and plug transparent 1x1 round plates into the gaps for a stained glass effect

A large arch creates the shape of a large window

Candlestick is made from a telescope, a LEGO Technic half-pin, and a minifigure screwdriver for the wick

Add some rodent residents to your spooky castle

Table leg attaches to the stud of a jumper plate on the floor

Combine tan and grey bricks for a weather-worn look

WINDOWS

For windows that look like they belong to a room that was built centuries ago, combine window frame pieces with latticed window elements. Surround them with grey arches and bricks to resemble stone blocks.

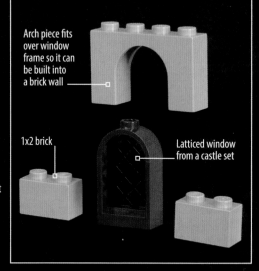

Arch piece fits over window frame so it can be built into a brick wall

1x2 brick

Latticed window from a castle set

OLD STONES

This part of the castle has been around for a long, long time. Slopes and unfinished edges make a stone wall look like it is falling apart and textured bricks add to the appearance of decay and disrepair.

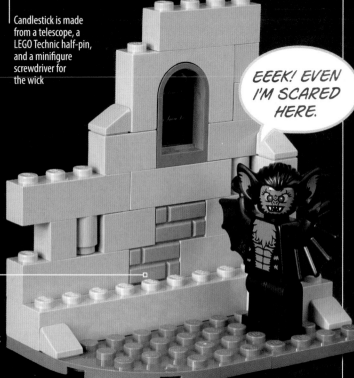

EEEK! EVEN I'M SCARED HERE.

GRAVEYARD

"Join us, Timmy," says the voice from under the ground. "Take a rest with us." There's nothing spookier than an old cemetery at midnight. Anything could pop out from under those headstones! When creating a creepy graveyard scene, make it look decrepit and crumbling by making the stones uneven and falling apart. Don't forget to add a forbidding crypt or tomb.

THE PERFECT FIT

To make a grave the right size for a minifigure, build it around the figure so it's guaranteed to fit! When building the headstone, combine grey log bricks with smooth bricks to create a weathered stone surface.

1x2 log brick

Bricks topped with smooth tiles in the corners of the grave let the cover rest in place without sticking

Build bricks-with-holes into the sides of the plots and click the sections together with LEGO Technic connector pins

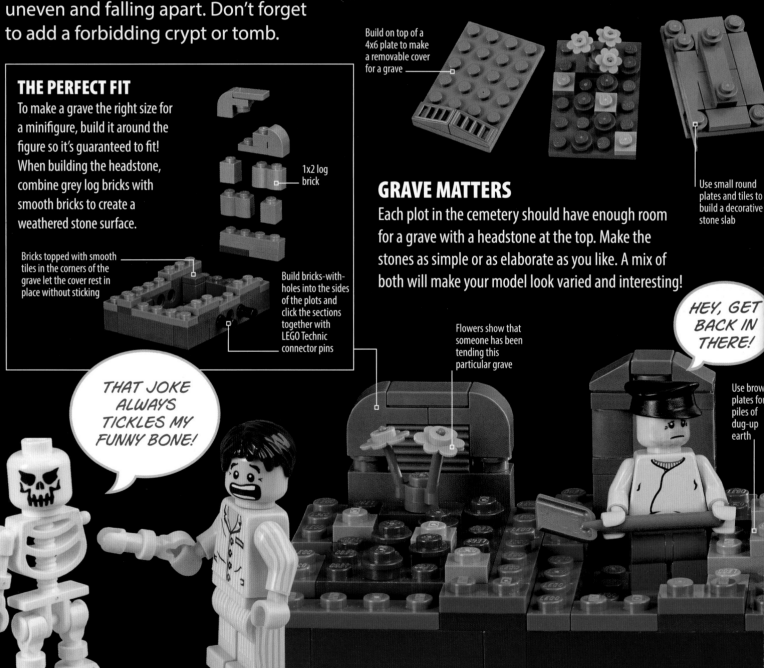

Build on top of a 4x6 plate to make a removable cover for a grave

Use small round plates and tiles to build a decorative stone slab

GRAVE MATTERS

Each plot in the cemetery should have enough room for a grave with a headstone at the top. Make the stones as simple or as elaborate as you like. A mix of both will make your model look varied and interesting!

THAT JOKE ALWAYS TICKLES MY FUNNY BONE!

Flowers show that someone has been tending this particular grave

HEY, GET BACK IN THERE!

Use brown plates for piles of dug-up earth

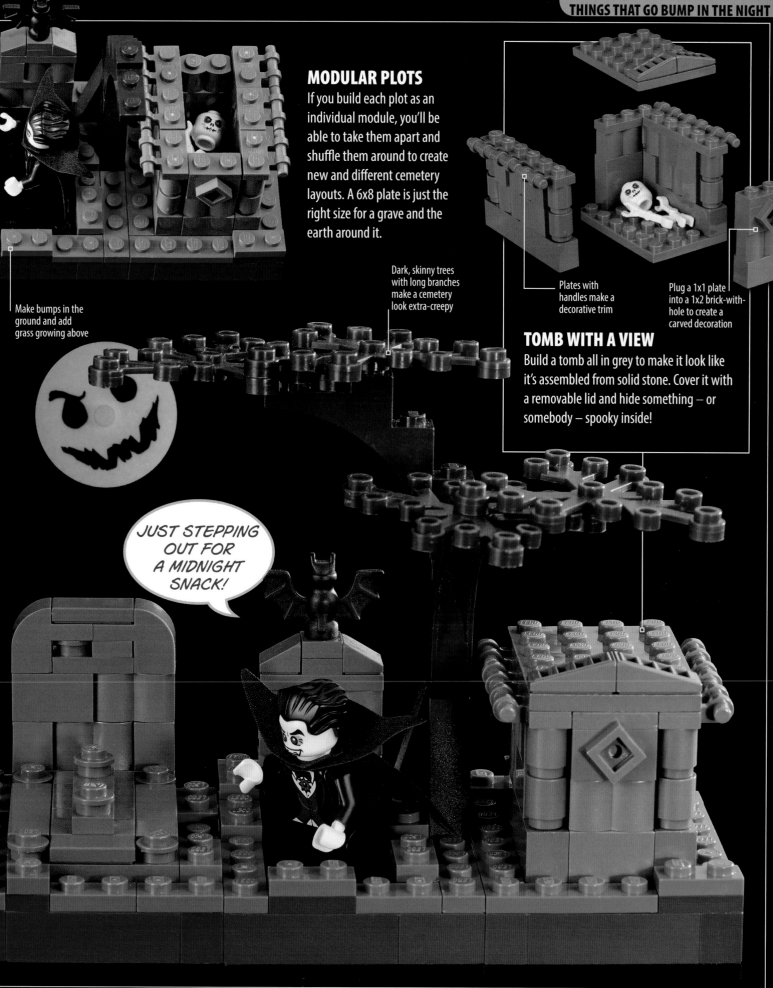

MODULAR PLOTS

If you build each plot as an individual module, you'll be able to take them apart and shuffle them around to create new and different cemetery layouts. A 6x8 plate is just the right size for a grave and the earth around it.

Plates with handles make a decorative trim

Plug a 1x1 plate into a 1x2 brick-with-hole to create a carved decoration

Dark, skinny trees with long branches make a cemetery look extra-creepy

TOMB WITH A VIEW

Build a tomb all in grey to make it look like it's assembled from solid stone. Cover it with a removable lid and hide something – or somebody – spooky inside!

Make bumps in the ground and add grass growing above

JUST STEPPING OUT FOR A MIDNIGHT SNACK!

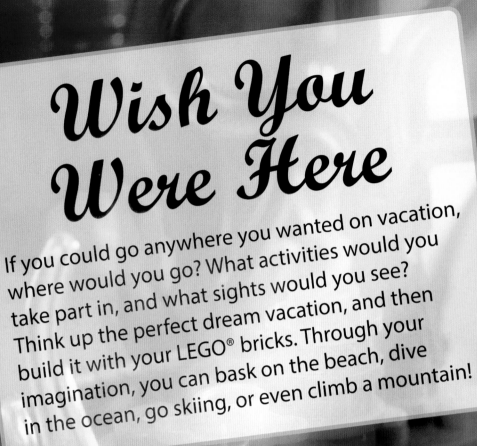

Wish You Were Here

If you could go anywhere you wanted on vacation, where would you go? What activities would you take part in, and what sights would you see? Think up the perfect dream vacation, and then build it with your LEGO® bricks. Through your imagination, you can bask on the beach, dive in the ocean, go skiing, or even climb a mountain!

DID YOU PACK YOUR TICKETS? INTERGALACTIC PASSPORT? RAY GUN?

ZORG

EARTH MISSION

Glax is a space-travel journalist who has just received a very exciting interstellar mission from his boss, Zorg. Glax is to travel to a remote planet called "Earth" and experience all of its best vacation spots and leisure pursuits, then write about it all for the Space Network. The entire galactic quadrant will be reading his daily reports! Glax's job has taken him all over the known universe, but this will be his first time on Earth. He hopes the locals are nice and he doesn't lose his luggage!

YEP, YEP, AND DOUBLE-YEP!

GLAX

HAVE A GREAT TIME!

Glax quickly discovers the sweet, cool concoction known as "ice cream"

MAKING VACATIONS
TIM JOHNSON

"I did a lot of online image searches to get references for what I wanted to build for my chapter. Sometimes the real thing didn't match what I saw in my head, so I went with what I'd imagined instead. The models that I like the best are the ones that are closest to my own experiences. I grew up in Australia and the blue beach hut (p.168) was heavily inspired by one my grandparents owned."

Space Network

6,846

Home Aliens Inbox

Wall

Photos

Info

Profile

Name: Glaxxico8791
Location: Pluuvonic Nebula
Occupation: Freelance tourist
Likes: Solar sailing
Dislikes: Wormholes

Friends 7,946,462

HANNO **ROX**

DOLO **ZORG**

YOXY **PX200-E**

ZX81 **COLIN**

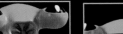

GLAX ... is somewhere special. Here's a hint: it's round and blue-green. Give up? It's Earth!

GLAX commented on his own picture

Here I am going up a mountain in a cable-mounted travel pod. When I get to the top, I will strap boards onto my feet and slide back down!

GLAX commented on his own picture

I have enjoyed resting in the rays of Earth's sun, next to an artificial body of water with an elevated launch platform. Note: human waiters do not enjoy being splashed.

ZORG commented on your picture
That strange Earth food looks a little like you, Glax.

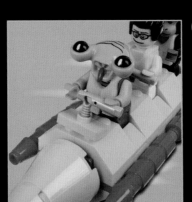

GLAX commented on his own picture

Today I explored the Earth ocean aboard a floating vehicle shaped like a giant piece of fruit. Later, I lay down on some sand until I turned from green to red. Humans have very strange hobbies!

GLAX commented on his own picture

BEACH HUTS

Greetings from Earth! Glax's holiday has begun with a trip to something called "The Beach," a sandy desert next to a large expanse of water. Humans must be partly solar-powered, because they sure enjoy lying out in the sun! Build a stretch of beach for your vacationing minifigures to enjoy. Include beach huts so they can relax in carefree comfort.

Brown bush pieces look like dry beach plants

REAR VIEW

HOME ON THE SAND

At a beach hut, vacationers can change into bathing suits, grab a snack, or snooze in the shade. To make one, build a small one-room house with lots of seaside details. Include a sandy beach around it!

Transparent slopes in the roof let the sunlight in

A key from the back of a wind-up LEGO® Minifigures character doubles as a latch

Rows of slopes and jumper plates create a festively striped roof

Hinged door hatch for a simple storage hut

A LEGO chain helps the hut's owners pull the open door back down

THIS IS ONE WAY TO GET OUT OF DOING THE WASHING UP!

Sand bank can be filled with pieces of any shape and colour, and then covered with tan plates or bricks

I THINK WE LEFT THIS FISH OUT IN THE SUN TOO LONG.

Window pieces without glass support the porch railing

Supports let huts sit level on top of a steep sand bank

Stack up round bricks and plates to build a minifigure-sized sand castle

Build up mounds of plates to make the beach bumpy and uneven

COOL BRICK

"I love the 1x4 bricks with grooves for creating textures. A wall of them resembles corrugated metal. If you leave the short end exposed in a wall, it looks a little like a window."

FRONT VIEW

A tile with a number identifies the vacation hut

SURF HUT

The surfers who own this hut have cheered it up by painting a mural on the back wall. Inside are shelves for their surfboards and clips to hold their favourite beach gear.

Mural is built on a small plate and attached to the interior wall using bricks with side studs

HUT CONSTRUCTION

Try building each hut as a separate mini-scene and then connecting their sections of beach together. They can be identical buildings in different colours, or totally individual designs.

Include beach accessories like shells, fishing poles, and swimming equipment

A small ladder provides quick and easy access

Tell a story with your scene. These surfers have just returned from a fishing trip in their rowboat. Time for a beach cook-out!

▶ QUICK BUILD

MICRO BEACH HUT

A big beach hut may take a while to assemble, but you can put together a micro-scale version in no time at all. When you've finished, build even more to make a whole ocean-view scene!

A bracket allows the doors to be attached sideways

Use jumper plates to centre the roof slopes

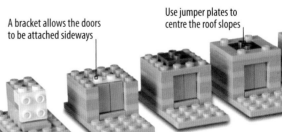

Build matching shapes with different doors and decorations

ICE-CREAM STALLS

While at the beach, Glax samples a unique human delicacy: a wafer rolled into a cone and filled with a frozen substance that has something to do with Earth cows. Believe it or not, it tastes much better than it sounds! Who doesn't love sweet, cold ice cream on a sunny day? Build a stall so your beach-goers can enjoy some of their own!

Arch is supported by columns built from 1x1 round bricks and plates

This ice-cream scoop started out as a LEGO® Ninjago nunchuk handle!

SMALL KIOSK

This stall is just big enough for a vendor and a freezer full of frozen treats. Give it a bright colour scheme and an eye-catching sign overhead, as well as a shade to block the sun on hot summer days.

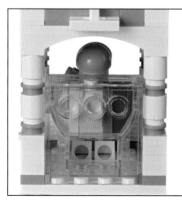

FREEZER
Inside the stall is a freezer full of ice-cream flavours. If you don't have this single transparent piece, you can build your own out of LEGO windows, tiles, and hinge pieces.

SIGNAGE

No sunbather will miss this sign! Its scoops are built around two brackets and two inverted brackets. An upside-down 2x2 cone is held on by a long rod piece.

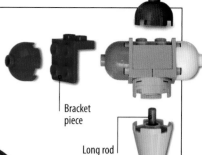

Bracket piece

Long rod

Hinge cylinder underneath the ice-cream sign snaps onto the back of the kiosk

Big scoops are 2x2 domes in different colours

Alternate curved bricks of the same shape to make a striped awning for the stall's roof

Transparent elements look like glowing lights

1x1 round plates underneath give the awning a fringe

1x1 round plates make good single-serving scoops

Build in textured bricks for detail

Hat comes from a LEGO butcher minifigure

Refrigerated display under the counter is made with two transparent windshield pieces

REAR SIDE VIEW

Transparent goblet for a dessert glass

A sink for cleaning up melted ice cream

The hut is built on a raised cement platform of grey plates, but sand has piled up around its base

AWNING CONSTRUCTION

The front awning is attached to the roof by click hinges, letting it fold down when the hut is closed at night!

Plate with click hinge

LARGE HUT

For a more crowded beach or resort, you'll need a bigger ice-cream stall. This one looks cool and classy with its extended awning, transparent counter and lots of dessert-making equipment. Its kitchen has something for every hot beach-goer!

I LEARNED TO DO THIS AT SUNDAE SCHOOL!

A 1x1 round plate attaches this LEGO® Technic ball-joint piece to its goblet cone

Beach umbrella pole plugs into the centre of a 2x2 round brick

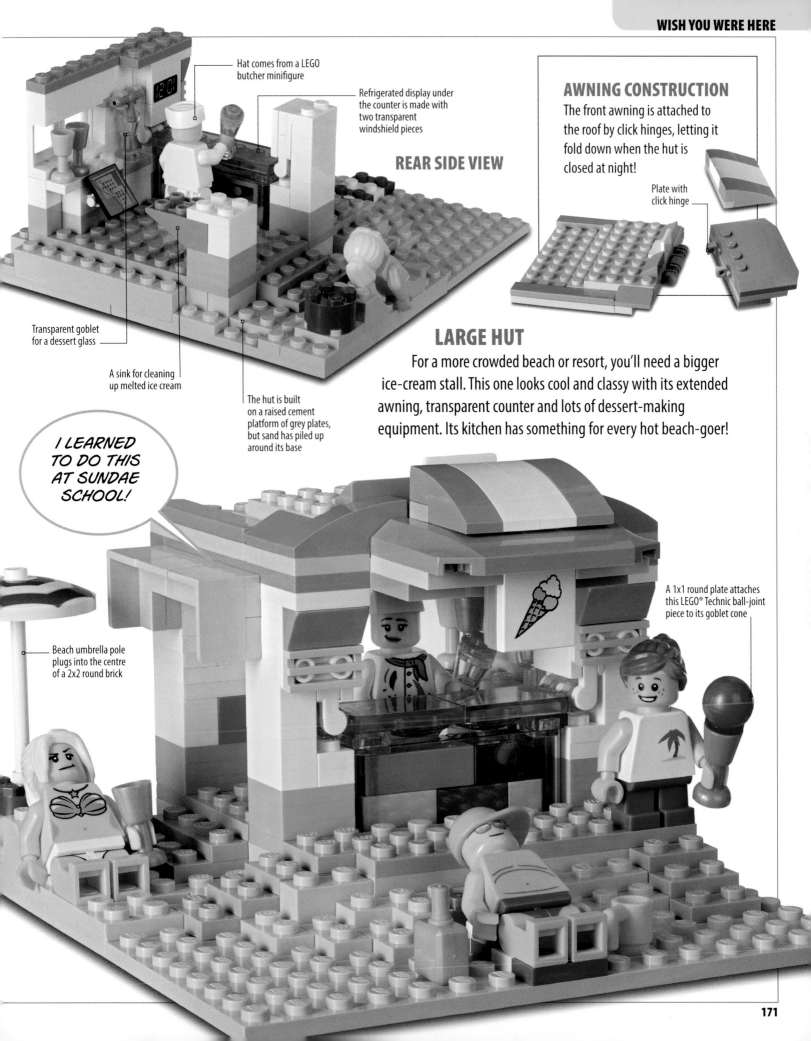

BEACH ACCESSORIES

Before visiting an Earth beach, Glax recommends that you obtain the appropriate equipment: a face-mounted apparatus to protect your ocular orbs and a personal seating device to avoid getting sand in your spacesuit. Here are some items that will make a trip to the beach even more fun.

A radar dish mounted on a group of 1x1 round plates provides a freshly scooped curve

If you don't have enough pieces in the same color, pick something similar for a ripple of colour

Scoops don't all have to be this size and shape – they can look any way you like!

Use a red 2x2 dome for a cherry on top, or smaller pieces for nuts and sprinkles

Make some of these pieces brown or black for chocolate chips

WHAT'S THE SCOOP?

How do you build a big scoop of ice cream? Make a round, bumpy shape out of 2x2 round bricks and place a circular plate or brick on top to hold them together.

KING-SIZED CONE

This giant cone is made by building ringed layers of 2x2 round bricks and log bricks that get smaller as they get closer to the bottom.

Use tan, brown, or white bricks for the cone

A plate layer every few rows makes the cone strong and sturdy

The upside-down cone at the tip is held on by a LEGO Technic cross-axle

ICE CREAM CONE

Why should minifigures have all the fun? Put your bricks together and build a life-sized ice cream cone for yourself. Just don't try to eat it – this colourful plastic treat is for play and display purposes only!

I'LL BET I'VE GOT THE BIGGEST ICE CREAM CONE IN THE WORLD!

Build a silly nose or eyebrows onto the frames to make a funny disguise!

I DON'T HAVE ANY HEARING DISCS TO HOOK MY GLASSES ON TO!

Half-arches should fit comfortably over ears

Use tinted window pieces for the lenses

BUILDER TALK

"Once you decide what to build, try searching the internet for images to inspire you. You could mix different details, using the shape of one image and the colours of another."

Use bricks with clips and bars to make folding earpieces

SUNGLASSES

They may not shield your eyes from the sun, but these full-sized sunglasses are still plenty cool! Build the frames out of thin plates to keep them lightweight and design them to fit the size and shape of your face.

REAR VIEW

Pick your favourite colours for the frames

An auto mudguard makes a handy nose-rest

Use lots of plates with clips and bars to replicate the flexible movement of fabric

DECK CHAIR

A portable deck chair is perfect for sitting out in the sun near the ocean or by the side of a pool. Just fold it up and take it along with you wherever you want to go!

Try building an even smaller deck chair so it's minifigure size.

Smooth tiles make the frame sections look like wooden beams

Place thin plates side-by-side to make a striped pattern

Build the parts of the frame first, then attach them together

Bricks with holes are connected together with LEGO® Technic pins for swiveling motion

REAR VIEW

173

BEACH BOATS

Glax observes some humans going out on the water inside small floating crafts that lack even basic antigravity propulsion. Perhaps this is an activity that he should attempt as well? Going out in a boat turns a trip to the beach into an adventure on the water, whether you're going fast or taking your time. Build one and try it out!

There are lots of other pieces that can substitute for this rectangular bar element

Auto mudguards create seats with comfy armrests

BOTTOM VIEW

I LIKE THE VIEW.

AND I LIKE THE EXERCISE!

PADDLE BOAT

A paddle boat moves when you turn its foot pedals. The more you pedal, the faster it goes! Build a paddle boat to be flat and stable for a comfortable ride. With two seats, friends can team up for twice the boating fun.

FRONT VIEW

Use long inverted curve bricks to make floatation pontoons

A car roof is a simple way to make the front of the boat, but you could build it out of plates instead

PEDAL POWER

The pedals are round bricks with fins from a rocket. They are connected together by a LEGO Technic cross-axle that passes through a pair of bricks-with-holes so the pedals can spin.

Curved bricks cover and hide the rotating pedal function

Use plates to lock the bricks-with-holes together on the top and bottom

Cross-axle

Pedal

Try building a spinning paddle-wheel under the boat, or one on each side!

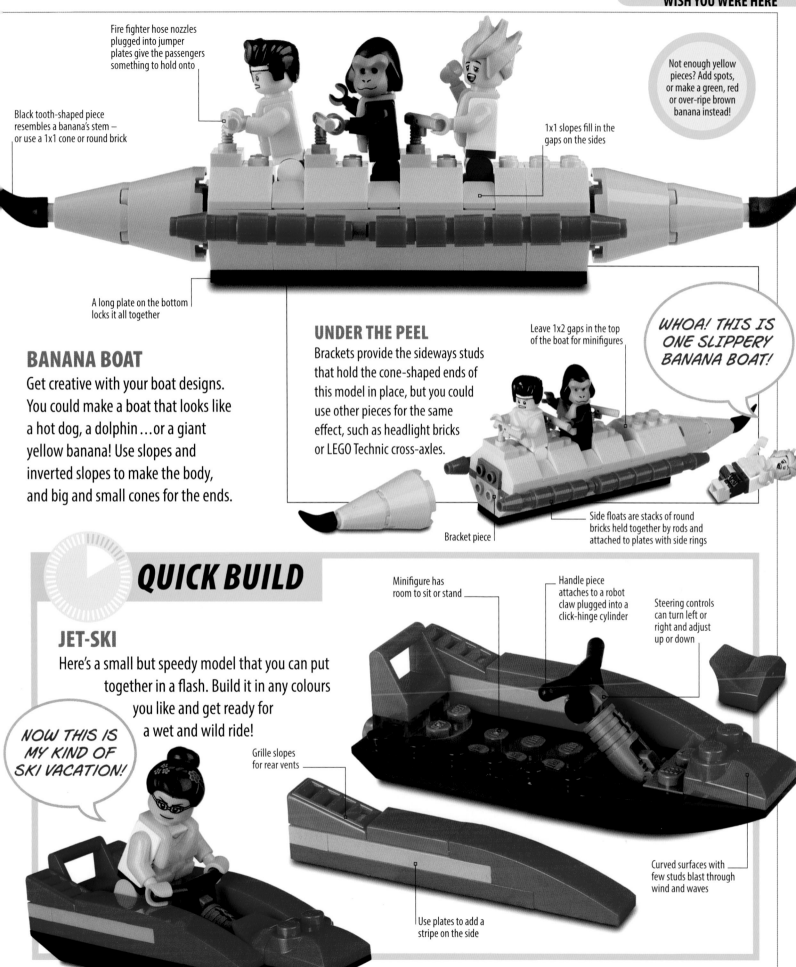

Fire fighter hose nozzles plugged into jumper plates give the passengers something to hold onto

Not enough yellow pieces? Add spots, or make a green, red or over-ripe brown banana instead!

Black tooth-shaped piece resembles a banana's stem — or use a 1x1 cone or round brick

1x1 slopes fill in the gaps on the sides

A long plate on the bottom locks it all together

BANANA BOAT

Get creative with your boat designs. You could make a boat that looks like a hot dog, a dolphin …or a giant yellow banana! Use slopes and inverted slopes to make the body, and big and small cones for the ends.

UNDER THE PEEL

Brackets provide the sideways studs that hold the cone-shaped ends of this model in place, but you could use other pieces for the same effect, such as headlight bricks or LEGO Technic cross-axles.

Leave 1x2 gaps in the top of the boat for minifigures

WHOA! THIS IS ONE SLIPPERY BANANA BOAT!

Bracket piece

Side floats are stacks of round bricks held together by rods and attached to plates with side rings

QUICK BUILD

Minifigure has room to sit or stand

Handle piece attaches to a robot claw plugged into a click-hinge cylinder

Steering controls can turn left or right and adjust up or down

JET-SKI

Here's a small but speedy model that you can put together in a flash. Build it in any colours you like and get ready for a wet and wild ride!

NOW THIS IS MY KIND OF SKI VACATION!

Grille slopes for rear vents

Use plates to add a stripe on the side

Curved surfaces with few studs blast through wind and waves

HOTEL POOL

After Glax's beach adventure, he discovers a building where individual hibernation pods can be rented for the night. Amazingly, it includes its own miniature ocean! A hotel swimming pool provides even more opportunities for vacation fun. Your minifigures can swim, splash, play water-tag, and even take a leap from the high diving board!

SWIMMING POOL

Build a big swimming pool for a vacation hotel! You can make rippling water by adding layers of transparent blue pieces over a base of blue plates. Include other familiar pool features, such as a diving board and a lifeguard. If you don't have enough pieces to build an entire pool, just make part of one!

Binoculars and a floatie ring are a lifeguard's most important gear

Place the lifeguard's seat on a raised platform so he can spot any trouble

NO FAIR. WHY CAN'T I GO FOR A SWIM TOO?

HEY MUM, BOBBY IS MAKING BUBBLES!

Use 1x2 wall elements to make ladder steps

Use small tiles and round plates to create waves

Attach the top half of a minifigure to the water surface to make it look like he is submerged in water!

I HOPE EVERYBODY DOWN THERE IS READY FOR A BIG SPLASH!

Coat the board with tiles —or leave two studs exposed at the end so you can attach a diving minifigure

An angled support beam makes a good base for a sturdy diving board

You could also build hand-rails with bricks or clips and bars

Clip a ladder to the back of the board so your minifigures can climb up to the top

Build pool signs with letter and number tiles

Try building a big splash under the diving board!

Build the water into the pool walls to keep everything locked together

SUN LOUNGERS

Build your hotel guests some sun lounger chairs so they can kick back, relax and catch a few rays by the pool. There are lots of different ways to make them!

WHERE'S THE "HOVER" BUTTON ON THIS THING?

Angled back — use a hinge to make it adjustable

Seat is low to the ground

PLAY

Look through your collection for pool-side accessories such as balls, swim fins, and beach umbrellas.

Build a lounger with or without armrests

MAKING A SPLASH

Glax's afternoon at the pool has left him soaked. He tries to dry himself by using a rapid-velocity acceleration ramp, but that only results in him becoming wetter! Make a towering waterslide and send your minifigures screaming with laughter into the water below.

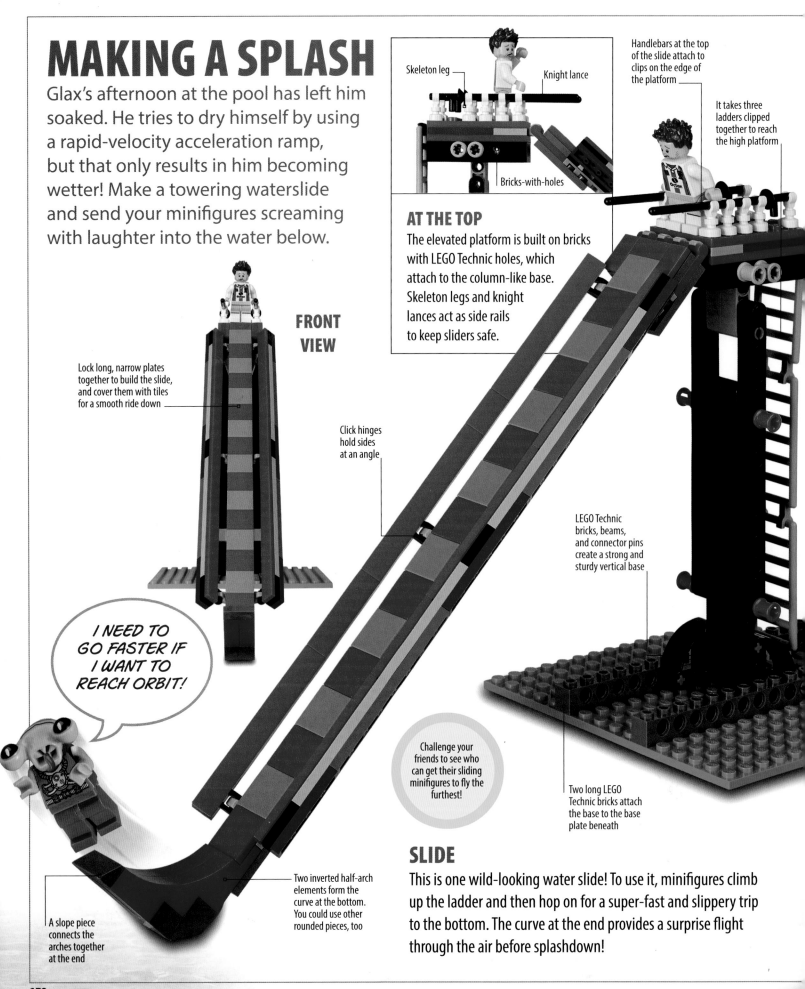

Skeleton leg

Knight lance

Handlebars at the top of the slide attach to clips on the edge of the platform

Bricks-with-holes

It takes three ladders clipped together to reach the high platform

AT THE TOP
The elevated platform is built on bricks with LEGO Technic holes, which attach to the column-like base. Skeleton legs and knight lances act as side rails to keep sliders safe.

FRONT VIEW

Lock long, narrow plates together to build the slide, and cover them with tiles for a smooth ride down

Click hinges hold sides at an angle

LEGO Technic bricks, beams, and connector pins create a strong and sturdy vertical base

I NEED TO GO FASTER IF I WANT TO REACH ORBIT!

Challenge your friends to see who can get their sliding minifigures to fly the furthest!

Two long LEGO Technic bricks attach the base to the base plate beneath

A slope piece connects the arches together at the end

Two inverted half-arch elements form the curve at the bottom. You could use other rounded pieces, too

SLIDE
This is one wild-looking water slide! To use it, minifigures climb up the ladder and then hop on for a super-fast and slippery trip to the bottom. The curve at the end provides a surprise flight through the air before splashdown!

SURFBOARDS

Surfboards come in lots of different sizes –
though you probably haven't seen too many
like this! There are official minifigure-scaled LEGO
surfboard elements, but you can also build your own out
of plates, boat parts and other long, flat and curved pieces.

WHOA. THESE
ARE SOME
RIGHTEOUS
BOARDS, DUDE!

The long, curved pieces at the
front and back come from
airplane, boat, helicopter,
and spaceship sets

The bigger you make
your surfboard, the more
colours and patterns you
can build into it

TOP VIEW

Use tiles for smooth,
flat surfaces on top

TOP VIEW

A LEGO Technic connector
pin connects this fin piece
to a plate-with-hole on
the board's underside

The bottom of this board
uses rectangular, angled
and even circular plates

The size of these surfboards is
determined by the size of the
special parts on the ends

TOP VIEW **BOTTOM VIEW**

BOTTOM VIEW

Construct
ramps and
obstacles for an
even bigger
challenge!

⭐ **CHALLENGE**

BAGGAGE CART STACKER

Have you ever tried to cross a busy airport with a cart full of
luggage? Build a simple base with wheels, add a brick to it,
and roll it over to a friend, who adds another brick and rolls it
back with a single push. Who will be the first to topple the truck?

Can you place your bricks in a
way that makes your opponent's
bricks off-balance?

Try building rolling bases
of different shapes, or using
different-sized wheels

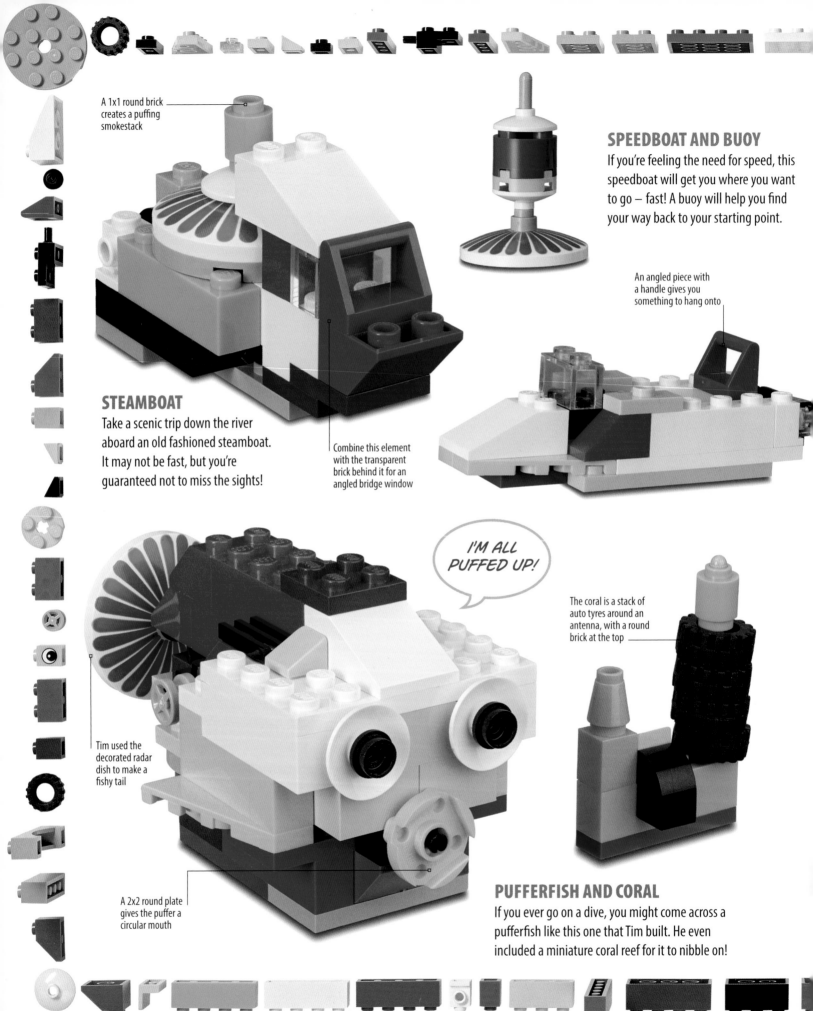

A 1x1 round brick creates a puffing smokestack

SPEEDBOAT AND BUOY

If you're feeling the need for speed, this speedboat will get you where you want to go – fast! A buoy will help you find your way back to your starting point.

An angled piece with a handle gives you something to hang onto

STEAMBOAT

Take a scenic trip down the river aboard an old fashioned steamboat. It may not be fast, but you're guaranteed not to miss the sights!

Combine this element with the transparent brick behind it for an angled bridge window

I'M ALL PUFFED UP!

The coral is a stack of auto tyres around an antenna, with a round brick at the top

Tim used the decorated radar dish to make a fishy tail

A 2x2 round plate gives the puffer a circular mouth

PUFFERFISH AND CORAL

If you ever go on a dive, you might come across a pufferfish like this one that Tim built. He even included a miniature coral reef for it to nibble on!

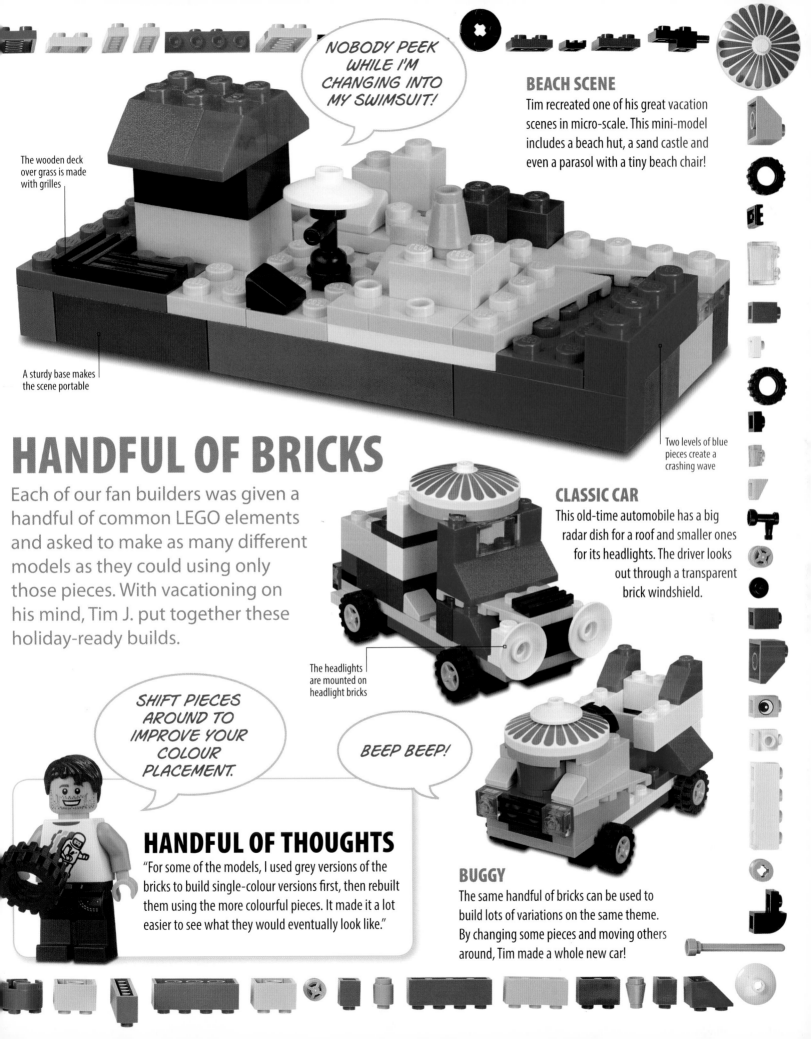

NOBODY PEEK WHILE I'M CHANGING INTO MY SWIMSUIT!

The wooden deck over grass is made with grilles

A sturdy base makes the scene portable

BEACH SCENE
Tim recreated one of his great vacation scenes in micro-scale. This mini-model includes a beach hut, a sand castle and even a parasol with a tiny beach chair!

Two levels of blue pieces create a crashing wave

HANDFUL OF BRICKS

Each of our fan builders was given a handful of common LEGO elements and asked to make as many different models as they could using only those pieces. With vacationing on his mind, Tim J. put together these holiday-ready builds.

CLASSIC CAR
This old-time automobile has a big radar dish for a roof and smaller ones for its headlights. The driver looks out through a transparent brick windshield.

The headlights are mounted on headlight bricks

SHIFT PIECES AROUND TO IMPROVE YOUR COLOUR PLACEMENT.

BEEP BEEP!

HANDFUL OF THOUGHTS
"For some of the models, I used grey versions of the bricks to build single-colour versions first, then rebuilt them using the more colourful pieces. It made it a lot easier to see what they would eventually look like."

BUGGY
The same handful of bricks can be used to build lots of variations on the same theme. By changing some pieces and moving others around, Tim made a whole new car!

BENEATH THE SEA

Diving under the sea is like exploring a whole different world. The fish remind Glax of some of his friends back home! Whether you're diving from a speedboat on the surface or swimming down near the sea floor, you're sure to see scenery and animals that you've never encountered before when you venture beneath the waves.

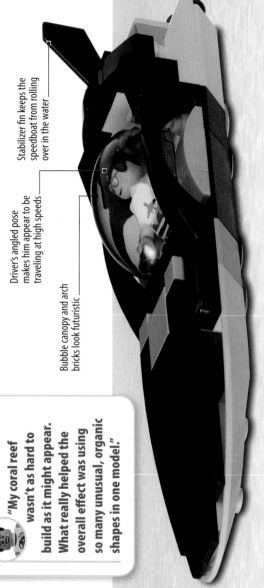

Stabilizer fin keeps the speedboat from rolling over in the water

Driver's angled pose makes him appear to be travelling at high speeds

Bubble canopy and arch bricks look futuristic

LUXURY SPEEDBOAT

For the ultimate in sea thrills, build a super-fast speedboat and hang on tight! Long curved and inverted-curve bricks make this boat's nose look smooth and streamlined. Give your speedboat a big engine and a windshield to protect the driver from water spray.

REAR VIEW

LEGO Technic balls attached to the ends of transparent flexible pipes

Use transparent pieces for rear lights

REAR VIEW

BOTTOM VIEW

Place round sliding plates on the bottom to coast across flat surfaces!

CLEVER CORALS

Coral structures should look unique. This one is built by clipping transparent blue axe heads onto a rod sticking out of a stack of 2x2 round bricks.

Use tentacles to create long, waving sea plants

SCHOOL DAYS

Build a floating school of fish by clipping them above a bar piece using robot or skeleton arms. Create even stranger ocean life with brushes from a LEGO® Friends set!

Blue brush head

Brown bar piece

CORAL REEF

Start your coral reef by adding bricks to a base plate to make an uneven sandy, rocky surface. Use some of your most unusual and colourful pieces to build different types of plant or coral. Ice cream scoops, barbell weights, and even lipstick create a colourful reef that any diver would want to explore!

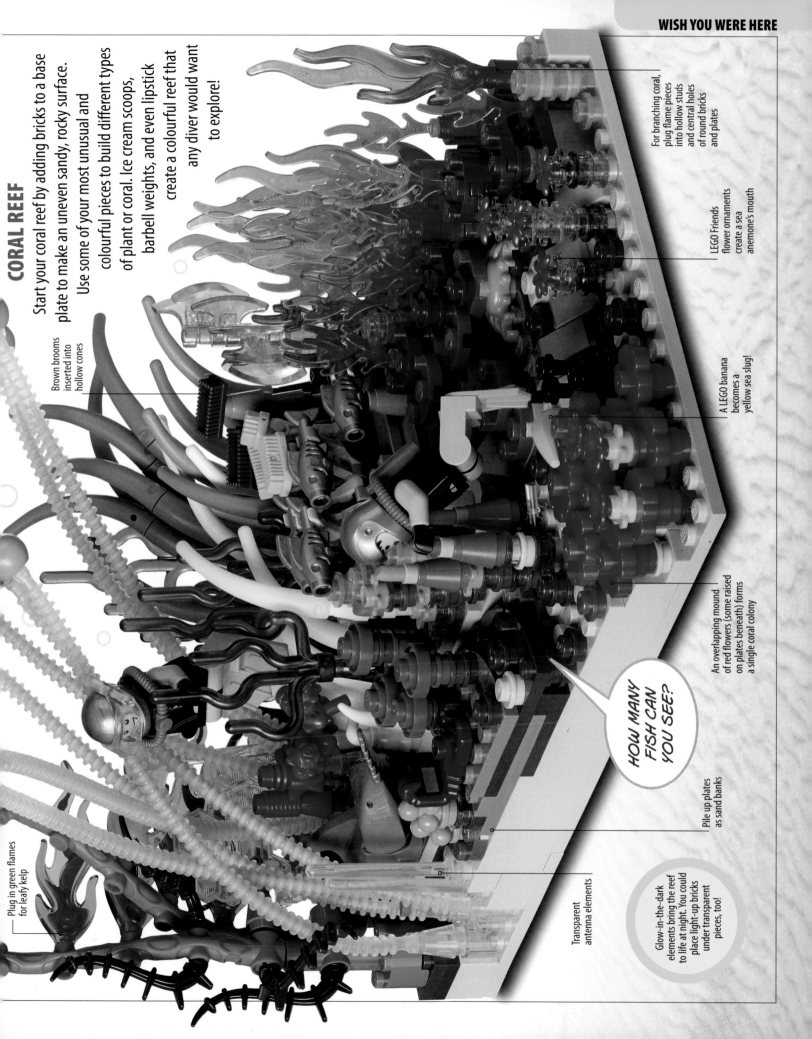

For branching coral, plug flame pieces into hollow studs and central holes of round bricks and plates

LEGO Friends flower ornaments create a sea anemone's mouth

A LEGO banana becomes a yellow sea slug!

An overlapping mound of red flowers (some raised on plates beneath) forms a single coral colony

Brown brooms inserted into hollow cones

Plug in green flames for leafy kelp

Transparent antenna elements

Pile up plates as sand banks

HOW MANY FISH CAN YOU SEE?

Glow-in-the-dark elements bring the reef to life at night. You could place light-up bricks under transparent pieces, too!

EXTREME SPORTS

Glax thinks he has finally discovered how humans get into orbit. They climb up mountains! For a real rugged outdoor adventure, try a day of rock-climbing – or let your minifigures do it for you! You can give them an extra thrill by building a bungee jump up at the top!

Turn the page to discover another way of getting down the mountain: hang-gliding!

WHEE! I'M ON TOP OF THE WORLD!

ROCK CLIMBING

Not everybody wants to relax on their vacation, so how about a bracing rock climb? This rock face is built with lots and lots of inverted slopes. A LEGO rope helps determined climbers reach the summit.

Make the surface rough and uneven to resemble a real rocky cliff

A LEGO rope piece features built-in bars for a minifigure to hang on to

Cracks and crannies provide hand-holds – or hiding places for critters!

Use a free-spinning LEGO Technic pin and two bricks-with-holes for the catapult's rotation point

WHATEVER YOU DO, DON'T LOOK DOWN!

Exposed brick studs make rocky surfaces look more real

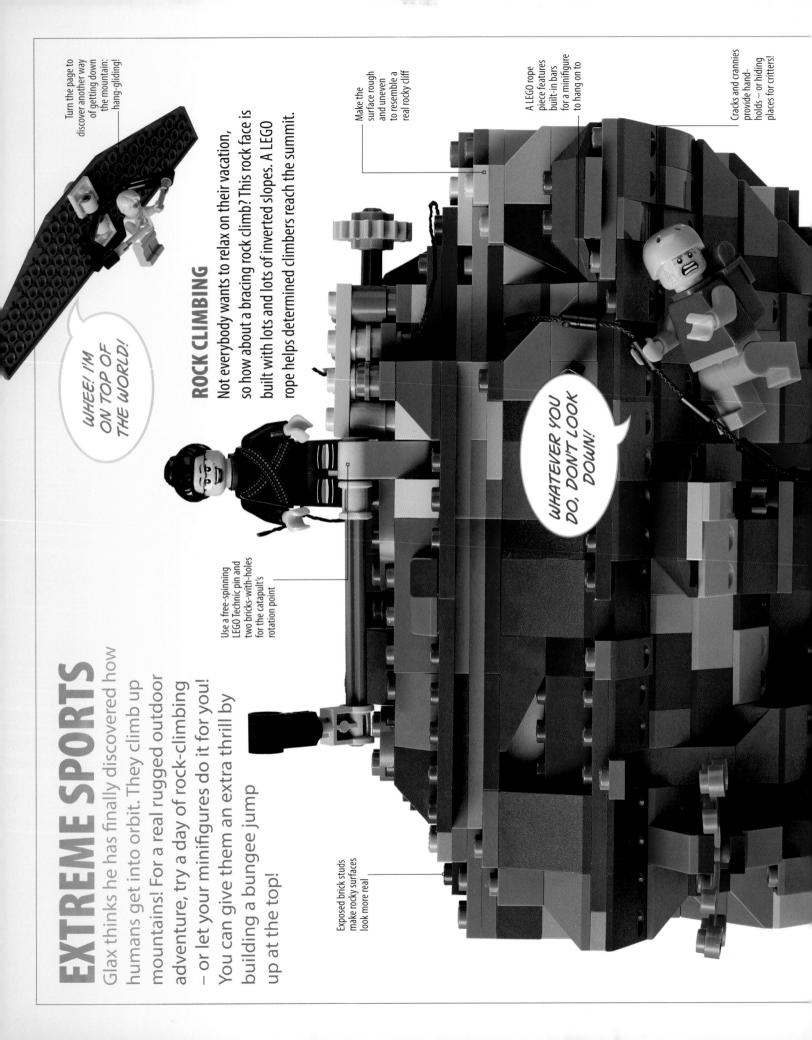

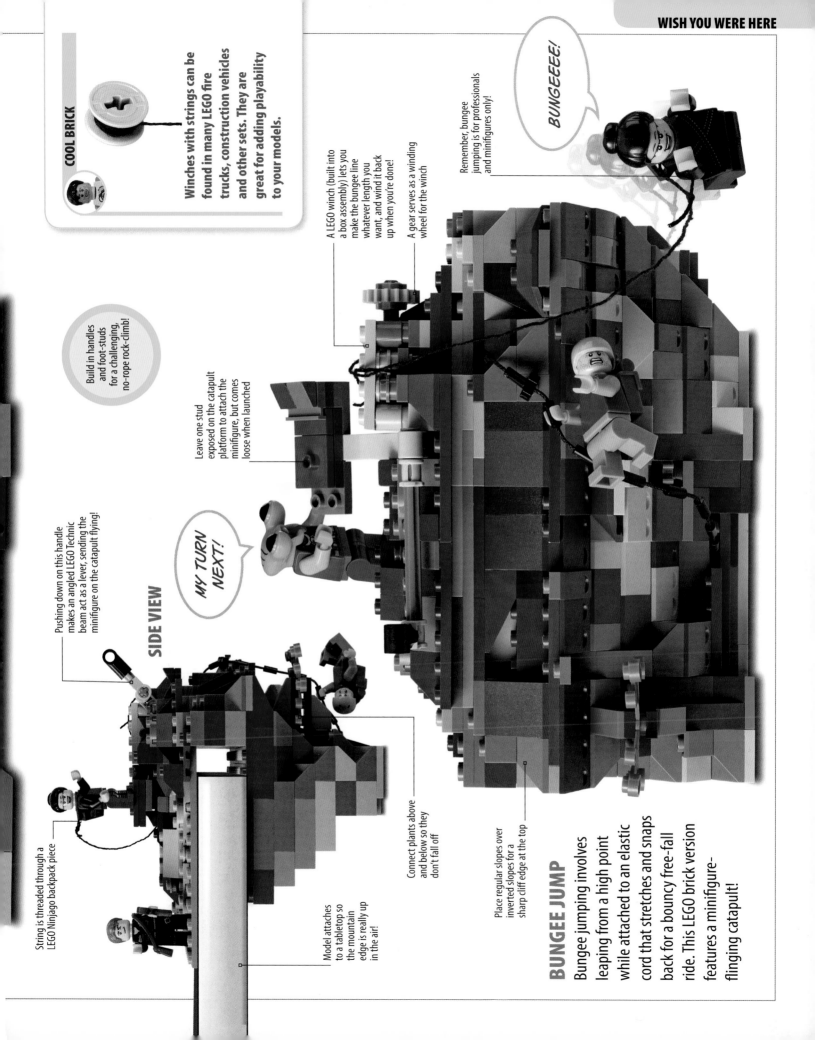

COOL BRICK

Winches with strings can be found in many LEGO fire trucks, construction vehicles and other sets. They are great for adding playability to your models.

BUNGEEEE!

Remember, bungee jumping is for professionals and minifigures only!

A LEGO winch (built into a box assembly) lets you make the bungee line whatever length you want, and wind it back up when you're done!

A gear serves as a winding wheel for the winch

Build in handles and foot-studs for a challenging, no-rope rock-climb!

Leave one stud exposed on the catapult platform to attach the minifigure, but comes loose when launched

Pushing down on this handle makes an angled LEGO Technic beam act as a lever, sending the minifigure on the catapult flying!

SIDE VIEW

MY TURN NEXT!

String is threaded through a LEGO Ninjago backpack piece

Model attaches to a tabletop so the mountain edge is really up in the air!

Connect plants above and below so they don't fall off

Place regular slopes over inverted slopes for a sharp cliff edge at the top

BUNGEE JUMP

Bungee jumping involves leaping from a high point while attached to an elastic cord that stretches and snaps back for a bouncy free-fall ride. This LEGO brick version features a minifigure-flinging catapult!

ADVENTURES UP HIGH

These humans cannot seem to decide whether they want to go up or down. Not only do they climb and bounce, but they even strap on giant wings and fly! Send your minifigures to even greater heights by building entire mountains for them to scale and colourful hang gliders to help them sail safely back down to the ground below.

MINIFIGURE MOUNTAIN

Let's hope your minifigures aren't afraid of heights, because they're going on an exciting mountaineering vacation! Use basic bricks to build a tall mountain — then take turns against your friends to race your minifigures to the top. To make your minifigures' mountain climb even more of a challenge, you could use small coloured pieces as distance markers, stopping your minifigures only at points of the same color.

Where in the world is your mountain located? Use different colors to create brown desert cliffs, green jungle slopes, or black and red volcanoes.

Use white bricks for a snow-capped peak

Small, colored pieces make distance markers

Build your mountain as tall as you want it to be!

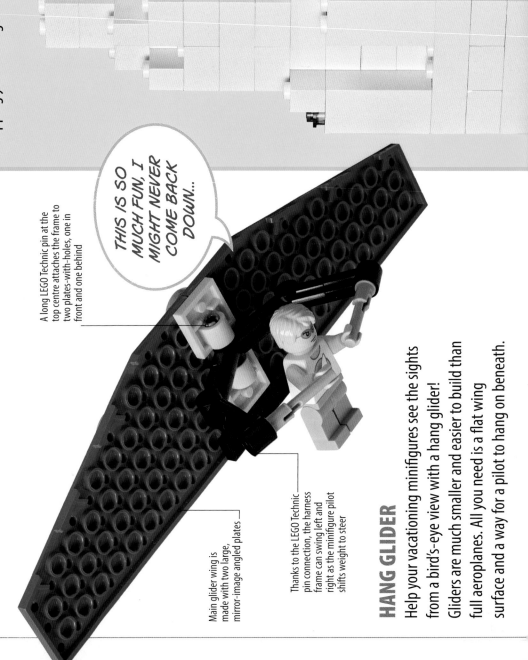

A long LEGO Technic pin at the top centre attaches the frame to two plates-with-holes, one in front and one behind

THIS IS SO MUCH FUN, I MIGHT NEVER COME BACK DOWN...

Main glider wing is made with two large, mirror-image angled plates

Thanks to the LEGO Technic pin connection, the harness frame can swing left and right as the minifigure pilot shifts weight to steer

HANG GLIDER

Help your vacationing minifigures see the sights from a bird's-eye view with a hang glider! Gliders are much smaller and easier to build than full aeroplanes. All you need is a flat wing surface and a way for a pilot to hang on beneath.

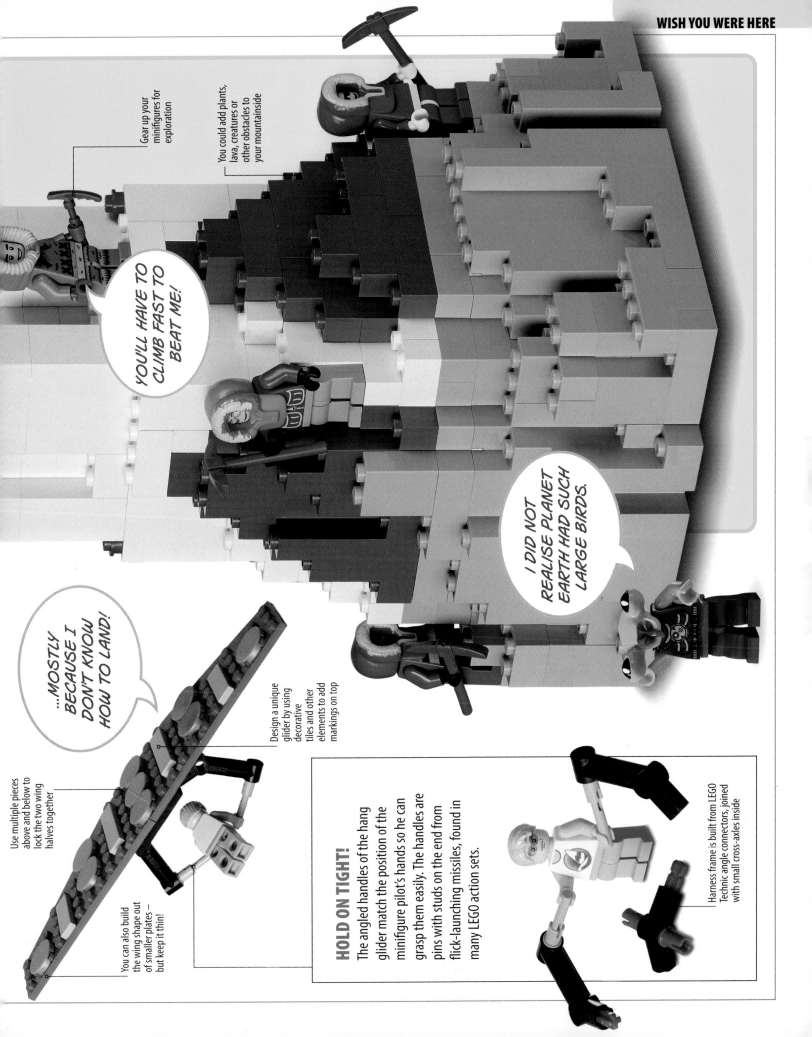

Gear up your minifigures for exploration

You could add plants, lava, creatures or other obstacles to your mountainside

YOU'LL HAVE TO CLIMB FAST TO BEAT ME!

I DID NOT REALISE PLANET EARTH HAD SUCH LARGE BIRDS.

...MOSTLY BECAUSE I DON'T KNOW HOW TO LAND!

Design a unique glider by using decorative tiles and other elements to add markings on top

Use multiple pieces above and below to lock the two wing halves together

You can also build the wing shape out of smaller plates – but keep it thin!

HOLD ON TIGHT!

The angled handles of the hang glider match the position of the minifigure pilot's hands so he can grasp them easily. The handles are pins with studs on the end from flick-launching missiles, found in many LEGO action sets.

Harness frame is built from LEGO Technic angle connectors, joined with small cross-axles inside

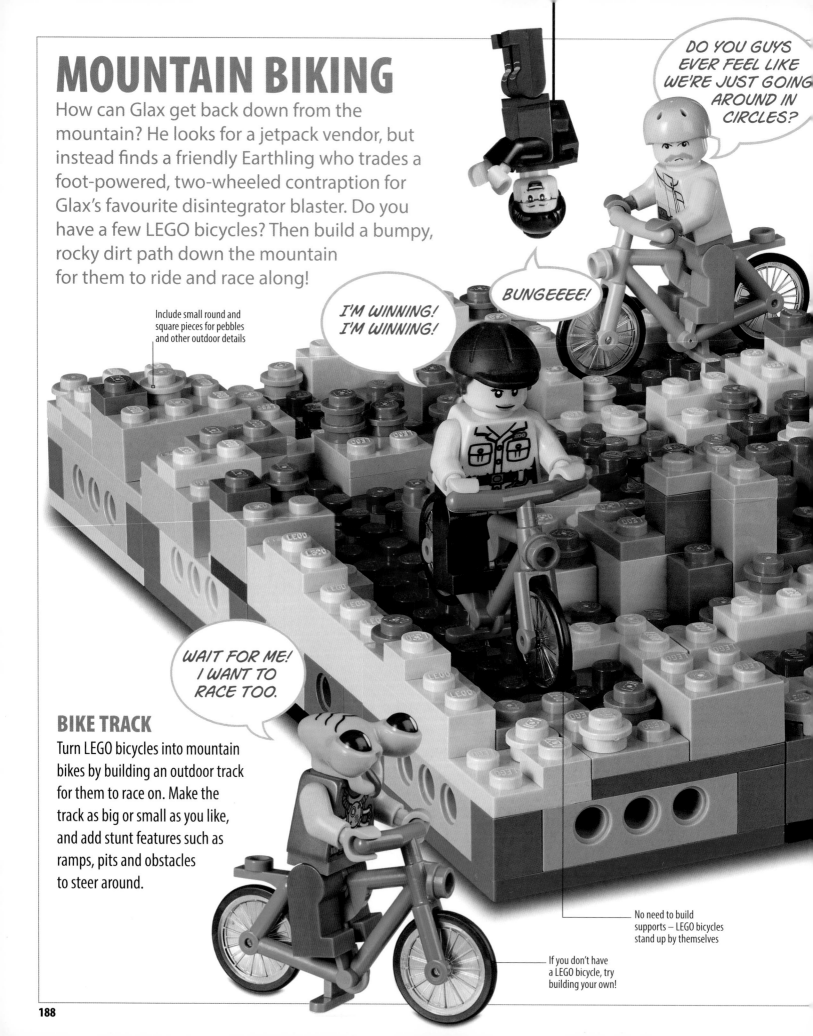

MOUNTAIN BIKING

How can Glax get back down from the mountain? He looks for a jetpack vendor, but instead finds a friendly Earthling who trades a foot-powered, two-wheeled contraption for Glax's favourite disintegrator blaster. Do you have a few LEGO bicycles? Then build a bumpy, rocky dirt path down the mountain for them to ride and race along!

Include small round and square pieces for pebbles and other outdoor details

I'M WINNING! I'M WINNING!

BUNGEEEE!

DO YOU GUYS EVER FEEL LIKE WE'RE JUST GOING AROUND IN CIRCLES?

WAIT FOR ME! I WANT TO RACE TOO.

BIKE TRACK

Turn LEGO bicycles into mountain bikes by building an outdoor track for them to race on. Make the track as big or small as you like, and add stunt features such as ramps, pits and obstacles to steer around.

No need to build supports – LEGO bicycles stand up by themselves

If you don't have a LEGO bicycle, try building your own!

Sturdy headgear is important when biking, especially on uneven terrain

WHEE!

TRACK LAYOUT

To make your track interesting, vary your paths – make straight lines, tight corners, T-junctions, crossroads, zig-zags and dead ends. You could also include growing plants, fallen tree trunks, and narrow streams or even rivers for the bikes to jump over!

Raised plates in the same colour as the trail create a realistic surface

Rearrange the sections to build a new course!

Use brown plates to make dirt trails

Consider building part of your trail out of slope bricks and racing your bikes to the bottom!

CONNECTING YOUR COURSE

To make a modular bike course, construct each section on a 6x6 plate with 1x4 LEGO Technic bricks on their sides. Connect the sections with LEGO Technic pins so that their paths line up to create a complete track.

If you don't have enough 1x4 LEGO Technic bricks, use two 1x2 ones instead

Since the middle will be covered, you can use any colours you want!

Fill in the corners with 1x1 bricks

WATER ADVENTURES

When the humans talked about "white water rafting," Glax did not expect to be floating down a rushing river at high speeds, narrowly avoiding many large rocks. This is even better than asteroid-surfing! Build a big raft or a kayak and send your most daring minifigures on a thrilling ride through the rapids.

Take a camping trip by storing backpacks and outdoor supplies in the kayak!

NO ONE BEATS ME TO THE FINISH LINE!

Place your paddler in the centre of the kayak for balance

BLUE KAYAK
This simple kayak is built around a pair of inverted curved wedge elements – a common piece that can be found in many LEGO sets. Plates arranged around the top give it a traditional kayak's partially covered deck.

A covered top keeps water from getting in

CAN'T YOU JUST ENJOY THE RIDE?

This double-ended paddle is made from a long bar and two sets of hinged pieces

KAYAK CONSTRUCTION
The space between the two curved wedges is filled by an inverted 2x4 double slope piece. Add more to make a longer kayak with room for extra paddlers!

Double angled plates match the shape of the wedges underneath

A two-stud-wide gap in the centre leaves room for a minifigure paddler

SIDE VIEW

Ends are 2x2 round bricks attached to the body from above and below

LIME KAYAK
This kayak design is a little more advanced. Its shape is made with curved slopes that are attached sideways to a 1x4 brick with side studs. Long tiles mounted on brackets in the centre lock the slopes in place.

Your kayak doesn't have to look the same at both ends. Use plates and tiles to make the front and back different

Curved arch brick

FULL OF AIR

A row of curved arch bricks almost all the way around gives the raft its rounded, air-filled appearance. You can also use angled slopes, or even make a ring of regular bricks.

A staggered front end helps the raft look angular, but not too pointy

BOTTOM VIEW

Sliding plates allow the raft to glide along easily

If you don't have this headgear, you could use construction helmets or astronaut helmets

You could add a motor here at the back!

REAR VIEW

I THINK I MIGHT HAVE GOTTEN ON THE WRONG BOAT!

Make sure there's enough space for a team of minifigures with oars or paddles

If you don't have enough oar elements, try building your own!

Use bright colours so your raft can be easily spotted in the water

WHITE WATER RAFT

This type of raft is usually inflatable and made of tough rubber, so your model should have rounded curves instead of square edges. Build it wide and low so it won't tip over in rough water!

The front is a little higher than the rest of the raft

SKIING

It may look like ice cream, but Glax finds Earth snow much less tasty, especially without chocolate syrup on top. On the other hand, it's great for skiing! Equip your minifigures with skis or snowboards and build them a snowy slope to slide down. Carry your skiers up to the top in an electric cable car and let the cold-climate adventures begin!

> ERM... I WAS HANG-GLIDING, BUT NOW I'M JUST HANGING.

Big windows will let your passengers see the snowy landscape

Use a printed tile for the ski resort's logo

Cable is a flexible LEGO tube, but you can use a long bar or even a string!

Bricks and plates with click hinges create a bent armature between the roof and the cable

If you don't have this piece you could use a window or a windscreen instead

BUILDER TALK

"If you're making a tall, sloped surface like a ski run, make sure you add filler bricks to support it from inside. Otherwise, you might have an avalanche on your hands!"

STAY CONNECTED

A plate with side ring provides a secure connection and lets the cable car slide up and down the tube — or use a clip instead!

Plate with side ring

CABLE CAR

Build an enclosed cable car to carry multiple minifigures up the slopes. It should be lightweight and sturdy enough to hang from the cable without coming apart. Add bricks inside so your skiers have benches to sit on, and leave plenty of space for skiing gear.

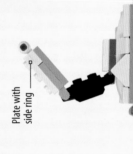

Hinged spaceship canopy opens to let skiers get on and off

A tile with caution stripes says "Watch your step!"

Add white pieces to the roof for a coating of snow

SKI SLOPE

You can build a ski slope of any size and shape – from an easy nursery slope for beginners to a steep mountainside for fearless experts. Find all of the white slope bricks in your collection and start building!

You could attach curved bricks to make gentler, more rounded snowdrifts.

If you don't have minifigure skis and ski poles, improvise! Use long, thin plates to make skis and rods or anything skinny with a handle for the poles

LEFT-SIDE VIEW

Sharp peaks look like mountains far off in the distance

RIGHT-SIDE VIEW

You could cover the ground with white tiles for the appearance of freshly fallen snow

Use multiple layers to connect white plates together to make a wide base

Add transparent blue pieces for icy details

It looks like some of these skiers need a little more practice

IT DIDN'T SHOW THIS IN THE HOLIDAY BROCHURE!

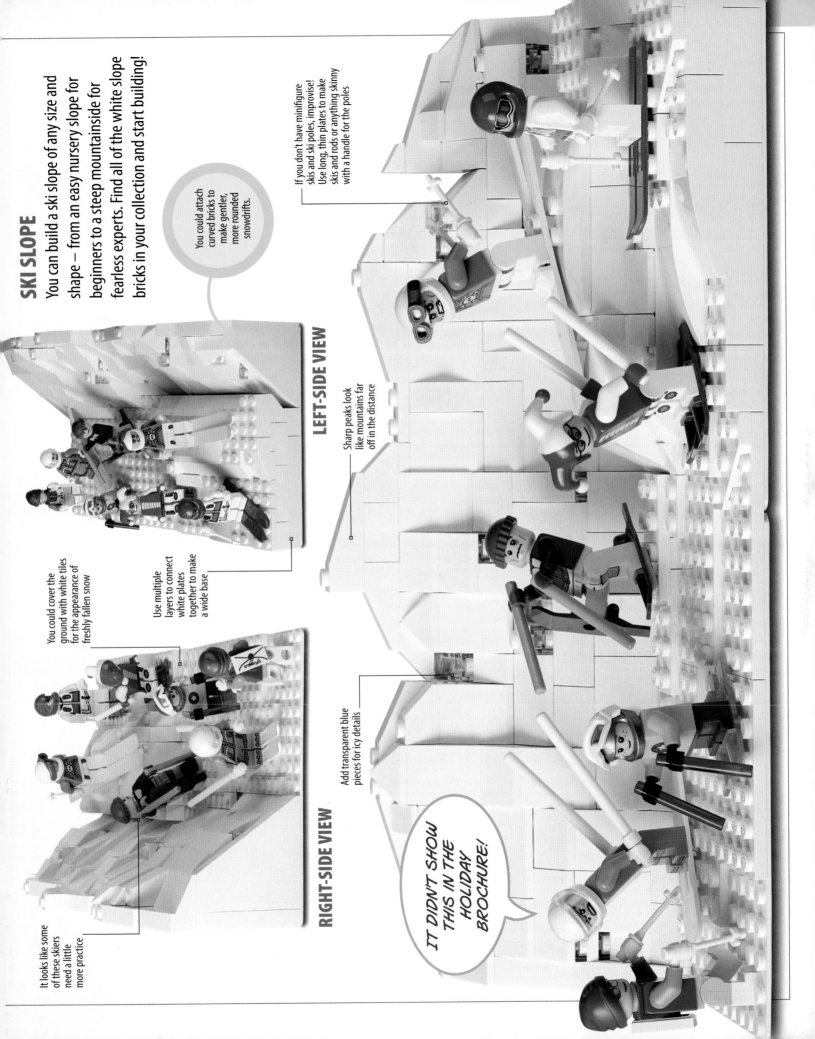

SNOW TRANSPORTS

What's the best way for an alien tourist to trek around on a snow-covered mountain? Earth technology has provided visitors with several useful options. Whether they choose to drive through the drifts on a snowmobile or surf down the slopes on a snowboard, it's a whole lot easier than using snow shoes to get where you need to go!

SNOWMOBILE

Who needs roads? When you have a snowmobile, you can go anywhere...as long as it's covered in snow! Give your snowmobile skis in front for steering, and a treaded tire in back for traction and power.

SIDE VIEW

Attach a four-stud-wide front end to a three-stud-wide back with jumper plates

A bracket lets you attach these curved bricks using sideways building

A clipped-on flap keeps snow from spraying on anyone behind the snowmobile!

Short minifigure skis are held by tap elements, which plug into 1x1 plates with side rings on the snowmobile

A hinge plate holds the controls at a comfortable angle

A long, free-spinning LEGO Technic pin holds the tyre in place

Use latticed elements to form a railing to keep the riders in place – or use regular 1x4 bricks

2x12 plate attaches to 1x4 bricks with side studs on the base

Strings attach to the outermost studs on 1x4 bricks with side studs

Curve made from four arch pieces attached to a 1x4 plate

TOBOGGANS

A toboggan is the perfect snow transport. It's fun, fast and you can fit a few minifigure friends aboard it if you make yours long enough. You need a wide, flat base, an upwards-curving front, spots for riders to sit or stand and strings for steering.

Curved wall element

SIDEWAYS SLIDER

The J-shaped nose of this toboggan is made from a tall, curved wall element. Most of the rest is built sideways, from a combination of bricks, plates and slopes.

SNOWBOARD JUMP

It's like surfing on a frozen wave! Give your snowboarding minifigures something to really jump about by building a snowy-looking stunt ramp. Assembling the slope is relatively easy, but the curve at the bottom may take a bit of clever construction.

HALF-PIPE

This stunt, the half-pipe, was built by connecting four large arches side-by-side with tiles and plates with clips. They attach to the rest of the snowboarding model upside-down!

TOTALLY AWESOME DUDE ...ER WHATEVER THAT MEANS!

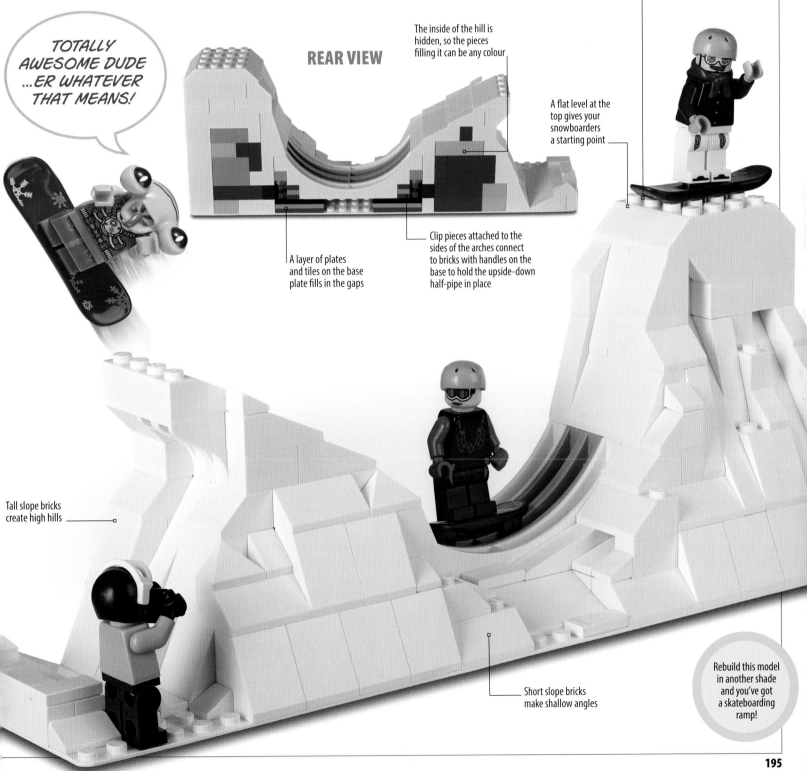

The inside of the hill is hidden, so the pieces filling it can be any colour

REAR VIEW

A flat level at the top gives your snowboarders a starting point

A layer of plates and tiles on the base plate fills in the gaps

Clip pieces attached to the sides of the arches connect to bricks with handles on the base to hold the upside-down half-pipe in place

Tall slope bricks create high hills

Short slope bricks make shallow angles

Rebuild this model in another shade and you've got a skateboarding ramp!

195

SKI HOTEL

Skiing may not be as cold as wading through the nitrogen streams of Pluton IV, but it's still nice to have somewhere to warm up at the end of a long day on the slopes. Build a lodge where your winter vacationers can relax and thaw out by the fire. If you're lucky, Glax won't have finished off all of the hot chocolate!

ALPINE HOTEL

Before you start building, do some planning. Pick out doors and windows you would like to use (or you could construct your own), and choose colours that look good together. Don't forget to think about the little details that will bring your hotel to life!

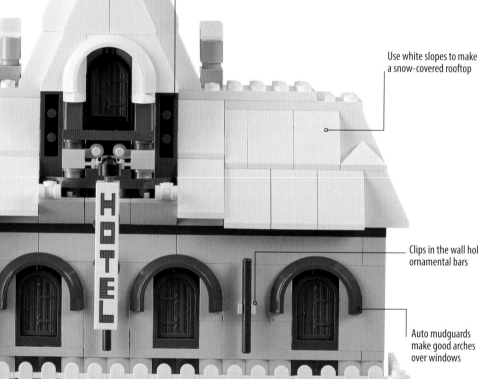

The undersides of bricks add their own interesting effects

Use white slopes to make a snow-covered rooftop

Windows with shutters help keep out the cold

Clips in the wall hold ornamental bars

Fence elements can also be a terrace's railing

Auto mudguards make good arches over windows

Plates between brick layers add decoration and support

ALL THIS SHOVELLING SURE KEEPS YOU TOASTY!

A lamppost with a telescope base helps late arrivals find their way to the front door

Stack extra white plates for deeper snow on the ground

Shovel the entrance so your door has enough clearance to swing open!

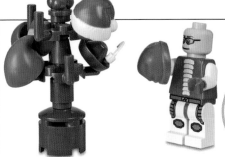

LOOKS LIKE SANTA HAS ARRIVED ALREADY!

HOTEL-BUILDING

If you only assemble the front of the hotel, you can keep the back open to move your minifigures around the different rooms and floors. Make sure the bottom floor is strong so that it doesn't fall apart as you add the higher levels.

Build in a peaked roof for a traditional Alpine-style building

HOME COMFORTS

Your hotel will need some amenities to keep the vacationers happy. Include things like chairs, telephones, cabinets, a fireplace and a hatstand for storing hats and ski equipment.

You can store all kinds of odd objects up in the attic!

Looks like this bat has found somewhere warm to stay for the winter!

The split flue carries smoke from the fireplace on the middle floor to the chimneys on the roof

Pillars and inverted slopes help bear the weight of the structures above them

Transparent yellow 1x1 round plates create soft interior lights

Stack log bricks to make traditional log columns and walls

Include a magazine rack in reception!

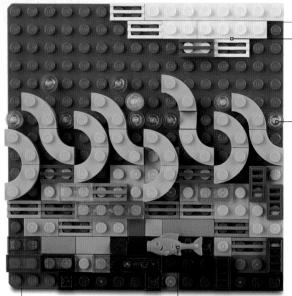

White pieces for a hint of cloud

Stacks of 1x1 round plates form bubbles and ocean froth

Use clips to attach fish and other objects or accessories

HOLIDAY POSTCARDS

Although Glax's holo-camera ran out of power (who knew the sockets were incompatible?), he has learned about the human custom of sending each other images of places where they have been. Build a one-of-a-kind vacation postcard using your LEGO pieces! You can design a flat mosaic, or add layers and accessories to make your postcard really pop.

OCEAN SURF

Start your postcard by picking a base plate (or putting several together) in the colour that you want for a background. You can make ocean waves with curved macaroni bricks and other water effects with transparent tiles and grilles!

You can use tiles to make a school of fish

Make waving lines of tiles for long strands of seaweed

Mix dark green pieces in for deeper water

Use round pieces to make organic, living shapes and forms

SHARK SCENE

Frame an animal in the postcard just like you would in a photograph. To make a shark's distinctive shape, try building an outline first and then carefully removing it to add the body colour underneath. When you put the outline back again, you'll have a coloured-in creature!

EVEN ALIENS LEAVE IT UNTIL THE LAST DAY TO WRITE POSTCARDS!

Your postcard doesn't have to be flat – use grille slopes to add some depth to the surf

Teeth are 1x1 slopes attached to the side studs of headlight bricks

Step-shaped angled bricks can be used to make undersea plants

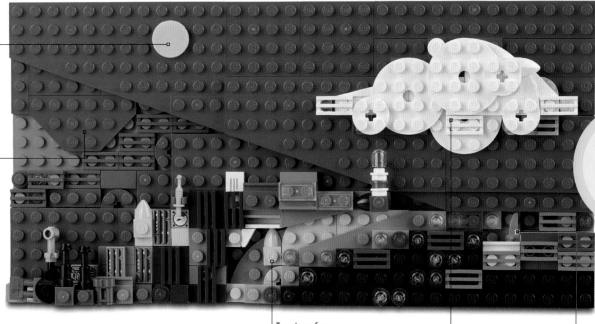

Sometimes simple works – like a bright yellow 2x2 round tile for the sun

Blue sky plates are layered on top of green hills in the background

Search for old postcards around your house and use them for inspiration!

Tan pieces for a sandy shoreline

Use round and angled plates to make clouds, with grilles for the wispy bits

With multiple layers, you can hide parts of elements to change them into something else – like letting the point of a gold pickaxe stick up as a sailboat's tiny sail!

SEASIDE TOWN

When you've got the hang of building postcards, try making one in a style that's a little more advanced. This scene of a small town by the sea uses layers of plates along with grilles, a letter, binoculars, a nunchuk handle, telescopes and even a doctor's needle to create three-dimensional details.

Striped lighthouse is a red headlight brick, three 1x1 round plates and a transparent bulb piece on top

Symmetrical geometric designs are a good way to practise building LEGO brick mosaics

Use one stud jumper plates to get your piece placement just right

BUILDER TALK

"These mosaic models look best at a distance because the shapes blend together better. While building, move away from your model to see if your additions look good."

Different shades of yellow make the sun look like it is blazing with light

Use 1x1 plates to make diagonal rays

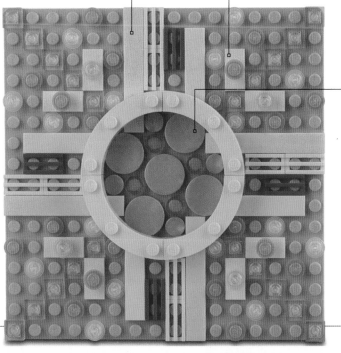

Gold-coloured elements make the centre even more radiant

THE SUN

Be creative with your postcards! While you should never look directly at the sun, you can still build your own version to enjoy. Use warm brick colours to make a circle and then add rays pointing in all directions.

HANDFUL OF BRICKS LIST

4x4 plate x 1

2x2 inverted slope x 1

2x2 brick x 3

2 x 4 brick x 2

2x2 plate x 2

1x2/1x4 angle plate x1

1x6 plate x 2

2x2 slope x 3

Antenna x1

1x2 slope x 2

2x3 slope x 1

1x1 slope x 4

1x1 brick eyes x 2

1x2 tile with top bar x 1

1x2 plate x 1

1x1 round brick x 1

2x4 angled plate x 2

1x3 brick x 2

1x2 curved half-arch x 1

4x4 round plate x 1

2x2 round brick x 1

DK
LONDON, NEW YORK
MELBOURNE, MUNICH and DELHI

For DK Publishing
Project Editor Hannah Dolan
Senior Designer Guy Harvey
Editors Jo Casey, Victoria Taylor
Designers Jill Bunyan, Sam Richiardi, Lauren Rosier, Rhys Thomas
Pre-production Producer Siu Chan
Producer Louise Daly
Design Manager Nathan Martin
Art Director Ron Stobbart
Publishing Manager Julie Ferris
Publishing Director Simon Beecroft

For the LEGO Group
Project Manager Mikkel Joachim Petersen
Assistant Licensing Manager Randi Kirsten Sørensen
Senior Licensing Manager Corinna van Delden
Designer Melody Louise Caddick
Building Instruction Developer Alexandra Martin
Model makers Stephen Berry, Yvonne Doyle, Rod Gillies, Tim Goddard, Tim Johnson, Barney Main, Pete Reid

Photography by Gary Ombler

First published in Great Britain in 2013 by Dorling Kindersley Limited
80 Strand, London WC2R 0RL
Penguin Group (UK)

10 9 8 7 6 5 4 3 2 1
001—187415—Sep/13

Page design copyright © 2013 Dorling Kindersley Limited.

A CIP catalogue record for this book is available from the British Library.

ISBN: 978-1-40932-751-6

Reproduced by Altaimage in the UK
Printed and bound by South China

Discover more at
www.dk.com
www.LEGO.com

Acknowledgements
Dorling Kindersley would like to thank: Randi Sørensen, Mikkel Petersen, Melody Caddick, Corinna van Delden and Alexandra Martin at the LEGO Group; Stephen Berry, Yvonne Doyle, Rod Gillies, Tim Goddard, Tim Johnson, Barney Main, Pete Reid and Andrew Walker for their amazing models; Daniel Lipkowitz for his inspiring text; Gary Ombler for his endless patience and brilliant photography; and Emma Grange, Lauren Nesworthy, Lisa Stock and Matt Wilson for editorial and design assistance.

1x1 brick x 7

4x6 plate x 1

1x1 headlight brick x 2

1x4 brick x 6

1x2 brick x 5
(including 1 transparent)

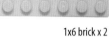
1x6 brick x 2

1x2 jumper plate x 3

2x3 brick x 1

1x1 round plate x 2

1x2x1 panel x1

1x4 plate x 2

2x2 radar dish x 2

1x1 cone x 1

Wide rim, wide tire, and 2x2 axle plate with 1 pin x 4

2x6 plate x 3

1x1 plate x 4

1x2 grille plate x 2

2x4 plate x 2

Tap x 1

1x6 arch brick x 1

2x2 round plate x 2

4x4 radar dish x 1

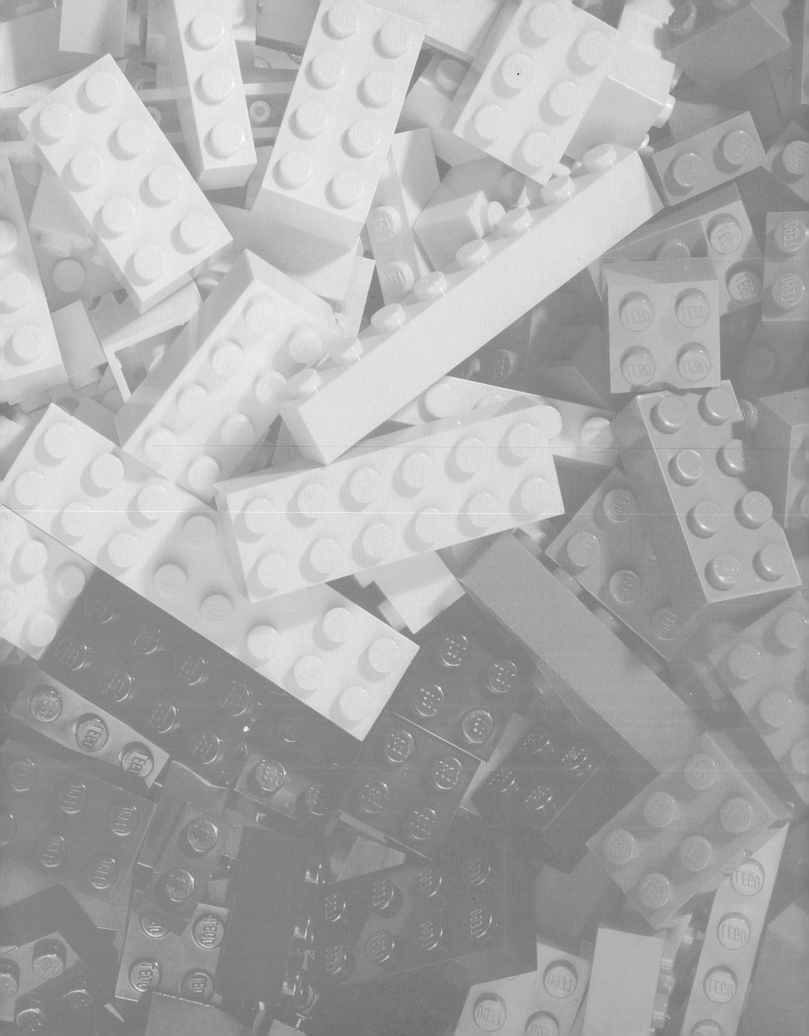